UNLOCKING
COMPLEX
TEXTS

A Systematic Framework For Building Adolescents' Comprehension

LAURA ROBB

SCHOLASTIC

New York • Toronto • London • Auckland • Sydney
Mexico City • New Delhi • Hong Kong • Buenos Aires

DEDICATION

In loving memory of my husband, Lloyd, and my parents, Sydney and Rachel Seidner

ACKNOWLEDGMENTS

Every book is a team effort, and deep satisfaction comes from working with others to solve problems, receive feedback, and discuss the effectiveness of teaching and learning practices. My infinite thanks goes to my editor, Joanna Davis-Swing. Her insights into the framework, her advice and counsel, and her terrific editing have enabled me to shape this book into one that I hope teachers will find useful.

My sincere thanks to middle-school students in Maine, Michigan, and Virginia who tested the reading passages, took early versions of the quizzes, and planned and wrote paragraphs that argued, explained, or informed. Their valuable work and self-evaluations enabled me to choose selections and adjust the lessons to meet a wide range of learning needs. Thanks to the teachers who took time to test some units and offer candid feedback, for without their teaching and comments, I would not have been able to revise the lessons to insure they met middle-school teachers' and students' needs. Sincere thanks to Patti Kobeck, Sue Leighton, Sandra Lowry, Jennifer Petzke, and Carol Sherburne.

To Fay Stump, my heartfelt appreciation and thanks for sharing two of her seventh-grade classes with me, and for providing valuable feedback during the three months we taught and planned.

Cover Designer: Jorge J. Namerow

All photos courtesy of the author.

Editor: Joanna Davis-Swing

Interior Designer: Sarah Morrow

Copyright © 2013 by Laura Robb

All rights reserved. Published by Scholastic Inc.

Printed in the U.S.A.

ISBN: 978-0-545-44906-9

1 2 3 4 5 6 7 8 9 10 40 19 18 17 16 15 14 13

Contents

Resources CD Contents

Foreword

by Jennifer Serravallo

In the fury to meet the demands of the Common Core State Standards, well-meaning people have suggested a bevy of nonsensical things, such as forcing kids to spend time with texts way too hard for them to understand, or asking young readers to slog through a dense text at a mind-numbing pace, annotating as they go. Laura Robb is the antidote to these misguided recommendations.

In her great new book, Laura Robb reminds us what research says and shares what teachers and students have done in real classrooms with real results. Laura has given teachers a much-needed combination of lessons, materials, and professional development to help them help their students unlock complex texts. This book is a must-have resource for so many reasons.

First, she lays out a pathway for teachers who want to teach students to read closely, carefully, and analytically—while still staying interested. That's got to come first: lessons that are fast-paced, rich, and feature materials that appeal to adolescents. Moreover, the units are structured to gradually release responsibility to students, helping them feel empowered and ensuring that the teacher isn't doing all the thinking work every day.

Second, Laura has given teachers the stuff they need to make the lessons a cinch to pull off. The accompanying CD contains a wealth of great materials, including anchor, on-level, and below-level texts for differentiation as well texts and booklists to help independent reading thrive; conference forms that help teachers assess and document students' application of reading strategies; writing about reading tasks with student samples to help teachers visualize the end product; and teaching tips peppered throughout that address concerns and questions that may come up as you try to implement her recommendations. The book also provides tables with suggested strategies for scaffolding struggling learners and help with troubleshooting.

Third, Laura Robb has faith in and respect for educators, and has said time and again that it is the skill of the teacher that matters most. With that in mind, she has structured her book in such a way that it is more than a collection of (really well-written) lesson plans; each unit plan follows a replicable sequence that educators can use to create their own curriculum. The lessons themselves span genres and purposes, and at the end of each chapter Laura has provided topics and questions so that you and colleagues can have professional conversations about the work. Ultimately, this book is not only a rich source of lessons—it is also professional development material.

Laura has thought of everything—such as how to balance the suggestions in this book with all the other demands in a middle school teacher's hectic schedule, how to organize yourself and take deliberate notes so that these ideas can work with even 100 students, and even how to use quizzes to teach test-taking skills.

So hold tight to what you believe and don't let yourself get distracted by some of the suggestions others have put out there about Standard Ten. Children can be taught to access complex texts in ways that are developmentally appropriate and engaging. Laura Robb knows the combination to the lock—and now she's given it to you.

CHAPTER 1

The Reader, the Teacher, the Text, and the Standards

"If I can't read it, how can I learn from it?" —eighth grader

"I can't do this," a young teacher said to me. "I've only used scripted programs, and now I'm supposed to teach informational texts and literature? I need help!"

This middle-school teacher, entering her third year, expresses the concerns of teachers all over the country regarding the search for the silver bullet that will reform education. Trained at college under the Reading First Initiative, this teacher, like thousands of others, lacks a broad knowledge of reading research, the theoretical underpinnings, and the student-teaching experiences that would enable her to teach reading and writing most effectively.

This literacy story is a cautionary tale for all school districts and states that have adopted the Common Core State Standards (CCSS). Mandated changes that aren't backed up with funding for ongoing professional study—that is, continual study to develop teachers' expertise in teaching reading to, and implementing the standards with, diverse student populations—will result in spotty improvement at best. Here's a staggering statistic to bear in mind: 1.3 million high-school students drop out each year because they can't read or write at a level that enables them to cope with school assignments; more than half are students of color (Alliance for Excellent Education, 2010). The eighth grader's lament—"If I can't read it, how can I learn from it?"—is a plea we all need to remember as we implement the Common Core State Standards (CCSS). Giving students complex and challenging materials they can't read will not improve their reading, and it discourages students from reading independently (Allington, 2002b). However, giving students complex and challenging texts at their instructional levels and then having them choose materials so that they read widely and independently will help students. It will enlarge their vocabulary, build background knowledge, and develop their fluency so they can accelerate reading and thinking power and cultivate a personal reading life—not to mention meet the demands posed by the Common Core State Standards.

Chapter Overview

In this chapter, we will examine the rigorous demands of the Common Core State Standards, particularly text complexity and text-based comprehension. We will see how the skills and strategies we have been teaching fit in with the new standards and how we may need to make some adjustments. We'll explore the role of writing in reading instruction and how it is essential for helping students meet the CCSS in reading. By the end of the chapter, you'll have a clear overview of the CCSS expectations. Then, in the next chapter, I'll outline a sensible instructional framework that helps students achieve the standards while still keeping their needs at the center of instruction.

The Common Core Reading Standards Unpacked

The Common Core provides ten reading standards for grades 6 to 12; there are separate standards for literature and informational texts, yet there is significant overlap, so we will consider them together. The standards are organized into three groups: Key Ideas and Details, Craft and Structure, and Integration of Knowledge. We'll address each group before turning to the final standard, which relates to the range of reading and text complexity.

Key Ideas and Details

The three standards in this group require students to determine accurately what the text says explicitly so they can draw logical inferences and analyze how various details and ideas relate to one other. The first two standards are nearly identical for informational texts and literature; the only difference is that for literature, students determine the theme or central idea, whereas for informational texts they determine the central idea. For the third standard, the literature version asks students to trace and analyze plot and character development, while the standard for informational texts asks them to trace and analyze the presentation of ideas. Let's take a closer look at each standard.

Standard 1: *Read closely to determine what the text says explicitly and to make logical inferences from it; cite specific textual evidence when writing or speaking to support conclusions drawn from the text.*

To meet this standard, students must be able to

- identify details
- retell the text
- reread and close read to clarify understanding
- skim to locate key details
- draw logical inferences based on text details
- use details from the text to support their ideas about the text

Standard 2: *Determine central ideas or themes of a text and analyze their development; summarize the key supporting details and ideas.*

To meet this standard, students must be able to

- identify central ideas and themes
- show how details convey the central ideas or themes

- trace the development of central ideas or themes
- summarize the text

For literature, students need an understanding of

- literary elements: plot, character, setting, theme, antagonistic forces, problems, resolution, conflict

For informational texts, students need an understanding of

- central ideas and supporting ideas

Standard 3: *Analyze how and why individuals, events, and ideas develop and interact over the course of a text.*

To meet this standard, students must be able to

- see connections between individuals, events, and ideas
- identify relationships between individuals, events, and ideas
- note how and why change occurs

For literature, students focus on plot and character development, particularly how characters respond to events and what they say and do. Students need an understanding of

- literary elements: plot, character, setting, conflict, resolution, antagonistic forces, problems
- cause-effect relationships

For informational texts, students focus on how the author presents information and develops ideas. Students need an understanding of

- organizational structures: cause-effect, problem-solution, compare-contrast, categorization, description, sequence, question-answer
- analogies

As we can see from this set of standards, no longer is learning the facts enough while reading informational texts. The facts are there for thinking and analysis. Our job is to show students how the facts can help them identify, analyze, and evaluate ideas.

For literature, students must move beyond retelling and summarizing to analyzing plot and character development, determining themes, and identifying central ideas. Certainly this is demanding work, but rich and rewarding work as well.

Craft and Structure

The craft and structure standards ask students to look closely at how the writer constructed the text, carefully considering word choice, sentence structure, and text structure. Students analyze the writer's choices, determining the effect each has on the text as a whole and evaluating the writer's point of view and purpose for writing the text.

Standard 4: *Interpret words and phrases as they are used in a text, including determining technical, connotative, and figurative meanings, and analyze how specific word choices shape meaning or tone.*

To meet this standard, students must be able to

- use context clues to infer a word's meaning
- use word parts, such as roots and affixes, to infer a word's meaning
- identify connotative and denotative meanings of words
- confirm definitions using available tools, such as glossaries and dictionaries
- recognize figurative language and understand how it affects meaning, visualization, and comprehension
- determine how word choices affect meaning and tone

Standard 5: *Analyze the structure of texts, including how specific sentences, paragraphs, and larger portions of the text (e.g., a section, chapter, scene, or stanza) relate to each other and the whole.*

To meet this standard, student must be able to

- identify text structures used in the piece, such as compare-contrast, problem-solution, and so on
- recognize and interpret text features, such as diagrams, charts, and so on
- understand genre characteristics, such as chapter headings, scenes, stanzas, and so on
- analyze how text structures, text features, and genre characteristics work together in a text to convey meaning

Standard 6: *Assess how point of view or purpose shapes the content and style of a text.*

To meet this standard, students must be able to

- identify the author's point of view
- identify the author's purpose
- retell the content of a text
- describe the style of a text
- analyze how the author's point of view and purpose affect what information is presented (content) and how it is presented (style)

For literature, students must be able to

- explain how the author develops the point of view of the narrator
- analyze how the author creates different points of view for different characters
- examine the effects of the various points of views, for example, creating suspense or humor

For informational texts, students must be able to

- describe the author's point of view and purpose for writing
- distinguish between the author's point of view, the reader's point of view, and other people's points of view
- analyze how the author distinguishes his or her point of view from others', paying attention to how the writer acknowledges and responds to arguments that differ from his or her own position

This set of standards requires that students read and reread text carefully, drawing on their knowledge of text structures, text features, and genre characteristics to analyze how a text works. Then students go a step further, considering the point of view and purpose of the author and evaluating how his or her perspective shapes the way the text was structured. This type of high-level thinking and analysis is challenging for students—and teachers! It's hard work, yet necessary for our students to become critical readers who can make informed decisions.

Integration of Knowledge and Ideas

Standard 7: *Integrate and evaluate content presented in diverse formats and media, including visually and quantitatively, as well as in words.*

To meet this standard, students must be able to

- compare and contrast different versions of a text
- identify and understand techniques used in various formats, such as lighting, camera angles, graphics, hypertext, and so on
- evaluate the effectiveness of various techniques, formats, and media for accomplishing the author's purpose

For literature, students must be able to

- identify and evaluate differences in how a story is portrayed in different media, such as a film version of a book

For informational texts, students must be able to

- assimilate information about a topic from various sources in diverse formats, such as a written text and a podcast
- evaluate sources

Standard 8: *Delineate and evaluate the argument and specific claims in a text, including the validity of the reasoning as well as the relevance and sufficiency of the evidence.*

This standard applies only to informational texts. To meet this standard, students should be able to

- trace an argument through a text
- identify claims
- identify the evidence provided for each claim
- determine whether evidence is relevant and sufficient to support a claim
- evaluate whether an argument is sufficiently supported by its claims and evidence

Standard 9: *Analyze how two or more texts address similar themes or topics in order to build knowledge or to compare the approaches the authors take.*

To meet this standard, students must be able to

- compare and contrast information or literary elements from multiple texts
- identify the authors' points of view
- evaluate how a central idea is developed
- find common themes
- compare and contrast logical inferences
- compare and contrast text structure and its effect on meaning

Range of Reading and Level of Text Complexity

Standard 10: *Read and comprehend complex literary and informational texts independently and proficiently.*

Of course, this is the ultimate goal for all our students. Focused lessons, guided practice, and plenty of time for independent reading are the way to help our students meet this goal.

Shifts in Thinking About Text Complexity

The final reading standard is "Read and comprehend complex literary and informational texts independently and proficiently." The CCSS offer a supplemental note about the range of reading expected:

> To become college and career ready, students must grapple with works of exceptional craft and thought whose range extends across genres, cultures, and centuries. Such

> **CCSS Tutorials**
>
> The units in this book provide the focused lessons and guided practice that students need. If you'd like more detail on how to apply the CCSS to literary and informational texts, please see the tutorials on the Resources CD.

works offer profound insights into the human condition and serve as models for students' own thinking and writing. Along with high-quality contemporary works, these texts should be chosen from among seminal U.S. documents, the classics of American literature, and the timeless dramas of Shakespeare. Through wide and deep reading of literature and literary nonfiction of steadily increasing sophistication, students gain a reservoir of literary and cultural knowledge, references, and images; the ability to evaluate intricate arguments; and the capacity to surmount the challenges posed by complex texts (CCSS 2010, p. 35).

The CCSS have provided guidelines for determining a text's complexity that fall into three categories: quantitative measures, qualitative measures, and reader and task considerations. We'll examine each in turn.

Quantitative Measures

Quantitative measures of text complexity examine characteristics of a text best analyzed by computer, such as sentence length and word frequency. Several methods exist that calculate a text's readability and assign it a grade level; the Common Core uses Lexile® measures for their guidelines. Revised grade-level expectations for Lexile® measures of texts students should be able to read are shown in the table below.

It's important to remember that a Lexile® measure refers to the readability of a text; a student's Lexile® level depends on her reading ability, not her grade level. So a seventh-grade developing reader might be able to comprehend texts at a Lexile® linked to fourth grade, while an advanced reader in that

GRADE-LEVEL BAND	OLD LEXILE® RANGES	CCSS LEXILE® RANGES
K–1	N/A	N/A
2–3	450–725	450–790
4–5	645–845	770–980
6–8	860–1010	955–1155
9–10	960–1115	1080–1305
11–CCR	1070–1220	1215–1355

(CCSS, Appendix A, p. 8)

same class can comprehend texts Lexiled for ninth or tenth grade. Word frequency, sentence length, and syntactic difficulty determine a Lexile® measure. A text that has long sentences or short sentences with subordinate clauses and few repeated words will be more challenging to understand and have a higher Lexile® measure (*http://www.lexile.com*).

Qualitative Measures

Using only quantitative measures to determine appropriate instructional material for students is not enough. It's also important to examine a book's content and concepts, and that's why the Common Core also includes qualitative measures: knowledge demands (what prior knowledge the reader must have of the subject), levels of meaning, structure, language conventionality, and clarity. To these measures, I add vocabulary, concepts embedded in a text, and inferential-thinking demands.

For me, text complexity also includes the concepts and content in reading materials. A book with a fifth-grade Lexile® score, such as *The Giver* by Lois Lowry, is appropriate for seventh and eighth graders because it deals with euthanasia and inhibiting sexual feelings. It's the content and the warnings for the future of our society that Lowry presents in her dystopian novel, and not the syntax and vocabulary, that determine its complexity.

Reader and Task Considerations

The CCSS's third factor in text complexity is the reader and the task she has to accomplish. Reader variables identified by the Common Core are motivation, knowledge, and experience. Task variables include the purpose and complexity of the task, such as the type of questions posed. When selecting an instructional text for a student, it's important to consider quantitative and qualitative measures as well as the task the reader must accomplish. Doing this provides teachers with the flexibility to match students to texts so that learning and accelerated achievement can occur, and students can develop the reading skill they require to meet the challenges of complex, grade-level texts.

Shifts in Thinking About Comprehension

In addition to increased text complexity demands, the Common Core emphasizes text-based comprehension—that is, being able to accurately state what a text says and use text details to support any idea about or analysis of a text. This is a change for many teachers.

At a recent workshop for middle-school teachers, I asked partners to read and discuss a poem about Japanese Americans after the bombing of Pearl Harbor. The poem, "In Response to Executive Order 9066: All Americans of Japanese Descent Must Report to Relocation Centers," by Dwight Okita, is written in the form of a letter to the government by a fourteen-year-old girl.

During the paired discussion, I invited participants to use the poem to find two or three themes and to support their thoughts with details and inferences from the poem. One teacher suggested this theme: "The Kamikaze pilots did not fear suicide as long as it was part of fulfilling a mission for Japan." When I asked for support from the text, he could not find details or inferences in the poem to back up this idea. "I know that happened at this time," he said. "It's my connection to the poem."

I agreed that this statement about Kamikaze pilots may have been true and relevant to the poem. However, for an interpretation of a text to be valid, the reader needs to cite details and logical inferences *from that text* to support it. That's text-dependent comprehension, and that is an aspect of reading the Common Core emphasizes, as we saw in Standards 1–3 above. It's what Louise Rosenblatt, in *Literature as Exploration* (1938, 1983) and later in *The Reader, the Text, the Poem* (1978), called valid interpretations of a text.

We've just moved through a period in the teaching of reading when teachers were encouraged to elicit personal connections from students, and these connections were considered valid interpretations even if the text did not support the ideas. Personal connections are fine; we all make them. To encourage text-dependent comprehension, however, we need to help students understand the difference between valid, text-based analysis, where the text supports readers' hunches, and an idea that the text sparked in the reader but that can't be validated by the text. Whether you are teaching developing, proficient, or advanced readers, it's helpful to find informational texts and literature worthy of reading and discussing—texts that have multiple interpretations that can be supported with text details and with logical inferences based on text details. Finding such texts can be a challenge, especially for developing readers, but it is well worth the effort, and in fact it's necessary if we want to help all our students achieve the ambitious goals set out by the CCSS (see pages 35–37 for suggestions on finding texts).

Writing About Reading to Boost Comprehension

The high-level comprehension and analytical thinking demanded by the Common Core requires we have our students write about their reading. Evidence demonstrating the powerful effect writing about reading has on comprehension is summarized in *Writing to Read* (Graham & Hebert, 2010), which includes a meta-analysis of research studies investigating the relationship between reading and writing. You can download the report at *www.carnegie.org/literacy*. Here, I will present the key findings and discuss how they relate to the CCSS.

1. **Have students write about the texts they read.**
   The first key finding is that writing about texts improves comprehension of those texts. In fact, "Writing about a text proved to be better than just reading it, reading and rereading it, reading and studying it, reading and discussing it, and receiving reading instruction" (p. 12). Clearly, writing about texts is essential if we want our

students to achieve high-level comprehension of complex texts. The report recommends these specific activities based on the research studies they analyzed (p. 11):

- responding to a text in writing (writing personal responses, analyzing and interpreting the text)
- summarizing a text
- taking notes about a text
- answering questions about a text in writing

2. **Teach students the skills and processes that go into creating text.**
   Since reading and writing are reciprocal communication processes, it seems intuitive that teaching about one improves the other. That is just what Graham and Hebert found in their meta-analysis; the report highlights these activities as particularly effective (p. 11):

   - teaching the process of writing, text structures for writing, and paragraph and/or sentence construction skills (improves reading comprehension)
   - teaching spelling and sentence construction skills (improves fluency)
   - teaching spelling skills (improves word reading skills)

3. **Increase the amount of writing students do.**
   Again, this feels intuitive; if writing about reading improves comprehension, the more students write, the better their comprehension will be. That's precisely what Graham and Hebert found in their meta-analysis. It's a compelling reminder that we should always include a writing component within our reading units.

Writing About Reading: The Common Core Connection

The Common Core State Standards are in concert with Graham and Hebert's recommendations for using writing to improve reading. The Common Core writing standards for grades 6 to 12 ask students to write about reading in order to develop analytical and inferential thinking, in support of the reading standards discussed on pages 9–13. Note that the writing depends on students' ability to comprehend texts by making logical inferences and selecting details, then using both details and inferences to support their writing. Let's take a look at the relevant writing standards. Again, these are the College and Career Readiness Anchor Standards; be sure to consult your grade-level standards as well.

Writing Standard 1: *Write arguments to support claims in an analysis of substantive topics or texts, using valid reasoning and relevant and sufficient evidence.*

Students can develop a thesis, claim, or position statement based on their reading and argue for or against it using inferences, details, and data from the texts.

Writing Standard 2: *Write informational/explanatory texts to examine and convey complex ideas and information clearly and accurately through the effective selection, organization, and analysis of content.*

These essays can grow out of a study of one text or of multiple texts on the same topic. Students have to select and connect information to demonstrate their comprehension and ability to think about and link ideas across texts.

Writing Standard 9: *Draw evidence from literary or informational texts to support analysis, reflection, and research.*

Students use evidence from the text to back up their analysis of a claim, describe their response to it, or explain it.

Practical Ideas for Integrating Writing About Reading Into Instruction

Here are practical suggestions for integrating writing about reading to improve comprehension that include Graham and Hebert's recommendations along with my own.

- *Summarize.* Students can summarize part or all of texts. Summarizing invites students to think about the text and select important details for writing a summary. On the Resources CD, you'll find reproducible forms that support students as they summarize: Somebody-Wanted-But-So (for literary texts) and Five W's: Who, What, When, Where, Why (for informational texts).

- *Take notes.* Note taking occurs in all subjects. Helping students take notes in their own words is doable as long as students have a purpose for reading. For example, with fiction, students might take notes on the events and people that change the protagonist. For informational text, students can note the points a writer uses to argue a position or explain information.

- *Write answers to questions.* Questions about a text can be teacher-created and/or student-created. I recommend that teachers model questioning techniques that ask students to interpret the facts and not just gather facts. Once teachers model, they can invite students to create their own open-ended questions that depend on the text for support, using verbs such as *how, why, evaluate, compare,* and *contrast.*

- *Plan and write analytical paragraphs and essays.* I have added this type of writing because it trains students to critically analyze texts, supporting the Common Core guidelines. Analysis of texts can include explaining why characters change; how different authors treat the same theme; how setting affects characters' decisions and solutions to problems; or how information can support the solving of problems, such as improving advance warning systems for earthquakes and tornadoes or evacuation plans that can save lives before a natural disaster strikes. You'll find a framework for teaching analytical writing on the Resources CD.

- *Plan and write informative/explanatory paragraphs and essays.* Students can also write to explain the arguments an author used, to explain and/or develop procedures for information they learned, and to inform an audience about information they read and discussed. I have included this type of writing because it depends on students' ability to comprehend and infer from texts and then write about what they learned to help themselves and others deepen their understanding of a complex topic, theme, or idea.

  Analytical writing and informative/explanatory writing also include writing that compares and contrasts multiple texts on the same theme or issue; comparing characters, themes, conflicts; and comparing the history in a piece of historical fiction to the facts about a specific era. (See my *Smart Writing: Practical Units for Teaching Middle School Writers* [2012] for more detail.)

- *Develop spelling and sentence construction skills.* Graham's research shows that bolstering these skills improves reading fluency because students can say and spell more words and learn to write and read complex and compound sentences. Spelling skills also improve decoding if students do word sorting and word study (see *Words Their Way* by Bear, Invernizzi, Templeton, & Johnson, 2011).

In this chapter we've taken a close look at the Common Core State Standards for reading and examined how CCSS conceptions of text complexity and text-dependent comprehension may cause us to shift some of our ideas about reading instruction. We've seen that writing about reading is key for fostering high-level comprehension, a fact the Common Core recognizes and mandates in its writing standards. In the next chapter, I will present the instructional framework I have developed to help students meet the demands of the Common Core.

Professional Study

One of Richard Allington's mantras is that the teacher is the key to student learning and achievement (2000, 2007). To help you reflect on your practice and develop your expertise as a teacher of reading, I end each chapter with questions and prompts. I recommend that you discuss these with a colleague, mentor, or coach, at a department or team meeting, or at a faculty meeting. Conversations will relate to the material presented in a specific chapter and will include professional materials I recommend teachers investigate and discuss. Sharing experiences, ideas, and lessons that worked and didn't work, as well as reading to learn more about best practices, can have powerful effects on our teaching.

DISCUSSION QUESTIONS AND PROMPTS

Since talk clarifies ideas and helps readers build new understandings, use the questions that follow to discuss the information in this chapter. Your conversations may spark new ideas on how to improve your classroom practice.

1. What are the positive points presented about the Common Core? What cautions are raised? Evaluate these cautions.

2. How do you see quantitative and qualitative measures affecting the texts you select and/or students choose? Why is it important to have both measures?

3. Explain text-dependent comprehension. How will this type of reading affect or change your teaching? Why is this kind of text support important to improving students' reading skills?

4. Discuss the research on writing to read and its effect on comprehension. How will this research affect your teaching of reading? Can you carve out more time for writing? Should you offer *Writing to Read* by Graham and Hebert to administrators in your school? Explain why this might help your decision to add more writing to your curriculum.

5. Review the tutorials on the Resources CD.

Professional Books to Investigate

Work with a colleague or several colleagues and decide on a book to read and discuss. You can find discussion guides for Scholastic (*www.Scholastic.com*) and Heinemann (*www.heinemann.com*) books on their Web sites.

- *Teaching Reading in Middle School: A Strategic Approach to Teaching Reading That Improves Comprehension and Thinking*, 2nd edition, by Laura Robb (Scholastic, 2010b)

- *What Really Matters for Struggling Readers: Designing Research-Based Programs*, 3rd edition, by Richard L. Allington (Allyn & Bacon, 2011)

- *What's the Big Idea? Question-Driven Units to Motivate Reading, Writing, and Thinking* by Jim Burke (Heinemann, 2010)

- *Words Their Way: Word Study for Phonics, Vocabulary, and Spelling Instruction*, 5th edition, by Donald R. Bear, Marcia R. Invernizzi, Shane Templeton, and Francine R. Johnston (Allyn & Bacon, 2011)

CHAPTER 2

An Instructional Framework for Meeting the CCSS in Reading

"We're being asked to change so quickly and there's not enough time to think through how the changes affect instruction and our students."

—ELA teacher with ten years of classroom experience

Questions. Teachers and administrators pepper me with questions. And they're all related to the Common Core State Standards in reading. Teachers wonder what makes a text complex and how they can assess students' application of the reading standards. As states and districts interpret the standards and teachers implement them, my advice is not to read the standards as rigid, inflexible guidelines, but to always keep in mind the needs of the children you teach. Below I share some of the questions that teachers and administrators repeatedly ask. I have included the answers I offer.

"Should we give students texts they can't read?"

When students can't read a book, they cannot understand it. They cannot comprehend the information, use information to make inferences from key details, synthesize across texts, evaluate an argument or line of reasoning, or deepen their knowledge of text structure. These are all goals of the CCSS that cannot be met unless the student can read the text. When faced with texts that are too difficult, students' reading becomes halting and disfluent, and they learn that reading is an unpleasant task to be avoided. In fact, when students can't and don't read, their reading skill slips backward instead of moving forward. To accelerate students' progress, a charge of the Common Core, we must find complex texts written at students' instructional levels and do the rigorous reading work with them. At the same time, we must build their vocabulary and background knowledge, and read aloud texts above their instructional levels to tune their ears to the syntax, vocabulary, and sentence length of challenging material.

"Why is building background knowledge now something to be avoided?"

Actually, the Common Core has revised its stance on activating students' prior knowledge—a good decision, especially with all the research on schema theory and the fact that prior knowledge affects comprehension. As P. David Pearson pointed out at the 2012 IRA Conference in Chicago, it's about finding a balance: 15 minutes on building prior knowledge and 30 minutes for sustained silent reading instead of the reverse.

I have developed a student-tested method for building prior knowledge independently before reading short, complex texts; this method also creates motivation for reading the text (see pages 28–31).

"Do we have to stick to the Common Core reading lists for grades five to eight?"

The list was compiled from the Common Core State Standards initiative as an example of texts that meet Common Core guidelines. The word "suggested" before each grade-level list makes it clear that school districts and teachers have the flexibility to select their own materials using quantitative and qualitative measures that meet the guidelines of the Common Core (see pages 14–15). Teachers will find suggestions for read-alouds of literature, poetry, and informational texts helpful but should not feel limited by them. You can find the CCSS list of suggested books by grade level in Appendix B of the English Language Arts Standards, and you can check out some of my suggestions on the Resources CD that accompanies this book. One note of caution: the CCSS list is not multicultural, which is a major drawback. Children need to see themselves in books, and teachers can and should find materials that reflect the populations they teach.

"Does independent reading have to be difficult and challenging?"

For me, independent reading is fun, enjoyable, even better than a movie—and the books are ones I choose! I read mysteries, biographies, informational texts, and historical fiction. No struggle. No frustration. No inability to recall and think across texts. By acquiring reading mileage using books students choose, they enlarge their background knowledge and vocabularies as they continually meet words in diverse contexts. Donald Graves encouraged teachers to get in touch with their literary lives and have middle-school students read for the same reasons we adults choose to read (1989). As we set goals for applying the Common Core State Standards to independent and instructional reading, it's necessary to recognize the importance of meeting individual students' needs in order to motivate, engage, and accelerate their reading skills.

Chapter Overview

In order to improve students' ability to read and write about complex texts and at the same time meet the Common Core State Standards for reading, I have developed a sensible framework for teaching the skills and strategies students need to read informational texts and literature. The lessons are explicit, range from fifteen to twenty-five minutes each day, follow an easy-to-teach pattern, and comprise the instructional piece of your reading block. You'll find these lessons in Chapters 3 to 9. In this chapter, I will present the instructional framework, including the lesson components and instructional routines that will help students develop their reading skills.

The Three-Part Instructional Framework

I've intentionally divided the instructional framework for teaching complex texts into three parts: teacher modeling, student collaborative practice, and independent student work. The progression of lessons from teacher modeling to student practice follows the gradual release model and provides the time and practice students need to develop proficiency with Common Core skills. It also allows plenty of opportunities for teachers to monitor and assess students' progress.

I have created seven units based on genre and built around a theme. Each unit contains five short, complex texts that are used for teacher modeling and student practice—with the exception of the short story and poetry units, which contain fewer texts. The thematic aspect allows students to develop vocabulary and background knowledge and have collaborative discussions even if they read different texts; I provide both on-level and below-level texts for the student practice lessons.

Let's take a closer look at each part of the framework.

Texts for Each Unit

- 1 anchor text for teacher modeling
- 1 grade-level text for guided practice
- 1 below-level text for guided practice
- 1 grade-level text for independent practice and assessment
- 1 below-level text for independent practice and assessment

1. **Teacher Modeling** Read aloud an anchor text, modeling the skills and strategies necessary to meet the target Common Core reading standards. For each unit, you will

   - develop a concept map to build vocabulary around the theme
   - model how to use the text to build prior knowledge
   - demonstrate how to close read and reread to identify key details, make logical inferences, understand vocabulary, and clarify confusing parts of the text
   - think aloud as you find themes and central ideas and apply other reading strategies
   - discuss genre characteristics of the anchor text
   - foster collaborative discussions about the anchor text
   - guide students to write a paragraph that argues a position or explains a concept based on the anchor text
   - model how to answer short, multiple-choice quiz questions

   As you model and interact with students, they will develop and enlarge their mental models of the CCSS reading standards and skills. Students will observe how to use close reading to solve reading problems; they'll experience how multiple readings improve comprehension and recall, and they'll deepen their understanding of how to use text details to make logical inferences.

2. **Student Collaborative Practice** Using a new text selection—either at grade level or below level based on their reading skill—students work with partners to practice the skills and strategies you modeled with the anchor text. They will

   - add to the concept map
   - use the text to build prior knowledge
   - close read to figure out new words and clarify confusing parts

Students Who Can't Comprehend a Text Independently

When students can't comprehend a text, they can't learn from it. For these students, try the following:

- Read aloud the below-grade-level text.
- Work on close reading of difficult words.
- Working with small groups or individual students, model how you figure out word meanings, and gradually release the responsibility to students.
- Listen to partners discuss and help them find the parts in the text that support their reasoning.

Modeling text-dependent comprehension and the thinking and problem-solving strategies good readers use can build students' self-confidence and provide them with a powerful mental model of reading.

The key to their progress, however, lies in the amount of independent reading these students complete. Help them find books they can read with 99–100 percent accuracy. Over the course of a year, encourage them to read 40 to 60 books that they choose themselves. Include magazines, blogs, e-books, and Internet articles in the mix; it's fine if the texts are short, as students will turn to longer texts once they have the stamina to concentrate, and they will develop stamina by independently reading texts they enjoy.

- reread and close read to identify key details and make logical inferences
- explore genre characteristics of the text
- engage in discussions about the text, the theme, and the central ideas
- plan and write a paragraph about the text
- complete a short, multiple-choice quiz on the text
- choose one quiz item and write a paragraph defending their answer using text-based evidence

Partnerships are valuable because they can increase students' self-confidence as students support one another. As pairs work together, you can circulate around the room answering questions and helping students find text details and make inferences that support their discussions and comprehension. It's also the ideal time to note which students will require one-to-one conferences to develop their skills.

3. **Independent Student Work** Provide students with new text at their instruction-al reading level. For each unit, I provide two selections to choose from, one for on- and above-level students, and one for students who can't read and comprehend the grade-level text independently. Students work through the same tasks but this time independently, allowing you to evaluate what they understand and to identify areas that require scaffolding. Students will

- use the text to build prior knowledge
- read and reread the text
- close read to figure out new words and clarify confusing parts
- reread and close read to identify key details and make logical inferences
- write a summary of the text and/or a paragraph that explains an idea or argues for a claim using text evidence
- complete a word map about the unit's theme
- write a paragraph or essay about the unit's theme, drawing on multiple texts (optional)
- receive scaffolding if needed
- complete a self-evaluation (optional—recommended three times per year)

At the end of each unit, I provide a Scaffolding Suggestions chart for intervention, follow-up teaching ideas, and ideas for extending students' thinking by asking them to use texts they've read to better understand community and world issues. You'll find each Scaffolding Suggestions chart on the Resources CD, along with a list of books related to the unit that you can investigate. There is also a Scaffolding Suggestions chart on the Resources CD with ideas for helping students with their writing.

Lesson Components

Each of the seven units in this book has the same lesson components, which I will describe here. Instructional routines are described in the next section.

Concept Map: Each unit is built around a theme or concept, and I suggest a concept to use as the basis of a concept map. You can create it on chart paper or on a whiteboard; you'll revisit it several times throughout the unit, so be sure it's easy to access. Concept mapping introduces students to denotative (literal) and connotative (associated) meanings of words. See a sample concept map on page 28.

Short Texts: Each unit includes five short texts, one that serves as an anchor text for teacher modeling—two at different readability levels for guided practice and two at different readability levels for independent practice. (The short story and poetry units are structured slightly differently.)

Text Complexity Grids: For each text, I provide a text complexity grid that evaluates quantitative and qualitative measures that contribute to a text's complexity. See the example grid below. In addition to the Lexile® measure, the grid provides my assessment of its qualitative measures: the content and vocabulary, background-knowledge demands, inferential thinking demands, and so on, so you can consider a wide range of data when deciding which students can read and learn from a text.

Text-Specific Discussion Prompts: Each selection in the teacher modeling and guided practice sections of a unit has text-specific discussion prompts that ask students to make inferences, find themes and central ideas using details from the text, and think deeply about the text.

Multiple-Choice Quiz: Each text (with the exception of the short stories, poems, and independent practice texts) has a five-item multiple-choice quiz that helps students practice for state tests and provides you with a quick and easy assessment of students' text-dependent comprehension. Questions are all high level, and I encourage teachers to have students note on the Quiz Answer Sheet which paragraph or paragraphs they used to find the answer. Doing this builds students' ability to use the text to pinpoint the best response to a question by skimming and rereading. I invite students to choose one of their answers and defend it in a short paragraph. The Quiz Answer Sheet has guidelines for planning and drafting the paragraph.

Text Complexity Grid

Selection from *The Great Fire* by Jim Murphy
Lexile®: 1000
Text Complexity: 1 = Accessible to 5 = Challenging

QUALITATIVE	1	2	3	4	5
Knowledge demands				X	
Author's purpose				X	
Meaning			X		
Text structure				X	
Language/vocabulary				X	
Concepts				X	
Inferential thinking demands				X	

Independent Practice and Assessment: To wrap-up each unit (except short story and poetry), I offer three ways to assess students. You can have students write a summary of the selection or a paragraph that explains an idea or supports a claim. You'll also find a Word Map for students to complete that assesses their knowledge of the concept/theme studied throughout the unit. Students can complete all three assessments, or you can choose which ones students do. For each type of paragraph, you'll find a rubric for grading on the Resources CD.

Book Lists: On the Resources CD you'll find a list of books that you can use if you have choices when developing your reading curriculum for the CCSS.

Instructional Routines

In each unit, students will work though the following instructional routines to develop their comprehension skills. Of course, you will initiate and model all of these routines first, reteaching as necessary.

Building a Concept Map

You begin the concept map by writing the concept in the middle of a web. Students add words and phrases to the map both before reading and throughout the unit, always explaining how the word or phrase connects to the concept. The concept map enlarges students' vocabulary and their understanding of the concept. The words and phrases on the map can also provide additional writing ideas, as long as students select ideas that relate to the text and that the text can support.

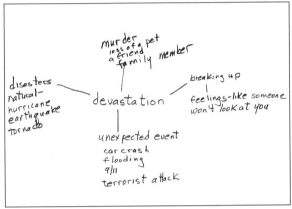

Early in the unit

Building Prior Knowledge

After proponents of the Common Core announced that teachers should not spend time activating and/or constructing students' prior knowledge, I felt frustrated and angry. Why? Because we know that prior knowledge—stored in the brain in schema—improves

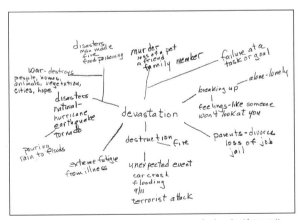

Later in the unit

students' comprehension (Anderson, 1984; Anderson & Pearson, 1984; Duke & Pearson, 2002; Marzano, 2004; Robb, 2008). Once my anger and frustration abated, I decided to develop a method that would put students in charge of building prior knowledge and setting a purpose for reading. This method develops middle-school students' independence and can support the reading they complete on mandated tests. The sample lesson on pages 29–31 and the student handout on page 261 outline the steps for you to model when teaching a unit and offers students the practice they need to absorb the strategy.

The Prior-Knowledge Strategy in Action

To demonstrate the effectiveness of this strategy, I will show how I work through the process using an excerpt from *Years of Dust: The Story of the Dust Bowl* by Albert Marrin (see the Resources CD for the complete selection). Here's how I think aloud for students:

> *The title is* Years of Dust: The Story of the Dust Bowl. *I don't know much about the Dust Bowl, but I do know the Rose Bowl football game and parade—but I don't think that will help me here. I will read slowly because this is new information to me. I will read the first and last paragraphs and the quiz items and talk to myself about what I have learned. Then I'll reread the first and last paragraphs because rereading improves recall and will help me remember more so I can jot down notes in my own words in a bulleted list. Writing the list in my own words or paraphrasing shows my understanding of the material.*

Years of Dust Excerpts

First Paragraph:

In April 1935, a reporter, Robert Geiger, set out by car across the Great Plains. As he headed east, heat waves made the air shimmer, causing him to squint. Temperatures rose to over one hundred degrees in the shade. There was nothing green visible in the fields; obviously no rain had fallen for many weeks. Then, while driving across Oklahoma, Geiger encountered a "black blizzard," an immense dust storm. He had never imagined, let alone experienced, anything like it before. It was as if nature had gone insane.

Last paragraph:

Depending on the season, the wind brings scorching heat and numbing cold. Summer winds whip out of the Mexican desert. Plains temperatures soar past one hundred degrees in the shade, and stay there for weeks, with no relief even at night. The dry heat is a killer. Streams vanish, leaving only a channel littered with dry stones. Animals die of thirst. Plants shrivel up, as if caught in the blast of a gigantic furnace. In summertime, railroads might have to stop service because the heat expands the steel tracks, putting them out of alignment.

QUIZ

Years of Dust: The Story of the Dust Bowl

Directions: *Circle the best answer.*

1. Why did Geiger coin the term "Dust Bowl"?

    a. to grab the public's imagination

    b. to capture the scale of the disaster by comparing it to a gala event

    c. to make fun of sports

    d. to describe how the Plains looked like a "black blizzard"

2. The phrases "darkness envelopes," "evil spirit," "billowing clouds of dust," and "howling winds" evoke what kind of mood?

    a. foreboding and threatening

    b. optimistic and positive

    c. somber and anxious

    d. tense and nervous

3. The word <u>tormented</u> in paragraph 8 means

    a. enchanted.

    b. exhausted.

    c. terrified.

    d. concerned.

4. Why do the winds blow so fiercely in the Plains, reaching over 100 miles an hour?

    a. There are no trees to block the wind.

    b. Temperatures vary so widely, reaching 100 degrees in the summer and freezing in winter.

    c. Miles of shoreline feed the winds.

    d. The area is unpopulated.

5. What does the author mean when he writes that dust storms "tore at the human spirit"?

    a. The dust got in people's lungs and made them ill.

    b. The storms seemed supernatural.

    c. People could think of nothing else except the dust.

    d. The storms frightened people and took away their ability to earn a living.

I read the paragraphs and quiz items aloud, then briefly retell, jotting notes as I go; you can write on chart paper or type on a computer and display on a whiteboard. Here are my notes:

- Takes place in 1935.
- Geiger, a reporter, is driving across the Great Plains.
- Over 100 degrees in shade—heat and sun make Geiger squint.
- "Black blizzards" happen in Oklahoma—a new experience for Geiger.
- "Black blizzard" is nature going insane.
- Extreme weather: brutal heat or extreme cold in different seasons.
- For weeks dry heat and no rain—it kills animals, plants shrivel, trains stop because tracks swell.
- Nothing green in the fields

I wrap up my think-aloud:

Now I have information that can help me comprehend the text. I know that the Dust Bowl has high temperatures and drought that can cause dust storms or "black blizzards." There is no green in the fields; I can infer that farmers are desperate because their animals die, their crops are ruined, and they cannot sell these to earn money. Goods cannot come into towns or go out when the trains don't run. Nature controls life. This background information will help me set a purpose for reading the entire selection, and my purpose and prior knowledge will deepen my comprehension of the entire piece.

Based on my reading and retelling, I want to set the following purpose for reading. From what I read about black blizzards, I want to find out what the Dust Bowl has to do with black blizzards. I also want to know why the extreme weather is dangerous to animals, people, and nature. I'll read the entire text with those questions in mind; they will help focus my reading.

Students can build their own prior knowledge and set purposes for reading with independent reading of long texts as well. With fiction and nonfiction, they read the title, study the cover illustrations, and read the first chapter. Not only does the strategy develop independence with learning, but it also offers students a way to build prior knowledge on a topic they know little to nothing about.

Rereading, Retelling, and Close Reading

Researchers support rereading as a fix-up strategy, and if rereading doesn't repair comprehension, students can close read to unpack meaning. A close reading invites

Tips for Teaching Students to Set a Purpose for Reading

Here are a few suggestions for showing students how to use a selection's title, their preview of a text, their written notes, and the unit's concept to set a purpose for reading.

Turn the title into a question(s):

- Why is the piece called *Years of Dust*?
- What kinds of stories will I learn about the Dust Bowl?

Use prior-knowledge notes to set a purpose(s):

- What does the Dust Bowl have to do with "black blizzard"?
- How do dust storms change people's lives?
- Why is extreme weather dangerous to animals, people, and nature?
- Why does the author say that nature has gone insane?

Use the concept map's theme to set a purpose:

- How does the concept of devastation relate to information in *Years of Dust*?

Notice the variety of purposes that students can develop. This is advantageous because with diverse purposes, discussions will be richer, as students' interpretations of the text will highlight different details and logical inferences.

students to study a confusing passage, sentence, or word by using context clues in the text. In addition, retelling can support students' recall of details in short, complex informational texts (Allington 2002a, 2011; CCSS Initiative, 2010; Fountas & Pinnell, 2006; Lipson, 2007; Tierney & Readence, 2000; Robb, 2010b). When I read a challenging text, rereading supports my recall of details, and once I have the details, I can use them to infer and find themes and central ideas. Rereading takes me deeper into a text and shows me language and ideas I didn't perceive after a first reading. To encourage rereading, the lessons in Chapters 3 to 9 ask students to reread and skim.

> As you model how to apply the CCSS reading standards, it's important to integrate rereading into your mini-lessons.

I tell students that reading a text several times is similar to their reasons for viewing a movie more than once. "It gets better every time I see it [the movie]," a seventh grader told me. "I see and hear things I didn't the first time." Middle-school students have definite reasons for re-viewing a movie. We need to give them the reasons for rereading, and the most effective way to do this is to integrate rereading into the lessons students complete.

Each time students read a chunk of a short or a long text, I ask them to first read to get the gist—a general idea of what the text is about—and complete an in-the-head retelling to make sure they are understanding the information. At this point, if there's little recall, I invite the student to reread, working on the hunch that the student's mind was somewhere else during the first reading. If there's still little recall after the second reading, then perhaps the text is too difficult and this is the ideal time to negotiate a change with the student.

Each unit has opportunities for students to practice close reading of a text to figure out the meaning of unfamiliar words or challenging passages; I've also included a handout for close reading that students can refer to while reading on page 262 and on the Resources CD.

Writing About Reading

In each unit, you'll explore a note-taking and drafting process for writing about the text that supports developing as well as advanced readers and writers; such planning and thinking an idea through is the foundation of good writing (Graham & Harris, 2005, 2007; Robb, 2010b, 2012). According to Graham, Harris, Perin, and Robb, students who put effort into the planning stage of writing—taking notes and collecting ideas before beginning to write—are engaging in deep thinking about a topic. Having thoughts and ideas on paper frees students to think about organizing their ideas and writing well. A seventh-grade special-education student said during a conference: "If my ideas are on paper, it's easier to write."

Chapter 3 serves as the launching unit; all the instructional routines and lesson components are introduced and taught there, so be sure to work through that unit first. Then you may select units that fit your curriculum and teach them in any order.

Fitting the Lessons Into Your Reading Block

The genre-based units provided in this book fit into the instructional part of your reading block. In 15 to 25 minutes a day, these lessons can help you teach students how to meet the CCSS by showing them how you think about texts. Use the remaining class time to teach your school's curriculum, provide extra support for students who need it, allow for independent reading, and confer with students.

I've designed the units to be flexible; if you do one lesson a day, each unit takes about four weeks. However, I also provide suggestions for combining lessons, and you can adapt them to suit your students' needs.

Integrating Your Required Curriculum

Here are some suggestions for integrating your required curriculum into a CCSS-aligned instructional approach. The 15- to 25-minute lessons in Chapters 3 to 9 are the instructional part of your reading class. The remaining time can be used in a variety of ways. Below, I've presented possibilities to choose from.

Basal Anthologies: If students all read at grade level, then use the anthology selections, but have students practice skills and strategies needed to meet the Common Core State Standards.

If your students have diverse instructional reading levels, consider using the basal selections as anchor texts for instructional read-alouds that model how to apply CCSS skills and strategies to different genres. Then, offer students complex texts within a genre at their instructional level that can improve their reading skill because the texts are accessible.

Required Book Studies: Middle schools often require teachers to use specific books with their classes; these texts can be fiction or informational. Considering the range of reading the Common Core recommends for middle school, required whole-class books do not meet the standard. Missing from these traditional types of texts are essays and functional writing.

One text will not meet the needs of all students, especially developing readers who cannot learn from a grade-level text. Adjustments to this type of curriculum include expanding the kinds of informational texts students read and finding alternative complex texts for students reading far below grade level.

Reading Workshop: For me, reading workshop is the ideal class organization for middle-school students because they have choices and responsibilities and can form partnerships that can improve text-dependent comprehension. Reading workshop gives you time to confer with individuals, pairs, or small groups and scaffold their reading to accelerate their progress. In a workshop, you can teach the genre-based lessons in Chapters 3 to 9 and then have students read long, complex texts at their instructional levels, as well as complete independent reading. I recommend that all instructional reading occur at school so you can observe, confer with, and support students; independent reading makes ideal homework.

At the same time, increase the number of long, complex texts available for students in your class library and your school's bookroom (see the Resources CD for a list of suggestions for finding funds to enlarge your class library). For more details on this type of differentiation, refer to my book, *Differentiating Reading Instruction*: *How to Teach Reading to Meet the Needs of Each Student*, 2008.

The Role of Independent Reading

In order to accelerate reading achievement, students need excellent instruction to help them learn from and think with complex texts; that's what the lessons in this book provide. In addition, it is critical that they complete a large amount of independent reading (Allington, 2011; Brozo, Valtin, Garbe, Sulkunen, Shield, & Pandian, 2012; Guthrie, Wigfield, Metsala, & Cox, 1999; Krashen, 2004; Robb, 2010b). To move forward and close reading gaps with their peers, students need to read 30 to 50 books a year at their independent reading level. Research has shown that students' reading achievement is directly linked to the amount of independent reading they complete. Those students reading below grade level can benefit from reading more than their peers who read at or above grade level. Independent reading materials can include traditional books, e-books, online articles, magazines, comics, plays, and graphic novels.

Finding Challenging and Motivating Complex Texts for Developing Readers

Recently, I did a model lesson in a school in Virginia with six special education students in fifth grade. The students were reading texts recommended by the state department of education—black-and-white texts that teachers photocopied for the group. The texts were not rich enough for students to find layers of meaning, the illustrations were dull and uninviting, and students weren't able to infer using them. This was, according to teachers, an inexpensive way to provide reading material for these students. Moreover, many felt that even if they had unlimited funds, it would be tough to find books for developing readers—students who need practice with below-grade-level texts—because instructionally they are three or more years below grade level.

It's true that finding materials for developing readers is difficult. Giving them books written for primary students can destroy their self-confidence and increase feelings of hopelessness about ever catching up with their on-grade-level peers. Here are some resources that can support your search for appropriate materials.

Curricular Materials

1. *Reading Advantage.* This is a curriculum published for developing middle- and high-school readers. In addition to instructional materials, kits contain magazines on motivating topics and a set of twelve books for independent reading. Books and magazines can be purchased separately; readability levels range from 2.0 to 8.0; interest levels are geared for grades 5 to 10. For more information, go to *www. greatsource.com* and search for "reading advantage."

2. *On the Record.* This is a reading, writing, and thinking curriculum for seventh and eighth grades, designed to engage students in thinking and writing about reading. There are mentor texts and reader's choice books; each book contains two contemporary biographies that include primary documents relating to four platforms about social justice: Defining Self, Becoming Resilient, Engaging Others, and Building Capacity. Dr. Alfred Tatum and Erin Gruwell are academic advisors for this curriculum, which also includes stretch texts—for improving students' reading of short, complex texts—and a rich online component. For more information, go to *www.scholastic.com/ontherecord*.

3. *XBooks.* This is a set of highly motivating books that align with the Common Core State Standards and stretch texts that improve students' reading of short, complex materials. Ideal for readers who struggle in middle school, *XBooks* is organized into five motivating themes: Strange, Tyrants, Medical, Forensics, and Total War. Each theme contains a mentor text and three additional reader's choice books that relate to the theme. Jeff Wilhelm and I served as academic advisors and helped develop easy-to-teach guidelines and a rich online component that will engage students, build academic and content vocabulary, and improve students' inferential thinking and writing. For more information, go to *www.scholastic.com/xbooks*.

4. *Action Magazine:* This magazine contains high-interest content for developing middle-school readers. Twelve biweekly issues contain true teen stories, a debate feature, Readers Theater plays, and much more. For more information, go to *http://classroommagazines.scholastic.com*.

5. *Choosing to Read: Connecting Middle Schoolers to Books* by Joan Kindig (2012). This professional book contains rich lists of books for a wide range of reading levels and interests. It's an invaluable resource!

Online Resources

1. **Bearport Publishing: Hi-Lo Books for Reluctant Middle-School Readers**
   Choices include high-interest nonfiction and fiction.
   http://www.bearportpublishing.com

2. **Scholastic's Book Wizard**
   Enables you to search for books by Lexile® measure, Guided Reading Level, topic, and genre. Each book has a summary of its content.
   http://www.scholastic.com/bookwizard

3. **Middle Grades Reading Network High Interest/Low Readability Books**
   Includes readability levels three, four, and five, but books will interest older middle-school students. Search for "Middle Grades Reading Network High Interest/Low Readability Books."

4. **High Interest/Low Reading Level Book Lists**

    Each book listed is matched with a reading level and interest level.
    http://www.schoolonwheels.org/pdfs/3328/Hi-Lo-Book-List.pdf

In addition to having books available for developing, proficient, and advanced readers, another way to boost comprehension is to invite students to write about reading.

Assessment

You can assess everything students do in your classes: written journal work, paired and small-group conversations, book talks, book reviews, writing about reading, book logs, homework, long-term projects, literature circles, research writing, quizzes, reading tests, notes based on your observations, conferences, and online responses on blogs and wikis.

Before continuing, ask yourself the two questions about assessment that follow. I find that having an in-the-head conversation with myself about topics such as assessment helps me clarify my practice with the goal of supporting students.

1. What do I need to assess to meet my school's grading requirements? Grading is a reality and schools have policies that teachers must follow. Considering the list above, you have plenty of opportunities for grading, although I hope that not everything on the list finds its way into your grade book—that can lead to grades taking precedence over the real purposes of assessment.

2. How can I use assessments to make instructional decisions for the class, small groups, and individual students? A letter or number grade will not answer this question, because the purpose of this type of formative assessment is to support students' progress and growth as readers and to adjust lessons to respond to students' needs. You can learn more about this type of assessment in my book *Assessments for Differentiating Reading Instruction* (2009).

Using Conferences to Assess Instructional Reading

Conferences are an excellent way of observing and assessing students' reading skills. Be a good listener during a conference and encourage students to explain their responses. Tell students your goal for the conference is to assess their application of the Common Core standard they have been practicing. Provide students with feedback based on the goal; feedback should first point out what a student has done well, and then pose a question that will focus the student on an area related to the goal.

For a detailed discussion of conferring, see the second edition of *Teaching Reading in Middle School*, pages 267–282 (Robb, 2010b).

For example, I might offer this feedback to a student about our conference on text structure: *You explained that the piece was in chronological order and summarized the key events in this informational text in clear, sequential statements* [positive feedback]. Then: *Can you explain how chronological order supported your comprehension of the life cycle of a frog?* [question that focuses students on an area to think about]. If the student cannot explain the "how," prompt her with questions. Your goal is to elicit the response from the student and not quickly jump in and give advice. To support the student, remind her of lessons you modeled and texts used for practice. If this doesn't work, model for the student why chronological order supports comprehension of a frog's life cycle. Then, schedule time for more practice with a peer or with you. Schedule another conference if you feel this is necessary.

On the Resources CD, I include conference forms that monitor progress with the CCSS for informational texts, for literature, and for writing about reading. You can use part of one of the text selections from the second or third part of the lesson cycle to assess students. For developing readers, you will have to find texts at their instructional level—texts they can read and learn from. The key point here is for students to use a text to think aloud, so you can observe their thinking process. Below is a conference form I

Conference Form: Inferring & Finding Themes With Informational Texts

Directions: Ask the student to read the selection silently, select details and use these to make logical inferences .

Text used: *Catherine the Great*

Observations *see attached*

The student can answer these questions/prompts:

_____ What makes an inference a logical inference?

_____ State two logical inferences you made using the selection.

_____ What text details did you use to help you make each inference?

_____ What are two themes you found in the selection? Provide the text evidence that enabled you to determine themes.

_____ How does the title enable you to figure out a theme? Explain.

Teacher's Feedback:

- Complemented on her recalling the inference the group discussed.

Notes About the Student's Ability to Infer & Find Themes

Needs support and practice with inferring and identifying themes

Check one : _____ Work with peer. ✓ Work with teacher.

_____ Can work independently.

Follow-up Conference on *3 follow up conf. in class* *schedule early morning – 20 min. meeting*

Additional Comments and Observations
need to model, prompt student, and practice, practice.
For last 2 class conf. – try working with a peer – feel the exchanges could be beneficial

---

Unsure of what an inference or logical inference is.

Unable to infer on own. Recalled that during discussion an inference was that (her) (Sophie's) mother was ambitious Mom wanted her [Sophie] to be a queen.

Could not think of an inference on own.

Unable to state themes.

Title – Maybe a theme is that she did good for people to be great.

Conference form and notes

filled out during a five-minute meeting I had with a sixth grader to assess his ability to infer with informational text and support inferences with text details.

[handwritten: Redo Reading Forms for Gr. 7.]

Monitor and Manage Independent Reading

Choice is the heart and soul of independent reading. Offering students choice allows them to select materials on topics that interest them and genres they enjoy. Help students understand that independent reading should be fun and enjoyable—texts they can read with 99–100 percent accuracy.

> To read more about class libraries, student activities for independent reading, book talking, and book reviewing see the Resources CD; also see the second edition of *Teaching Reading in Middle School*, pages 255–269 (Robb, 2010b).

For students to have access to books, be sure to continually build the collection in your classroom library (see the Resources CD for suggestions). A rich class library enables students to find new reading material. Encourage students to choose two to four independent reading texts and store these in a cubby or on a bookshelf in your room. Read more about monitoring and managing independent reading in Chapter 10 and on the Resources CD.

Using Conferences to Assess Independent Reading

I try to discuss an independent reading book with each student two or three times a year—and complete my first round of conferences by the end of the first six weeks. These are brief, three- or four-minute meetings. If your class is self-contained, you can do this more often. If you have 100 or more students, then twice a year is a reasonable goal. These conferences, along with the conferences that monitor students' ability to apply the Common Core reading standards to instructional and challenging texts, can help you assess and evaluate students' progress.

[handwritten: Conference every trimester 1st by 6 weeks.]

Professional Study Conversations

Engage in a discussion with a peer partner, your team, or your department about the elements of the lesson cycle you explored in this chapter. Return to this discussion after you have taught your first lesson cycle, and again after you've taught two or three additional units, to share adjustments, the writing students completed, and the parts of the lessons that worked well for you and students.

Professional Books to Investigate

- *Assessments for Differentiating Reading Instruction* by Laura Robb (Scholastic, 2009)
- *Differentiating Reading Instruction: How to Teach Reading to Meet the Needs of Each Student* by Laura Robb (Scholastic, 2008)
- *The Differentiated Classroom: Responding to the Needs of All Learners* by Carol A. Tomlinson (ASCD, 1999)

On the Resources CD

- Tutorial: Applying the Common Core Reading Standards for Literature
- Tutorial: Applying the Common Core Reading Standards for Informational Texts

CHAPTER 3

Reading Informational Texts

"My students read novels, especially fantasy," an eighth-grade teacher told me during a pre-coaching meeting she and I had. "We don't have many informational texts in our reading resource room to choose from, and I'm not totally comfortable teaching them." Middle-school teachers around the country have similar concerns because novel units have long been the steady diet of middle-school students. Researchers such as Nell Duke (2003, 2004) and Donna Ogle (2007, 2011) have called for a greater focus on reading informational texts, a call that is reinforced by the expectations of the Common Core State Standards. Researchers agree that a shift in emphasis from fiction to informational texts will enable middle-school students to meet the challenges of high school and college reading, as well as prepare for the type of reading they will encounter when they enter the workforce

(Beck & McKeown, 2006; Duke, 2004; Duke & Pearson, 2002; Guthrie, Wigfield, & Klauda, 2012).

This shift is the primary reason I recommend beginning with a unit that guides students through reading informational text. This unit will serve as your launching unit, introducing many of the routines and strategies you will use throughout the other instructional units in this book.

The Launching Unit

I've organized this launching unit around the theme of devastation; all units are built around high-interest themes to facilitate differentiation and thinking across texts, a key CCSS goal. As you model and think aloud about the anchor text—an excerpt from Jim Murphy's *The Great Fire*—students will observe how you apply the skills and strategies necessary for meeting the CCSS for informational texts (see pages 9–13 for a full discussion of the standards):

- making logical inferences
- finding themes
- understanding text structure
- pinpointing words and phrases in a piece that connect to themes and set a tone or mood
- using discussion questions to help students recall details, make logical inferences, and identify themes

Close Reading

During the launching unit and all other units you teach, you will model close reading, a strategy the CCSS values for teaching students to access complex texts. I've prepared a student handout, Close Reading Guidelines, that students can use as a reference after you've modeled the strategy and provided guided practice opportunities (see page 262 and the Resources CD for a reproducible copy of these guidelines and page 53 for how I introduce them during the lesson).

A Word About Text Features

Unlike history, math, and science textbooks that contain features such as diagrams, maps, charts, and so on, the selections in this unit are literary nonfiction and follow the CCSS guidelines pertaining to informational texts that integrate text structures such as cause-effect, sequencing, and description. To support your use of textbooks and articles rich in text features such as diagrams, maps, charts, and so on, see the Resources CD, where you'll find a list of these features along with explanations that you can use to introduce and/or review the features with students.

Text Structure and Purpose

Informational texts have four purposes: The text can argue for a position or opinion; present information on a topic; provide procedures or directions; or explain the why behind an event, such as a hurricane or war. Short informational texts and informational books can contain one or several of the following organizational structures: description, sequence or chronological order, problem-solution, question-answer, cause-effect, and compare-contrast.

Scheduling

Each unit in this book can be completed in four weeks; I wanted each lesson to take 15 to 25 minutes so that teachers with 45-minute class periods have time each day to return to their district's curriculum or hold a reading workshop. If you have longer class periods or are on a block schedule, then feel free to combine lessons so that you can complete units in about three weeks.

Each unit section opens with a text complexity grid for the anchor text and student selections. *All text selections are on the Resources CD.*

> Here are lessons you can easily combine. These are only suggestions. Combine those lessons that you believe will best support your students.
>
> - Lessons 4 and 5
> - Lessons 6 and 7
> - Lessons 9 and 10
> - Lessons 14 and 15

Model How to Read Informational Text

In this first set of lessons, you will use an anchor text to model key skills and strategies that readers use when tackling complex informational texts. Since this is the launching unit, you will also introduce several routines and strategies that are incorporated into all the units, such as building prior knowledge from the text, creating a concept map, close reading, making logical inferences from key details, engaging in pair-share collaborative discussions, and analytical writing.

Text Complexity Grid

Selection from *The Great Fire* by Jim Murphy
Lexile®: 1130
Text Complexity: 1 = Accessible to 5 = Challenging

QUALITATIVE	1	2	3	4	5
Knowledge demands				X	
Author's purpose				X	
Meaning			X		
Text structure				X	
Language/vocabulary				X	
Concepts				X	
Inferential thinking demands					X

LESSON 1

Getting Ready to Read

In this first lesson, you introduce a protocol that enables readers to generate knowledge about a topic by strategically previewing the text. You also begin a concept map for the theme of devastation, which you'll add to throughout the unit.

Materials

- Excerpt from *The Great Fire*, displayed on the whiteboard from the Resources CD
- Students' notebooks
- Building Prior Knowledge handout (see page 261 and the Resources CD), class set
- Chart paper and markers for taking notes and generating the concept map

Teaching the Lesson

1. Discuss with students why it is important to build prior knowledge before reading an informational text. Point out that sometimes they will encounter an informational passage in a testing or other situation where they will have to tackle the text with no teacher or peer support, so it's important that they know how to build prior knowledge from the text itself in case they know nothing about the topic. I say something like this:

   We've talked before about why it's important to build prior knowledge before reading a new text. What are some of the reasons? [Take a few student comments.] *When we read a text together as a class, I often provide some background knowledge for you, or you might work with a peer to discuss the topic and share information. But sometimes you'll be asked to read a text on a new topic in a situation where you won't have a teacher or friend to help, such as when you're taking a test. So today we're going to learn about a way to work with the text itself to generate some background knowledge so that you are better prepared to read and understand the text.*

2. Distribute the Building Prior Knowledge handout and display the excerpt from *The Great Fire*.

3. Model how to use the steps on the handout to build prior knowledge independently. Here's what I say:

   As you'll see on the handout, the first thing you do is read the title to set your reading rate. I'll read slowly since I don't know much about the Great Fire. Next, read the first paragraph if it is long, or the first two paragraphs if they're short; then read the last paragraph and any questions or discussion prompts

> You can display both pages of the excerpt by going to the View menu in Adobe Reader and selecting Page Display, then Two Page View.

at the end of the text. This step is especially important when you're taking an exam. Okay, I'll show you how this works for this excerpt from The Great Fire. *Follow as I read these parts aloud to build my background knowledge.*

4. Read aloud the first two paragraphs, the last paragraph, and the quiz items. Then model how you retell the details you remember from the text, jotting down notes as you go. Here's what I say and write on chart paper after previewing the text for my seventh-grade class:

The author says Chicago was a city ready to burn. It contained many buildings made out of wood—even buildings that didn't look like they were actually wood underneath. In the poor and middle-class sections, people lived close together, so the wooden structures were close together, and residential areas had businesses intermixed with homes. The O'Learys had built an addition to their home, so their lot was mostly wood. The last paragraph says a gusty wind spread flames from the O'Learys to their neighbors—thankfully, a neighbor woke them up and they escaped.

- In the late 1800s Chicago was ready to burn because most of the buildings were made of wood.
- A fire started in Chicago in a fence and shed. Winds were gusting, so the fire could spread.
- The word *smoldered* might have to do with the fire.
- The title means that at this time in Chicago there was a great fire.

5. Ask students to add any other ideas to the list from the text. Here's what my seventh-grade students added:

- Even if the outsides of buildings looked like marble, stone, tin, or copper—this was just a painted covering. Under this, they were made of wood.
- Wood burns.

6. Tell students that today the class will start a concept map by thinking about the concept of devastation in *The Great Fire*. They will revisit the map as they read other informational texts in the coming weeks (see Chapter 2, page 28, for more about concept maps). Write "devastation" on a sheet of chart paper and invite students to turn to a partner and take two or three minutes to discuss what they know about the meaning of this word. It's okay if no words or phrases come to mind. The class will continue to build the map after listening to *The Great Fire*. Most associations students make with *devastation* will be connotations. The denotative meaning is "destruction."

7. Ask pairs to share the words and phrases they discussed. Accept any word or phrase that students offer as long as they can link it to the concept; write their words and phrases on the concept map. For example, a seventh-grade girl offered breaking up with her boyfriend; another girl suggested parents divorcing. Each clearly explained how these were devastating. I suggest that at this point in the lesson you keep the focus open-ended, to broaden students' idea of devastation.

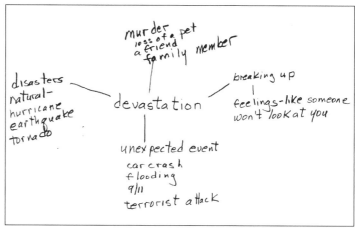

Early in the unit

8. Add a few phrases of your own to get students focused on fire. For example, I wrote "fire burns buildings; fire hurts people; fire destroys." Then I asked students to discuss how these phrases related to devastation.

9. Read aloud the selection from Jim Murphy's *The Great Fire* so students get the gist or some of the ideas in this piece. I tell students that this is a first reading, and their purpose is to get an overview and a few of the ideas and details in *The Great Fire*.

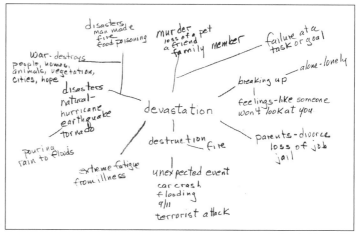

Later in the unit

10. Ask students to pair-share and discuss the gist of *The Great Fire*. Then invite partners to share their thoughts with the class.

Wrap-Up

Provide positive feedback on students' listening skills and their contributions to the concept map.

Taking the time to have students connect their ideas to the concept can enlarge students' prior knowledge, vocabulary, and analytical thinking.

Identifying Genre Characteristics and Setting Purposes

In this lesson, students explore characteristics of informational texts and set a purpose for the second reading of *The Great Fire*.

Materials

- Excerpt from *The Great Fire*, displayed on the whiteboard from the Resources CD
- Students' copies of Building Prior Knowledge handout
- Students' notebooks
- Prior-knowledge notes generated in Lesson 1
- Concept map started in Lesson 1
- Chart paper and markers

Teaching the Lesson

1. Display the text on the whiteboard. Invite students to talk with a partner to identify the genre characteristics of *The Great Fire*, an informational text. If your students are unfamiliar with the term *genre*, remind them that it refers to a specific kind of literature; texts within a genre typically share certain characteristics.

2. Circulate among students to listen to their brief conversations. Responses such as those in italics can let you know students have identified characteristics of informational texts: *I know Jim Murphy writes nonfiction; there is lots of information about buildings in Chicago and the number of fires; I don't see a narrative— there's no plot or characters; he's presenting an explanation of why Chicago was ready for a fire, and that's nonfiction.*

3. If students miss an important characteristic of the genre, take some time to point it out to them (see box above for a list of characteristics of informational texts). Tell them that knowing a genre's characteristics can help them determine the

> ### Genre Characteristics of Informational Texts
>
> - Are written to argue, inform, or persuade
> - Contain one or more text structures such as cause-effect, sequence, description, compare-contrast, problem-solution, question-answer
> - May contain text features such as photographs and captions, diagrams, charts, illustrations, maps, and sidebars
> - Contain technical vocabulary
> - Are written by an expert or authority on topic
> - Are nonfiction

genre of an unfamiliar text, which can in turn help them know what to expect from the text.

4. Have students reread the notes you made in Step 3 of Lesson 1 and review the Building Prior Knowledge handout.

5. Next, ask pairs to set a purpose for listening to *The Great Fire,* consulting the handout as necessary. If this is new to your students, you may want to discuss the various options for generating a purpose statement. Here are some suggestions to help students set purposes:

SETTING A PURPOSE FOR READING

It's essential for readers to set a purpose before they read a text to focus their attention on the key points in the text.

   - Turn the title into a question as a purpose to read: *Why did the author call this* The Great Fire*?*

   - Derive a purpose from prior-knowledge notes. Here are some purposes seventh graders set, based on the prior-knowledge notes I shared on page 46: *Read to learn why in 1871 Chicago was a city ready to burn; read to learn how wood and wind caused the great fire.*

   - Use the "devastation" concept map to set a purpose: *Read to learn how* The Great Fire *connects to devastation.*

6. Ask students to jot down their purpose for reading in their notebooks under the heading, "Purpose for Reading *The Great Fire.*"

7. Have students pair-share and discuss their purposes for reading, then invite a few students to share different purposes.

8. Read the selection out loud and have students follow with their purposes in mind. Explain that this is a second reading and that hearing the selection twice will enable them to recall more details from the text.

9. Ask students to identify details in the text that relate to their purposes for reading. As you circulate, offer help to students as they recall relevant details, encouraging them to reread parts of the text as necessary.

10. Return to the "devastation" concept map. Invite students to pair-share and contribute words and phrases to the map, based on the second reading. Make sure you ask them to connect their words and phrases to the concept and provide specific examples so the entire class benefits from their thinking.

Wrap-Up

Point out the positive discussions students had and acknowledge the number of ideas added to the "devastation" concept map.

Making Inferences and Finding Themes

In this lesson, you model how to use key details from the text to make logical inferences and find themes. Afterward, pairs practice this skill as you listen in and provide support.

Materials

- Excerpt from *The Great Fire*, displayed on the whiteboard from the Resources CD
- Students' notebooks

Teaching the Lesson

1. Display the excerpt from *The Great Fire* on the whiteboard and tell students that today's focus is to use text details to infer and find themes. If your students are new to inferring or could use a review, provide a quick definition: to infer is to combine what the text says with what you know to find meaning not directly stated in the text. Often inferences can help you identify themes in the text. A theme is suggested by details from or inferences about a text and can be generalized to apply to all humankind, not just the characters in the story.

   > You can use the passages from *The Great Fire* that I suggest in the lesson, or you can select your own passages.

2. Ask students to follow along as you reread the second and third paragraphs, beginning with "The situation…" and ending with "…the yards."

3. Present a think-aloud to show how you use specific text details to infer and find themes. Here's what I say:

   I can infer that wood was cheap and readily available in Chicago in the mid-1800s, because buildings in both poor and wealthy areas were made of wood. Building were built so close together that fire would spread quickly. Since businesses were interspersed among residential homes, and the business buildings were wood and contained combustible materials such as paint, lumber, gas, and furniture, I can infer that there was no one in charge of planning Chicago's residential and business areas. To keep homes safe, I infer, businesses with combustible materials should have been in separate areas. One theme from this passage is that failing to plan can lead to disaster. Notice that the inferences and theme aren't stated in the text. I had to use the information from the text and my own knowledge to infer.

4. Display and read aloud the fourth paragraph. Invite students to pair-share and use the information in this paragraph to make one logical inference and find a theme. Here's what seventh graders offered:

   • Quick solutions made Chicago more combustible (inferences). To deal with marshlands and mud they had hundreds of miles of sidewalks and streets made of wood.

   • Quick solutions can have unexpected consequences—people should think things through (theme).

5. Reread aloud the last three paragraphs of *The Great Fire*. Then invite pairs to infer, find themes, and discuss their inferences and themes with the entire class to show how key details supported inferring and finding themes.

Wrap-Up

Acknowledge students' ability to use text details to infer and find themes in *The Great Fire*.

LESSON 4

Interpreting Language and Discussing Text Structure

In this lesson, students focus on the language of the text, exploring how it relates to the concept of devastation and the themes and inferences discussed in the previous lesson. In addition, you will model how to identify text structure and discuss why understanding a text's structure can help readers comprehend a text more deeply.

Materials

• Excerpt from *The Great Fire*, displayed on the whiteboard from the Resources CD
• Students' notebooks
• "Devastation" concept map

- Key words from a few paragraphs written on chart paper (see Step 2)
- Chart paper and markers

Teaching the Lesson

1. Display the "devastation" concept map and invite students to add words and phrases from *The Great Fire*. Ask them to connect their ideas to the concept with specific details from the text and/or their experiences.

2. Choose 10 to 20 words and phrases from a few paragraphs of *The Great Fire* that relate to the themes and inferences that you and students identified in Lesson 3. Before the lesson, I write these words on a sheet of chart paper:

   jerry-built, highly flammable tar, disguise, wooden framework, fast-burning wood, interspersed, roads and sidewalks out of wood, lumberyards, mills, paint factories, 600 alarms, six fires every day, unrelenting summer sun, unusually dry, steady wind, gusty, dried out, swirling wind, smoldered, a thousand yellow-orange fingers

3. Display the words and ask students to reread them and pair-share to connect the language to themes and logical inferences in the text. My students linked the words and phrases to the inference that Chicago was a combustible city in 1871 and the gusty winds, drought, and sun helped the fires start. "Knowing the weather," Anthony said, "should have made them [builders and planners] think of building with stuff instead of wood."

4. Explain to students that in addition to selecting words or phrases that relate to themes in *The Great Fire*, it's important to understand the organization and structure of this selection. Here's what I say:

   Murphy opens with a position statement: "Chicago in 1871 was a city ready to burn." And then he presents evidence to prove this claim, starting with downtown buildings and then moving to poor and wealthy residential areas, and finally to the wooden streets and sidewalks. He uses foreshadowing, a literary technique, in the second paragraph when he mentions the O'Learys and their wooden barn built on a small lot and then returns to the barn in the last paragraph. Foreshadowing prepares readers for the fire starting in the O'Learys barn, at the end of the selection, and also helps them visualize the small lots and buildings crammed together. Then Murphy switches to background information about fires in other cities and in Chicago during that time. He explains his opening statement with lots of details and then lets readers understand that wooden buildings were common in other cities at that time.

In the first three paragraphs, Murphy uses descriptive details to categorize buildings in downtown Chicago, in middle-class and poorer sections, and in wealthy sections. Categorization is a subtle way to compare building construction in the three areas. In the fourth paragraph, problem-solution is the text structure: the problem is buildings constructed on wet marshland, and the solution is wooden sidewalks and roads. The fifth paragraph, which chronicles fires in Chicago, is organized chronologically. The last paragraph is descriptive and demonstrates cause-effect, as Murphy shows how gusty winds helped spread the flames.

5. Invite students to pair-share and discuss why it's important to understand a text's structure. Here's what seventh graders said:

   • It can help with my writing.

   • When I reread, the structure helps me organize my thinking.

   • Knowing structure makes me remember more from rereading.

   • Knowing structure helps me skim to find details.

Wrap-Up

Provide positive feedback on students' discussion of language and text structure.

LESSON 5

Close Reading and Adding to the Concept Map

In this lesson, you will introduce the strategy of close reading; students will practice after you model. Then students will add words and phrases to the concept map.

Materials

• Excerpt from *The Great Fire*, displayed on the whiteboard from the Resources CD

• Students' notebooks

• Copies of Close Reading Guidelines (see page 262 and the Resources CD), class set

- "Devastation" concept map
- Chart paper and markers

Teaching the Lesson

1. Distribute the handout and display the excerpt from *The Great Fire*. Model the strategy called close reading. Here's what I say:

   If you come upon a new word and can't figure out the meaning, or you encounter a sentence or short passage that confuses you, a close reading can help you use context clues to determine meaning and "unconfuse" a confusing passage.

   In The Great Fire, *I'm unsure what the term "combustible knot" in paragraph 4 means. I reread the sentence that contains the term, but I'm still unsure. I'm going to slow down my reading rate to do a close reading and consider phrases and individual words and think about how these connect to each other.*

   Here's the sentence: "On the day the fire started, over 55 miles of pine-block streets and 600 miles of wooden sidewalks bound the 233,000 acres of city in a highly combustible knot."

   To close read, I examine one phrase at a time. I get the first group of words—it's the day the fire started. I get wooden sidewalks. Pine-block streets—it said before that there were elevated streets make of wood—pine-block must be a kind of wood. I know bound *means tied, so maybe the sidewalks and elevated streets were tied around all the acres of land. I think combustible means it can burn. Here, it's tons of wood that could burn. I think that author uses the word* knot *because you tie a knot and the wood was like a knot around the land ready to burn.*

   Notice how I use what I know and remember along with clues in the sentence to figure out the phrase.

2. Read aloud the Close Reading Guidelines handout, discussing how you followed the steps in your close reading. Encourage students to paste the handout into their notebooks and consult it as necessary.

3. Have partners practice close reading to figure out the meaning of *unrelenting*. Highlight this sentence from paragraph 5:

   "Trees drooped in the unrelenting summer sun; grass and leaves dried out."

4. Circulate among students as they pair-share and prompt them with questions such as: *What happened to the trees? What happened to the grass and leaves? What made this happen? Can you connect these ideas to "unrelenting sun"?*

5. Explain to students that close reading can help them figure out difficult words or even whole sentences that confuse them.

6. Highlight this sentence from paragraph 1:

   "Many of the remaining buildings looked solid, but were actually jerry-built affairs."

   Have partners use close reading to deepen their comprehension of the sentence.

7. Circulate among students as they pair-share and prompt them with questions such as: *How can the phrase* looked solid *help you figure out* jerry-built*? How does understanding* jerry-built *add depth to your understanding of the construction of the buildings?*

8. Display the concept map, and invite students to pair-share and offer words and phrases for you to add to the map. Always encourage students to connect their suggestions to the concept of devastation.

Wrap-Up

Point out how well students applied the close reading strategy to figure out difficult words and sentences. Acknowledge how well they connected words and phrases to the concept of devastation.

LESSON 6

Collaborative Discussions

In this lesson, you review how to make inferences; then students work in pairs to discuss text-specific questions, rereading, skimming, and close reading as necessary to find evidence to support their ideas.

Materials

- Excerpt from *The Great Fire*, displayed on the whiteboard
- Students' copies of Close Reading Guidelines
- Students' notebooks
- A class set of discussion questions for each student (see page 57 and the Resources CD)

Text-specific discussion questions ask students to skim and close read to comprehend. In addition, because the questions are at a high level, discussing them can help students infer.

Teaching the Lesson

1. Organize students into pairs. I try to pair students whose instructional levels are no more than one year apart, so they have something to give one another. Students reading three or more years below grade level can work together with your support.

2. Have students take out their copy of the Close Reading Guidelines.

3. Explain to students that they're going to answer some questions about *The Great Fire* that require them to infer and use close reading to think deeply about the text.

4. Ask students to pair-share and discuss everything they recall about making inferences and close reading.

5. As you circulate among the students, listen in and spotlight any responses that will help the class by asking partners to share their thinking.

> The purpose of having students discuss text-specific questions is to give them practice with finding evidence in the text to support their answers, a key CCSS skill. The practice also enables them to succeed on the short quiz at the end of each selection and have more details and inferences to bring to their summaries and/or paragraphs.

6. Show students how to close read a passage to deepen comprehension and make an inference.

   I need to close read Murphy's statement that builders "disguised" buildings with brick exteriors in paragraph 1. I want to use the meaning of disguise *to help me infer. Costumes at Halloween and parties can disguise who you are—it's like the costume covers up your real self. When builders disguise wooden buildings to look like brick, stone, or metal, I can infer that the builders were dishonest because they wanted people to think the buildings were made of bricks and thus fireproof. The brick was fake and builders intended to deceive people into thinking the structures weren't made of wood when they really were.*

7. Distribute copies of the discussion prompts to students. Have partners discuss the prompts and find text evidence by skimming and rereading to find relevant passages. Encourage students to use the Close Reading Guidelines for any parts that confuse them.

8. Tell students that these prompts are specific to *The Great Fire* and require that they use information in the text to infer or to interpret information by explaining it, just as you did with the word *disguised*.

9. Give pairs five to ten minutes to discuss the prompts for *The Great Fire*. Encourage them to jot down notes and specific paragraph numbers that they used to find evidence. Circulate to listen in and extend or shorten the time as needed.

10. Invite pairs to share their answers and, if they close read a part of the text, have them explain how close reading helped them infer.

Wrap-Up

Point out what worked well during the paired discussions and while students gathered information for their notes. Compliment them on their recall and application of inferring and close reading.

DISCUSSION PROMPTS FOR *THE GREAT FIRE*

1. Why does the author say, "Chicago in 1871 was a city ready to burn"?
2. Why did buildings in poorer and middle-class districts contribute to the chance of a fire?
3. Explain whether it was wise or unwise to build Chicago on soggy marshland that flooded every time it rained.
4. Explain whether Chicago's weather did or did not contribute to a chance of fire.
5. Why did Dennis Rogan try to wake up the O'Learys?
6. Find a theme in this selection and support your suggestions with text evidence.

LESSON 7

Assessment: Test-Taking Strategies

In this lesson, you model how to strategically answer quiz items and find support in the text. Then students complete the quiz with a partner or in a small group.

Materials

- Excerpt from *The Great Fire*, displayed on the whiteboard from the Resources CD
- Copies of *The Great Fire* quiz (see the Resources CD), class set
- Building Prior Knowledge notes from Lesson 1
- Copies of the Quiz Answer Sheet (see page 263 and the Resources CD), a class set
- Quiz Answer Key for *The Great Fire* (see page 267 and the Resources CD)

Teaching the Lesson

1. Distribute *The Great Fire* quiz. Display *The Great Fire* and read it and the quiz items aloud. Ask students to raise a hand if they feel any part confuses them and a close reading is necessary. If so, close read each section to support students.

2. Review the Building Prior Knowledge notes.

3. Model how you answer the first quiz item, making sure to identify where you find support for your answer in the text. The model is thorough, so you can observe my thinking. Adapt to the needs of your students. Here is my thinking:

Quiz item number one reads: Which statement best expresses the main idea of the text? *First, I think about what the main idea of the text is, based on my reading and our discussions. I'd say the main idea is that Chicago was primed for a big fire in 1871. Now I'm going to read the possible answers on the quiz.* A: Don't use wood for any buildings in a city. *That's definitely not the main idea, so I'm just going to cross that off.* B: Winds can spread fires quickly and help fuel a major disaster. *That's a possibility.* C: A city with mostly wooden structures can quickly go up in flames. *That's close to what I initially thought, with just a little more detail, so that's a strong possible answer. Finally,* D: Fires can quickly get out of control. *That's true, but certainly not the main idea. So B and C are possibilities; let's reread them.* [Reread answers B and C.] *I'm leaning towards C because it's more specific; now I'm going to go back to the text to check that answer and find evidence for it. Skimming through paragraph 1, I find the details about the majority of buildings being made of wood, even buildings that didn't look like it. There were other structures made of wood too—I'm skimming—here in paragraph 4 are the details about the wooden sidewalks and streets. I am confident that C is the best answer, so I write that on my answer sheet, and I write 1 and 4 to show where I found the evidence for my answer.*

4. If you feel your students need extra support, you can model how you answer the second quiz item as well.

5. Give students the Quiz Answer Sheet. Tell them to write their name, the date, and the title of text at the top. Then have them record the answer(s) for the item(s) you modeled answering for them, writing the letter of the answer in the first column and the number(s) of the paragraph(s) containing the evidence they used in the second column.

6. Pair students with partners and have them complete the remaining quiz items, rereading the text from the whiteboard as necessary. If you have students who cannot read the text

independently, work with them in a group, rereading passages for them so they can complete the quiz.

7. When students have finished, call out the answers from the Quiz Answer Key as students self-check, and discuss where the evidence was located, or collect the quizzes and grade them yourself.

Wrap-Up

Acknowledge students for successfully skimming and rereading *The Great Fire* to locate the paragraphs that helped them find the best answers to the quiz items.

> Note that students will *not* be writing a paragraph about one of their answers during this lesson because the focus is on helping students practice the test-taking strategies modeled.

LESSON 8

Writing About Reading

There are two options for the writing about reading lesson: students may write a summary of the text or a paragraph explaining how the author's thesis or position was supported through key details in the text. Depending on the needs of your students, you may choose to have the whole class work on the same assignment; assign topics to students so you have two groups, one working on a summary, the other on an explanatory paragraph; or allow students to choose which assignment they would like to complete. If you have one group of students working on a summary and a second group explaining the thesis, you will meet with one group to explain the assignment while the other works independently; when the first group gets started, you will meet with the other group to go over the task. Since writing a summary is the simpler task, appropriate for students who may be struggling, meet with that group first so they have extended time to work.

This lesson requires more time; you can allot an entire class period, or allow students to work on it over two or three 20-minute sessions.

Materials

- Excerpt from *The Great Fire*, displayed on the whiteboard
- Students' notebooks
- Additional paper for writing the summary or paragraph
- Copies of the 5W's Organizer (see the Resources CD), enough for the students writing a summary
- Copies of Guidelines for Writing a Summary (see page 266 and the Resources CD), enough for students writing a summary

- Copies of Elements of a Paragraph handout (see page 265 and the Resources CD), enough for students writing a paragraph
- Copies of the Rubric: Informational Text Summary (see the Resources CD), for students writing summaries
- Copies of the Rubric: Paragraph (see the Resources CD), for students writing paragraphs
- Sticky notes

Teaching the Lesson

1. Determine which students will work on which assignment, either by assigning them a topic or allowing them to choose. For my seventh-grade class, I assigned writing a summary to my below-grade-level readers, and writing an explanatory paragraph to my on-grade-level students. To avoid confusion, make a list in your plan book or a notebook, detailing who's writing a summary and who's writing an explanatory paragraph.

Displaying the text in two-page view makes it easier for students to reread the text; see page 45.

2. Introduce the writing about reading task, explaining how the lesson will work. I say something like this:

   Today we're going to be writing about the text we've been working with. Writing about our reading deepens our comprehension and strengthens our analytical thinking because we're returning to the text for evidence, and we have to express our thoughts clearly and logically in writing. There are two types of writing assignments we'll work on. One group will write a summary, and a second will write a paragraph showing how Jim Murphy supported his thesis. I'll meet with the summary group first to go over the assignment. The rest of you will write a paragraph; you may read independently until I finish. Okay, summary students, please meet me in the front of the room.

TEACHING TIPS — STRATEGIES FOR STUDENTS

All students, but especially struggling readers and English language learners, benefit from having guidelines that ask them to plan before drafting and that spell out what the teacher expects from the assignment.

Tell students to read their paragraphs out loud to listen for missing words, punctuation needs, and sentence sense. Help them understand that reading out loud and listening to what they've written can support revision.

---

3. Gather students who will write a summary and distribute the 5W's Organizer, the Guidelines for Writing a Summary, and the Rubric: Informational Text Summary. Introduce the assignment by saying something like this:

Summarizing is an important skill because it helps you choose the most important information from a text and say it in your own words. This process helps you remember the information. Writing a summary informs your reader of the text you have read.

To help you plan and write a summary of an informational text, use the 5W's Organizer, which guides you to identify the key information in the text: the Who or What, the When and Where, and most important, the Why. Jot down important details from the text for each of these, and you'll be well on your way for writing a summary.

After you've filled out the organizer, use the Guidelines for Writing a Summary to draft your summary. Let's review the directions from that handout, along with the criteria on the rubric, which you can use to revise your writing.

Walk students through the handouts. See page 63 for a sample completed summary.

4. Gather students who will write the explanatory paragraph and distribute the Elements of a Paragraph handout and the Rubric: Paragraph.

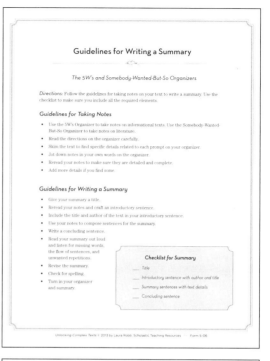

Introduce the assignment by saying something like this:

Today you're going to write about this statement from The Great Fire*: "Chicago in 1871 was a city ready to burn." First, you will take notes in your notebook, recording at least four pieces of evidence from the text to support that statement. When you have your notes, you'll use the Elements of Paragraph handout to write your paragraph, which will have the following parts:*

- *a short title that captures the reader's attention*
- *an introductory sentence that gives the title and author of the text, in this case, Jim Murphy and* The Great Fire*. This sentence should also express the point you want to make in your paragraph. For example, for this assignment, you might write:*
  In The Great Fire, *Jim Murphy explains why Chicago in 1871 was a city ready to burn.*
- *text-based evidence. Here's where you'll transform your notes into sentences that support and develop your main idea.*
- *concluding or wrap-up sentence that restates your main point and adds details that leave your reader thinking about your idea*

You can use the checklist at the bottom of the handout to make sure you've included all the elements you need and the rubric to help you revise your writing.

See page 64 for a sample paragraph.

5. As students write, circulate to observe them taking notes and then drafting a summary or paragraph.

6. Sit side by side with students who require extra support. Acknowledge the positive aspects of a student's work first. When possible, use questions rather than statements to address areas that need more work. Questions honor and empower students. Write helpful suggestions on sticky notes and give them to students as a reminder of your conversation. Remind students to use their rubric to guide their revision.

7. Gauge students' progress to determine how much time to allow for the writing.

Wrap-Up

Compliment students on their detailed plans and their summaries and paragraphs.

If you feel students need additional modeling before moving on to the guided practice portion of the unit, work through Lessons 1–8 again using the excerpt from *Years of Dust* as the read-aloud text (see the Resources CD).

Writing a Summary Using the 5W's Organizer

The 5W's Organizer is a helpful tool for planning a summary of an informational text. It guides students to identify the key details of a text: who or what it is about, what happened, when it happened, where it happened, and why it happened. For the why component, ask students to identify the causes behind the event and to make connections to community and world issues.

Once students have completed the organizer, they should generate a topic sentence that states the main idea of the text they are summarizing and includes the title and author of the text. Then students turn their notes into complete sentences. The student handout Guidelines for Writing a Summary outlines the steps for students and provides a checklist for students to use to check their work. Use the Rubric: Informational Text Summary from the Resources CD to evaluate summaries. It's also a good idea to give students a copy of the rubric beforehand so they can revise their writing.

Name: Megan   Date: 3/11

5W's Organizer

Directions: Read the explanation of each of the W's. Take detailed, specific notes under each heading. Write your summary on a separate sheet of paper.

Title: The Great Fire   Author: Jim Murphy

WHO or WHAT is this about?
The Great Fire

WHAT did the person do? Or WHAT happened?
There was a huge fire that spread throughout the city.

WHEN did this happen?
1871

WHERE did this happen?
Chicago

WHY did this happen? Think of causes behind the events and make connections to community and world issues.
- buildings were mostly wood – even those that looked like something else – and they were built close together
- sidewalks and roads were made of wood because of marshy ground
- it had been a hot dry summer
- it was very windy that day

Notes for summary

Megan

The Great Fire by Jim Murphy explains that the conditions in Chicago in the summer of 1871 were perfect for a big fire. First, most of the buildings in the city were made of wood. Even some churches and other buildings that looked like copper or stone were just wood painted to look that way. The buildings were also built close together. Since Chicago was built on marshy ground, they made roads and sidewalks out of wood so it wouldn't be so muddy. That summer had been very hot and dry, and that day was windy. So when the fire started, you can see that the weather and wooden buildings built close together made Chicago go up in flames.

Summary

Writing a Paragraph Using the Elements of a Paragraph Handout

The Elements of a Paragraph handout describes the components students should include when they write a paragraph about their reading. It also includes a checklist students can use to confirm they've included all required elements. See the sample notes and paragraph written using the handout below. Use the Rubric: Paragraph from the Resources CD to evaluate paragraphs. It's a good idea to give the rubric to students beforehand so they can revise their writing.

Maddie W.

① gusty, swirling wind - fuel a big fire.

② Most of the buildings, roads & sidewalks were made of wood.

③ the summer before was "unusually dry"

④ many trees lined the streets of Chicago

Notes for explanatory paragraph

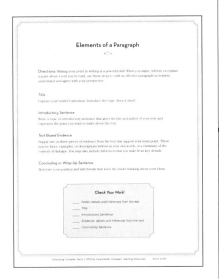

Maddie W.

Burning to the Ground

Chicago was a place that was just asking for a fire. The author argues this with many different ways.

First, most of the buildings & roads were made of wood, not nessisarily the safest thing. Chicago is named the windy city for a reason; it's got strong, gusty winds that are perfect for spreading a fire. The summer before the great fire was unusually dry, so it wasn't hard for sparks to catch one of the many trees or bushes that lined the streets of Chicago.

The great fire in Chicago was a tragite, & purhaps if they hadn't built most of the city in wood, or just gotten a bit of rain, the whole fiasco could've been avoided.

Explanatory paragraph

Guided Practice With a New Text

In this next series of lessons, you start releasing responsibility to students, reviewing and coaching as they practice the skills and strategies you modeled with *The Great Fire* excerpt. Assign students a text based on their reading level; text complexity grids for each selection appear below. Then work through the lessons at a pace that's reasonable for your students and schedule, allowing one to two weeks depending on students' needs.

Text Complexity Grids

Selection from *Blizzard!* by Jim Murphy
Lexile®: 1100
Text Complexity: 1 = Accessible to 5 = Challenging

QUALITATIVE	1	2	3	4	5
Knowledge demands				X	
Author's purpose				X	
Meaning			X		
Text structure			X		
Language/vocabulary			X		
Concepts			X		
Inferential thinking demands					X

Selection from *Dead Men Floating* by Danielle Denega
Lexile®: 720
Text Complexity: 1 = Accessible to 5 = Challenging

QUALITATIVE	1	2	3	4	5
Knowledge demands					X
Author's purpose				X	
Meaning			X		
Text structure			X		
Language/vocabulary			X		
Concepts			X		
Inferential thinking demands					X

Building Prior Knowledge and Setting Purposes

In this lesson, students receive a new passage; they preview and read for the gist with peer support. They also have the opportunity to add words to the "devastation" concept map.

Materials

- Copies of excerpt from *Blizzard!* for students reading at or above grade level (see the Resources CD)
- Copies of excerpt from *Dead Men Floating* for students reading below grade level (see the Resources CD)
- Students' notebooks
- "Devastation" concept map
- Chart paper and markers or interactive whiteboard

Teaching the Lesson

1. Review the method for building prior knowledge you modeled with *The Great Fire* excerpt (see pages 45–46). I have students suggest the number of paragraphs to read on the first page and remind them to read the title, the last paragraph, and the quiz items.

TEACHING TIP — STRATEGY FOR STUDENTS

If you have students in middle school who cannot read Dead Men Floating *independently, read it aloud to them. Make sure you find dozens of independent reading books and magazines for them. These can be e-books, high-interest, and easy reading books (see pages 35–37 and the Resources CD), as well as buddy reading books that students read with a student in the primary grades.*

Robert Smith
Block # 1

1. The Missouri River had to much water and then it started a flood.
2. They wanted to find the bones and put them back in their coffins.
3. They had a hard time find and put them together
4. They wanted to see if they had broken leg or something
5. They had dead bodies all over the place

Prior-knowledge notes for Dead Men Floating

Managing Groups Who Are Reading Different Texts

When you have two groups of students reading different selections and you want to meet with one group at a time, make sure that students in each group have work they can do independently. For example, students can complete independent reading, work on the summary or paragraph they started at the end of Lesson 8, or reread a short complex text. While the *Blizzard!* group works on their own, you can work with the group reading *Dead Men Floating*. Then switch, so that you are supporting the *Blizzard!* group while the other group works independently.

To ensure students don't interrupt you, provide them with a way to solve problems without asking you for help. (Make sure they understand that they can interrupt your work with a group in case of illness or some other emergency.) I organize students into reading partners and post these suggestions on chart paper:

If you are stuck while working independently then:

- Try again on your own.
- Ask your partner for help.
- Find something you can do, such as independent reading.
- Place your name on the chalkboard under "Needs Help."

I tell students that before switching groups, I will help students whose names are on the chalkboard. I find that with a method for problem solving, students usually can work through an issue that at first seemed challenging.

2. Distribute the copies of the texts to students. Have them preview their text to build prior knowledge. Remind students to make a list of what they learned from the preview in their notebooks.

3. Ask students to reread their lists and use the information to set purposes for reading. Remind them that to set purposes they can use the title, notes in their list of prior knowledge, or the concept of devastation. Have them write their purpose in their notebook. Circulate and support students who need extra help.

> Encourage students to read the selection two times to deepen their recall and comprehension.

4. Have students read the selection silently, using their prior knowledge and purpose for reading to get the gist or general idea of the text.

5. Ask students who read the same passage to pair-share to discuss the gist of their selection and connect it to devastation.

6. Circulate and listen to partner talk to determine whether students have the gist. If some students seem confused, support them by helping them close read and/or reread.

7. Display the concept map and invite students to add words from their selection to the "devastation" concept map. Always ask students to connect their word or phrase to the theme of devastation.

Wrap-Up

Point out what students did well with building their prior knowledge and setting purposes. Highlight the words and phrases students added to the concept map.

LESSON 10

Close Reading

In this lesson, students practice close reading to clarify meaning.

Materials
- Students' copies of *Blizzard!*
- Students' copies of *Dead Men Floating*
- Students' copies of Close Reading Guidelines
- "Devastation" concept map
- Chart paper and markers or interactive whiteboard

Teaching the Lesson

1. Organize students into partners who are reading the same text.

2. Refresh students' recall of close reading; review the guideline sheet with them and discuss the benefits of the strategy. Remind students to use close reading when they come across a word or phrase they don't understand or a part that confuses them.

3. Have students reread their selection silently, keeping in mind the previous day's purpose for reading and using close reading to clarify any difficult vocabulary or concepts. For your students who can't read *Dead Men Floating* independently, you'll read the text aloud and ask them to raise their hands when they hear a word or sentence that confuses them, so you can model close reading. Otherwise, you can select words and sentences to show the benefits of close reading.

4. Ask pairs to share how close reading helped them figure out a difficult word or a

passage that confused them. In my class, a pair of seventh graders shared how close reading helped them figure out the meaning of *pummeled* in the opening paragraph of *Dead Men Floating*. "We found clues in the sentence and paragraph. If rivers flooded and homes were destroyed and bridges and roads washed out, then *pummeled* must mean that the storms were hard, hard rain that did a lot of damage."

Since the CCSS values close reading as a primary fix-up comprehension strategy, take the time to let students share how they used it. The goal is to enable students to see how useful close reading is.

5. Have partners discuss their purposes for reading. Encourage partners to share places they close read to help them clarify meaning.

6. Invite students to pair-share to add words and phrases to the concept map.

Wrap-Up

Provide positive feedback to students for concentrating on reading silently, and for using close reading during paired discussions about unfamiliar words.

LESSON 11

Collaborative Discussions

In this lesson, partners work together to answer text-specific questions about the informational text they read independently. They will use the evidence they find to make logical inferences and find themes.

Materials

- Students' copies of *Blizzard!*
- Students' copies of *Dead Men Floating*
- Discussion Prompts (see page 71 and the Resources CD)
- Students' copies of Close Reading Guidelines

TEACHING TIP — SCAFFOLDING STUDENTS' READING

Support students who can't read the text independently by first pointing to the section in the text that answers the discussion question and then rereading that section for them.

Teaching the Lesson

1. Pair students with partners who have read the same text. Gather students who can't read *Dead Men Floating* independently and work with them.

2. Display the discussion prompts on a whiteboard or give a copy to each student. Invite partners to use the prompts to discuss *Blizzard!* or *Dead Men Floating.* Facilitate discussions with your group of struggling readers.

3. Invite students to reflect on their discussions and record in a T-chart the themes they found, along with the text details and inferences that led them to the themes. Here's how I introduce the T-chart:

   A T-chart helps you organize your thinking on paper. Writing down a theme you've identified and recording the details and inferences from the text that support the theme show that you can use text evidence to identify a theme. Showing your analytical thinking by providing text evidence is a sign of deep understanding. Let's look at an example before you get started.

4. Share the sample T-chart below, which is based on the anchor text, *The Great Fire*. Tell students to notice how you cite specific text evidence to support the theme.

THEME (*The Great Fire*)	INFERENCES/TEXT DETAILS
1. Lack of careful planning when building cities can create dangers for people and infrastructure.	1. Greed motivated builders to use wood because it was cheap and accessible.
	2. Buildings downtown and in residential areas made of wood
	3. Flammable paint factories, lumberyards, and mills mixed in with residences—bad planning
	4. Sidewalks and roads in marshy areas made of wood

5. Ask pairs to make a T-chart in their notebooks and record two themes they identified in their discussion, along with the text details and inferences that support each theme.

6. Invite partners to share their inferences and themes with the entire class. Their input provides additional models for using details to infer. As students share, have them cite the text details they used to infer and find themes.

Wrap-Up

Acknowledge students' focused discussions and their ability to use text evidence to infer and find themes.

DISCUSSION PROMPTS FOR *BLIZZARD!*

1. Why do you think Sam's aunt and uncle sent him out into the raging storm?

2. Compare and contrast Sam's feelings when he first went out into the storm to when he tried to get home.

3. Why do you think Murphy includes the words of the policeman and the traveler Sam meets?

4. How does the word *clawed* in the last sentence of the selection give you a visual picture of what Sam was doing?

5. What is the theme of this passage? Can you find more than one? Make sure you cite text evidence to support your response.

DISCUSSION PROMPTS FOR *DEAD MEN FLOATING*

1. Explain what you have learned about the power of large amounts of water.

2. Why were the people of Hardin so upset by the fact that corpses and skeletons were floating everywhere?

3. Why did the remains from more than 600 coffins pose such big problems?

4. What are antemortem profiles and how could these help identify bodies?

5. Why does the author compare the scene after the Missouri River flooded to a horror movie?

6. What is a theme that emerges from *Dead Men Floating*? Defend your response by citing text evidence that supports your thinking.

LESSON 12

Interpreting Language and Discussing Text Structure

In this lesson, students focus on the language of their informational text, connecting words and phrases to inferences, themes, and tone. Then they consider the text structure of the piece.

Materials

- Students' copies of *Blizzard!*
- Students' copies of *Dead Men Floating*
- Students' notebooks

- "Devastation" concept map
- Chart paper and markers or interactive whiteboard

Teaching the Lesson

1. Pair students with partners who are reading the same text. Ask pairs to identify eight to fifteen key words and phrases and connect them to an inference, the tone of the piece, or a theme.

2. Have partners volunteer to share their key words and connections. Here are words a pair of sixth-grade students selected for *Dead Men Floating*: *devastation, pummeled, floodwaters, wreckage, worst natural disaster, haunt, dead rose up, human remains, powerless, raging flood, 600 coffins, 3,400 bones.* The pair concluded that words such as *haunt, dead rose up, human remains, 600 coffins,* and *3,400 bones* created a macabre, scary tone. They also said that words like *pummeled, floodwaters, wreckage, powerless,* and *raging floods* show the huge destructive power of water and how people had no control of the rain and floods.

3. Ask partners to reread *Blizzard!* or *Dead Men Floating* to examine the text structure. (You'll reread *Dead Men Floating* aloud to developing readers.) Write the questions below on chart paper or type them into your computer and project them onto a whiteboard to help guide their discussion: *How did the writer set the scene and place you in the text? How did the writer organize information from beginning to end? Did the writer give background information? At what point in the text did you read background information? Did the writer include real people? Were there narrative elements such as dialogue, inner thoughts, conflicts, or problems to be solved?*

4. Invite partners to share with the class what they noticed about their text's structure. Here's what students in my sixth-grade class found:

   The *Blizzard!* group explained that narrative was a strong part of the text structure as the blizzard is seen through the eyes of Sam, a ten-year old, slogging through the snow to purchase the items his aunt needed. Everything that happens is conveyed through Sam's experiences. This structure connects readers to the blizzard and people, like the policeman who Sam meets. The text is organized in chronological order—Sam leaves home, and at the end he returns home.

   The *Dead Men Floating* group explained that they were drawn into the storm and its damage in the first paragraph. Events were recounted in chronological order and had lots of details that showed the destruction the storm caused; they said the detail about the cemetery was "gross" but riveting. The writer uses people to show how the storms affected them. He brings in Dean Snow, the coroner of Hardin, to help make the connection to science, describing the formation of a DMORT team and making antemortem files. Students thought the scientific information was easier to understand since a real scientist explained it.

5. Post the concept map, and have partners pair-share to generate words and phrases connected to *devastation* and add them to the map. Have students connect their ideas to the concepts.

Wrap-Up

Point out how well partners collaborated to find words and phrases from their selection and then linked these to an inference or a theme. Compliment students on their discussion and understanding of text structure.

LESSON 13

Assessment

Students complete the quiz that follows their text selection. Students have already read the items during their preview in Lesson 1 and should be familiar with them. In addition to answering the multiple-choice items and identifying paragraphs that support their answers, students will choose one item and defend their answer in a brief paragraph— they may not choose a vocabulary item.

Materials

- Students' copies of *Blizzard!*
- Students' copies of *Dead Men Floating*
- Quiz Answer Sheet (see page 263 and the Resources CD), class set
- Additional paper
- Quiz Answer Keys for *Blizzard!* and *Dead Men Floating* (see page 267 and the Resources CD)

> Students choose one quiz item and defend their answer in a paragraph.

Teaching the Lesson

1. Give students the Quiz Answer Sheet. Review the directions, reminding students to skim and reread the text to confirm their answers. Answers go in the first column; the numbers of the paragraph(s) that contain evidence for their answers goes in the second column.

2. Discuss the paragraph students will write to defend one of their answers; *they can use the guidelines on the Quiz Answer Sheet to plan and draft the paragraph, which they will write on a separate sheet of paper.* Tell them that they may not choose to write about the vocabulary item.

3. Have students write their name and the title of their text on the Quiz Answer Sheet; then have them complete the quiz independently.

4. Support students who have difficulty reading *Dead Men Floating* independently by rereading the selection for them. Then read the quiz items and answer choices one at a time and have students select the best answer.

5. When students finish, call out answers to the quiz and have students self-correct and turn their papers in, or collect the quizzes and grade them yourself.

6. Separate the quizzes into two piles: students who scored a 4 or 5, and students who missed three or more multiple-choice items.

7. Read the paragraphs students wrote to defend one of their answers. Check the response to make sure it has details from the text and follows the framework in the Guidelines for the Assessment paragraph. Make note of students who have difficulty and plan time to scaffold their learning.

Help students who struggled with the paragraph portion of the quiz by working with them in a small group. Show them how to take notes on evidence from the text and then write a brief paragraph that explains their thinking about a question, incorporating the answer from the quiz along with their own text evidence.

Wrap-Up

Acknowledge students for returning to the text and skimming or rereading before selecting an answer and for defending one of their answers.

LESSON 14

Writing About Reading: Note Taking

Students return to the discussion questions and choose one to write about in a paragraph. In this lesson, they collect evidence from the text and record it in their notebooks in preparation for writing the paragraph.

Materials

- Students' copies of *Blizzard!*
- Students' copies of *Dead Men Floating*
- Sets of Note-Taking Guidelines for *Blizzard!* and *Dead Men Floating* (see pages 75–76 and the Resources CD)
- Students' notebooks
- "Devastation" concept map

Management Tip

If you have developing readers and a teacher working with you, he or she can work with students who read Dead Men Floating *while you work with those who read* Blizzard!. *If you're the only teacher in the classroom, support one group at a time (see box on page 67 for more details).*

Teaching the Lesson

1. Explain that today students will write about the text they have been reading, either exploring a discussion question in greater depth or finding details to answer a question about their text. Distribute the Note-Taking Guidelines for *Blizzard!* and *Dead Men Floating*; you may also want to display them on the chalkboard or project them onto a whiteboard.

2. As students writing about *Blizzard!* work independently, support students answering questions about *Dead Men Floating*. Because this group consists of developing or struggling readers, give them a quote from the text that returns them to parts of *Dead Men Floating* to visualize the quote and explain what it means. Include prompts that help students take notes.

3. Invite students to add words and phrases to the "devastation" concept map.

Note-Taking Guidelines for *Blizzard!*

1. Choose one of the following prompts to write about in a paragraph:
   - Compare and contrast Sam's feelings when he first went out into the storm and when he tried to get home.
   - How does the word *clawed* in the last sentence of the selection give you a visual picture of what Sam is doing?

2. Write your selected prompt in your notebook.

3. Skim and reread to find key details that will serve as evidence for the point you want to make in your writing. Record these in your notebook.

Louisa J

4. The author chose the word because:
- It expresses the difficulty
- It shows what the conditions were
- Describes his emotions
- Creates imagery
- Illustrates Sam's fatigue
- shows that he has been brave but. he can't take it any more
- Describes how big the snowstorm is

Sample notes

Note-Taking Guidelines for *Dead Men Floating*

1. Consider this sentence from *Dead Men Floating*: "The dead rose up from the cemetery."

2. Discuss the following questions with other students who have read the same text:

    *   *What pictures does this sentence create in your mind?*

    *   *What does this sentence mean?*

    *   *How and why did this happen?*

3. Write these questions in your notebook. For each one, jot down details from the text that help you answer the question. You'll need to skim and reread to find the details you need.

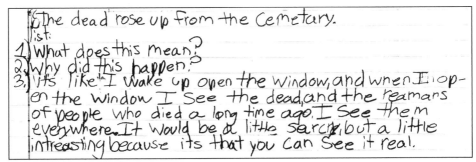

The dead rose up from the Cemetary.
1st:
1) What does this mean?
2) Why did this happen?
3) Its like I wake up open the window, and when I op-
en the window I See the dead, and the reamans
of people who died a long time ago. I See them
everywhere. It would be a little scary, but a little
intreasting because its that you Can See it real.

Sample notes

Wrap-Up

Acknowledge students' efforts in taking detailed notes on *Blizzard!* and *Dead Men Floating.*

LESSON 15

Writing About Reading: Drafting

In this lesson, students write an explanatory paragraph about their text, drawing on the notes they took in the previous lesson and consulting the Elements of a Paragraph handout. Students will need more than 20 minutes to complete the writing; I suggest allowing 30 to 45 minutes for the task.

Materials

- Students' copies of *Blizzard!*
- Students' copies of *Dead Men Floating*
- Students' copies of Elements of a Paragraph handout (from Lesson 8); you will need to make copies for students who wrote only a summary in Lesson 8 (see page 265 and the Resources CD)
- Students' copies of the Rubric: Paragraph (see the Resources CD)
- Students' notebooks
- Notebook paper for drafting a paragraph

Teaching the Lesson

1. Ask students to take out their Elements of a Paragraph handout and review the elements:

   - Title
   - Introductory sentence
   - Text-based evidence
   - Concluding sentence

   Pull students who have not used the handout before into a small group and introduce it to them using the guidelines on pages 61–62.

2. Suggest to students who are writing about *Blizzard!* that they restate the prompt they chose and turn it into an introductory sentence. They can also craft an original introductory sentence.

Louisa J

Clawing Through a Blizzard

Imagine yourself trudging through snow taller than you, as you suffer through the fright of a winter storm. In *Blizzard*, Sam is being challenged by the forces of nature. The question. How does the word clawed in the last sentence of the selection give you a visual picture of what Sam was doing? Mainly, it expresses the level of difficulty Sam faced coming home. It shows the level of fatigue and exhaustion he is battling with. Also, it symbolizes that he has faced lots of struggle and his bravery has at last paid off. Not only does it show Sam's emotions, but it creates the imagery of the size of the snowstorm. So, next time we have a blizzard, some of us could be clawing up the steps after a long day of snow!

Sample paragraph for Blizzard!*; see notes on page 75*

Josue R.

Rise of the-died

The author dead men floating writes "The dead
rose up from the Cemetary." What it means
is they came up. The died came up from the
Cemetary because in 1993 in Spring it Started
to rain in the midwestern in the United States.
Rivers in the Midwestern overflow thier
banks, A place called Hardin was Six miles
(ten Kilometers) north to Missouri River, The flood
hit the town. When the flood hit the town
the Cemetery was covered with water,
The cemetery was Small and was in lowlying
area in 1828, When the flood hit the Cemetary, the Coffins were dug up from the
ground, the coffins broke open, Human bones
were through fields and Streets, Some bones
8 miles (29 km) away,

*Sample paragraph for
Dead Men Floating;
see notes on page 76*

3. For students writing about *Dead Men Floating*, provide a topic sentence to help them get started: In *Dead Men Floating*, Danielle Denega helps us see the results of the flood by stating: "The dead rose up from the cemetery." Students can opt to use this introductory sentence or craft their own.

4. Instruct students to use their notes from the previous lesson to write a complete paragraph, following the guidelines on the handout. Remind them to use their rubric to revise their writing.

5. Circulate and support students as necessary. Always begin by noting the positives a student has achieved, and remember to phrase suggestions as questions, to honor and empower your students.

6. Collect the paragraphs and assess them, using the rubric. You can note errors in spelling, usage, and punctuation, and use this data for writing mini-lessons and in one-to-one conferences.

Wrap-Up

Provide positive feedback and compliment students for using their notes to craft their paragraphs.

Independent Practice and Assessment

In the last segment of the unit, students work with a text independently, so you can assess their progress, scaffolding or extending their learning as appropriate.

Text Complexity Grids

"The Fury of Fire" by Kristin Lewis

Lexile®: 960

Text Complexity: 1 = Accessible to 5 = Challenging

QUALITATIVE	1	2	3	4	5
Knowledge demands				X	
Author's purpose				X	
Meaning			X		
Text structure				X	
Language/vocabulary				X	
Concepts				X	
Inferential thinking demands				X	

"Dust Bowl Disaster" by Alex Porter and Kristin Lewis

Lexile®: 760

Text Complexity: 1 = Accessible to 5 = Challenging

QUALITATIVE	1	2	3	4	5
Knowledge demands				X	
Author's purpose				X	
Meaning			X		
Text structure				X	
Language/vocabulary				X	
Concepts				X	
Inferential thinking demands				X	

Reading a New Text Independently

Have students work on their own, as this is an assessment that will help you determine students' strengths and needs. They will build prior knowledge and read the text independently. For the assessment, you have three options: students can write a summary, compose an explanatory paragraph, or complete a Word Map about the unit's concept. I recommend that each student do at least one writing activity and complete the Word Map.

Set aside five or six consecutive days for the assessment. You will probably need two 30- to 45-minute classes for students to build prior knowledge, read for the gist, reread for deeper understanding, and complete the Word Map. Over the next three or four days, take about 35–45 minutes to have students complete the writing. If a few students need more time for taking notes and writing, give them the extra time.

Materials

- Copies of "The Fury of Fire" for students reading at or above grade level (see the Resources CD)
- Copies of "Dust Bowl Disaster" for students reading below grade level (see the Resources CD)
- Students copies of Building Prior Knowledge Handout (from Lesson 1; see page 261 and the Resources CD)
- Students' copies of Guidelines for Writing a Summary
- Copies of the 5W's Organizer (see the Resources CD), for students writing summaries
- Students' copies of the Elements of a Paragraph handout
- Copies of Writing Topics for each assessment text (see the Resources CD), for students writing paragraphs
- Copies of the Word Map (see the Resources CD), class set

> **TEACHING TIP — SCAFFOLDS FOR DEVELOPING READERS**
>
> To help students who can't read "Dust Bowl Disaster" independently, read the title, the first two paragraphs and the final paragraph of the text to build their prior knowledge. (You might have to read parts twice.) Then have students list what they learned. Next, tell students that you will reread the entire selection as they follow along; reread it again if necessary.

- Students' copies of the Rubrics for Informational Text Summary and Paragraph
- Students' notebooks
- Additional notebook paper for writing summaries and/or paragraphs

Teaching the Lesson

1. Have students take out their copy of the Building Prior Knowledge handout while you distribute the assessment texts and copies of the Word Map.

2. Remind students to use the strategy they have practiced to build their prior knowledge and jot down a list of what they learned from their preview in their notebook. Tell them that on the first two days of the assessment, they should preview the text to build prior knowledge, then read for the gist. Encourage them to reread the text for deeper comprehension before they complete the Word Map.

3. Invite students to complete the Word Map, specifying how many characteristics and examples you want them to provide to demonstrate their understanding of the concept.

4. On the next day, ask those students who will be writing a summary to take out their Guidelines for Writing a Summary handout. Give them a 5W's Organizer and the rubric you will use to assess the summary.

5. Ask those students who will be writing a paragraph to take out their Elements of a Paragraph handout. Distribute the Writing Topics list and the rubric you will use to assess the paragraph.

6. Invite students to reread and take notes for their summaries or paragraphs. Have them work through the writing process outlined on the Guidelines for Writing a Summary handout or the Elements of a Paragraph handout, consulting the corresponding rubric to check their work.

7. When students finish, have them turn in their work. Assess it using the rubric.

Interpreting Assessments

The paragraphs can show you whether students can make logical inferences and find specific text details from the selection. See the Scaffolding Suggestions chart on pages 84–85 to help you support students with reading issues.

To scaffold students who require writing support, use the Scaffolding Suggestions for Helping Students Write Summaries and Paragraphs chart on the Resources CD.

Following Up the Assessment

Based on your assessment of students' writing, you can determine how many days to spend scaffolding and extending their learning. I recommend allowing at least one day for students to revise their writing based on your feedback; during that time, you can meet with your most-struggling readers. Then you may choose to spend additional days working in small groups, scaffolding students who need it and extending the learning of those who are ready for more challenges.

Supporting Students Who Require Scaffolding

The chart on pages 84–85 offers scaffolding suggestions based on students' writing, your observations as they read and discuss texts, and your conferences on independent and instructional reading. Consult the Scaffolding Suggestions for Helping Students Write Summaries and Paragraphs on the Resources CD if students need help with their writing. Support students with similar needs by working with groups of two or three. When students struggle and are unsuccessful with the assessment, work one-on-one with them.

At first, when you scaffold, you might do all or most of the modeling and thinking aloud. Follow-up conferences should gradually turn over to the student the responsibility for learning. You can do this gradual release by pairing the student with a peer, by continuing to confer to observe the student's thinking, or by having the student work independently and then share her thinking with you. This can occur in two or three short conferences (see forms on the Resources CD for conducting and documenting conferences). However, some students will need several conferences, and you might have to return to the skill as you move on to another unit.

Texts to Use for Scaffolding

Students can use the text read for their independent assessment (page 79), or an informational text you have selected. You'll find excellent informational texts in these

Scholastic magazines: *Action, Science World, Scope,* and *Storyworks.* You'll also find two extra informational texts on the Resources CD.

Suggestions for Helping Students Think Across Texts

After students who were successful on the assessment revise their writing, you may want to follow up their learning by challenging them to think across the texts they have read during the unit; this task supports the Common Core State Standards 7 to 9 for reading informational texts. Once students have read, discussed, and analyzed each text in this unit, they will be able to find common themes and ideas among them. You can use the suggestions below to help students complete across-text thinking.

- Compare the text structure of two pieces.
- Connect the themes in two or more pieces to the concept of devastation or a related idea on the concept map.
- Use details and inferences in two or more selections to discuss and compare people's reactions to natural and man-made disasters.

Ideas for Inquiry and Problem Solving Beyond the Text

If you have time to extend the unit, ask students to devise questions based on their reading, or use the questions below to spark an inquiry.

- What problems in towns and cities and among people do natural disasters cause?
- What do scientists need in order to improve the amount of warning time they can give people for twisters, earthquakes, and hurricanes?
- What must cities do to create efficient evacuation plans? Give an example of a city with an excellent evacuation plan.
- What kinds of medical care need to be in place in areas that have natural disasters?

TOP-NOTCH INFORMATIONAL TEXTS

On the Resources CD you will find a list of ten informational texts to review for your class and/or school library.

Students can use the texts they've read during the unit and/or research new texts to explore the issues raised by the questions, which are all connected to the theme of devastation. Students can write a short paper to share their results, participate in a class discussion or debate, write and present a speech, create posters displaying what they've learned—the possibilities are varied, and I find allowing students to choose their mode of presentation motivates and engages them.

CLOSING THOUGHTS AND QUESTIONS TO DISCUSS

You can continue professional study by discussing with a peer partner or a group of colleagues the parts of the lessons that worked and the parts that need refining. Here are some questions to guide your conversations:

- Why did some students have difficulty making logical inferences with informational texts? What kinds of interventions helped them move forward?

- How can you use informational text structure to inform your writing workshop? Would any of these short selections work as a mentor text? Choose which ones might work and explain why.

- How do your students feel about informational texts? How can you help them include more informational texts in their choice reading?

- How can studying students' notes and paragraphs help you better understand their comprehension? Their ability to write a clear and compelling paragraph? What kinds of mini-lessons and support do you need to provide in the next unit?

Scaffolding Suggestions for Helping Students Read Informational Texts

STUDENT'S NEED	POSSIBLE SCAFFOLD
Building prior knowledge: Takes sketchy notes that lack specific details and/or student copies author's words	• Ask the student to build prior knowledge during a conference and share the details recalled. Point out that he can reread the section to enhance recall of details. • Have the student paraphrase the details orally after reading each section of the preview and then write notes in her own words. • Read slowly and reread if the student has no prior knowledge.
Reading for the gist: Shows limited of the main details after the first reading	• Ask the student to read the selection again and then state the gist. • Ask the student why he thinks recall is difficult. • Change texts if the student doesn't have the gist after the second reading—text might be too difficult.

STUDENT'S NEED	POSSIBLE SCAFFOLD
Making logical inferences: Is unable to use text details to find unstated meanings	• Model, in a conference, how you use a section of text to infer. Have the student reread a different section, and you select the key details. Ask the student to use these details to infer. • Continue to practice until the student can select details and use them to infer.
Finding themes: Is unable to use details and what happens in the text to figure out theme	• Show the student how you select important details and use these to figure them out. • Turn the process over to the student. • Continue to model and think aloud until the student can pinpoint themes.
Choosing key words in a text and using them to infer and connect to ideas in the text: Can choose word and phrases but can not use these to generalize about tone, theme, or author's purpose	• Return to the modeling you did using *The Great Fire*. Show the student how you use words that are similar and connected to determine tone and connect the words to theme and the author's purpose. • Ask the student to reread the list of words and group words with similar meanings. The student rereads a group and tries to figure out the tone or mood the words create and/or links the group of words to a theme.
Analyzing text structure: Has difficulty understanding the techniques the author used to organize the text	• Ask the student to determine whether the piece argues for or explains a point as Murphy did in *The Great Fire* or whether the structure supports explaining and informing. • Divide a text into sections and have the student decide whether a section argues, explains, or informs.
Vocabulary and context clues: Needs support in using text clues to figure out the meaning of unfamiliar words	• Point out the sentence a word is in doesn't always contain the clue for figuring out its meaning. Show the student how you often have to reverse and read several sentences that came before as well as read sentences that come after the sentence that contains the word. • Have the student show you which parts of the text helped her figure out a word's meaning. • Provide lots of practice using context clues with peer partners so the student can apply this strategy to independent and instructional reading.

CHAPTER 4

Reading Biography

Jon is an eighth grader reading at a fourth-grade instructional level. His English teacher and I are working together to find sports books that Jon can read independently because he loves sports. At school, he plays varsity soccer and basketball, and he loves to watch football, baseball, and tennis on television. Matt Christopher has become one of Jon's favorite authors. Recently, I gave Jon several picture-book biographies and invited him to choose two. He selected *Muhammad Ali: The People's Champion* by Walter Dean Myers and *There Goes Ted Williams: The Greatest Hitter Who Ever Lived* by Matt Tavares. When I saw him next, I sat side by side with him at the conference table. "I loved the Ted Williams," he told me. "The batting stats in the back were what I love to read about. The best part was when he [Williams] crashed his bomber plane in World

War Two. It went up in flames, but he walked out. Man, it was cool that he chose the crashing and not ejecting."

"What made the crashing better?" I asked.

"He could break his legs if he jumped," Jon said. "And he might not be able to play baseball and run fast."

Jon continued to talk about Ted Williams and his batting. "I never thought I would enjoy a picture book now [in eighth grade]," he said. "I'm almost done with the Muhammad Ali book. Got any more about sports?"

Jon was clearly hooked on picture-book biographies about sports heroes. Moreover, he was excited about reading and chatted about the book with little to no prompting from me. Here's what I see as the winning strategy with reluctant readers: Tap into a student's interests and passion, find books he can read with ease, offer choice, and you'll nurture and cultivate his independent reading. At the same time, the student will move forward because he's reading and comprehending!

Like Jon, whose passion was sports, many students have interests that provide you with opportunities to invite them into the world of biography. Biography is the story of a person's life researched and written by another person; it can cover a person's life from birth to death or it can focus on just a part of it. Biographical subjects can be alive or dead, from the present day or the ancient past. Regardless of the era, a person featured in a biography has generally done something to change the world—in a positive way, like Marie Curie, or in a negative way, like Adolph Hitler. Biographical texts can be books or short pieces of two to four pages, like those by Kathleen Krull.

Biographers complete intensive research using primary sources, such as the subject's letters, speeches, interviews, or diaries, along with secondary sources, such as news articles and other books written about the person. Therefore, a biographer makes choices of what to include in his or her book and what to omit. Often, these choices represent the writer's view or opinion of the person and can skew the reader's thoughts. Many biographies contain elements of fiction, like dialogue and plot that writers reconstruct using primary sources (written by the person) and secondary ones (written about the person by others).

I've organized the short biography selections in this chapter around the concept of obstacles, a theme that middle-school students can relate to. As they explore who they are and how they fit into this world, middle-school students, like the men and women they will read about in this unit, will have to cope with internal and external obstacles. In this unit on biography, I will model how I apply the Common Core State Standards for reading to a short biography of Woodrow Wilson by Kathleen Krull. I'll do all of the following:

- infer why and how a person changes over time
- determine the central idea and how it develops
- identify connections between events and how events are related
- understand the author's purpose and point of view
- recall details
- make logical inferences
- identify themes

Here are lessons you can easily combine. These are only suggestions. Combine those lessons that you believe will best support your students.

- Lessons 1 and 2
- Lessons 4 and 5
- Lessons 9 and 10

Lessons 1 to 7

Model How to Read and Analyze Biography

In this set of lessons, you will use an anchor text to model key skills listed above and strategies that readers use when tackling complex biographies.

Text Complexity Grid

"Woodrow Wilson" by Kathleen Krull

Lexile®: 1320

Text Complexity: 1 = Accessible to 5 = Challenging

QUALITATIVE	1	2	3	4	5
Knowledge demands				X	
Author's purpose				X	
Meaning			X		
Text structure				X	
Language/vocabulary				X	
Concepts					X
Inferential thinking demands				X	

Getting Ready to Read

In this first lesson, you use the protocol modeled in Chapter 3 to generate knowledge about "Woodrow Wilson" by strategically previewing the text. You also begin a concept map for "obstacles," which you'll add to throughout the unit.

Materials

- "Woodrow Wilson," displayed on the whiteboard from the Resources CD
- Students' notebooks
- Students' copies of Building Prior Knowledge handout (see page 261 and the Resources CD)
- Chart paper and markers for note taking and generating concept map

Teaching the Lesson

1. Have students take out their Building Prior Knowledge handout; display "Woodrow Wilson."

2. Review how to build prior knowledge of a topic independently using the short biography of Woodrow Wilson. I say something like this:

    We're reading a new text today, a biography of Woodrow Wilson. Many people these days are not familiar with Woodrow Wilson, so let's take a moment to build our knowledge by previewing the text, using the same procedure we used in our informational text unit; consult your Building Prior Knowledge handout if you need to review the steps. Follow along as I read the first two paragraphs and the last paragraph, along with the five quiz items at the end of the text.

3. Read the first two and last paragraphs aloud, then think aloud about all the details you recall. Explain to students that talking about details they remember lets them know whether they recall enough details or need to reread to gather more.

4. Write on a sheet of chart paper what you learned from previewing "Woodrow Wilson." Here's my list:

    - Though Wilson didn't make sense of the alphabet until he was nine, he read tons of books—he spent more money on books than on clothes. I can infer that he valued reading and learning from books.

- Wilson was president of the United States during World War I.
- He was highly educated, and when he taught he was popular among students.
- He was president of Princeton University and governor of New Jersey. I can infer that he enjoyed politics and public service.
- He died at age 67.

5. Ask students to add any other ideas to the list. Here's what eighth-grade students added:

- Wilson was courageous and ready to meet death because his machinery—or body—was worn out.
- He overcame a big learning disability.

6. Tell students that today the class will start a concept map by thinking about the concept of "obstacles" in "Woodrow Wilson." They will revisit the map as they read other biographies in the coming weeks.

7. Write the word *obstacles* on chart paper. Introduce the term and invite students to pair-share words and phrases related to it. I say something like this:

Obstacles can be within or outside of a person. Obstacles can be feelings, thoughts, other people, and events. Turn to your partner and take two or three minutes to discuss obstacles; try to find words and phrases that relate to this concept. It's okay if no ideas come to mind. We'll revisit the concept map several times during our study.

8. Ask students to share the words they came up with; accept any word or phrase students offer as long as they can link it to *obstacles*. My eighth-grade students offered these suggestions: *your emotions, an illness, a handicap.*

9. Read "Woodrow Wilson" aloud to help students get the gist of some of the ideas in the short biography.

10. Ask students to pair-share and discuss the gist of "Woodrow Wilson." Then invite partners to share their thoughts with the class.

> Taking the time to have students connect their ideas to the concept can enlarge their prior knowledge, vocabulary, and analytical thinking.

Wrap-Up

Acknowledge students' listening skills and their contributions to the concept map.

Identifying Genre Characteristics and Setting Purposes

In this lesson, students explore the characteristics of biography and set a purpose for the second reading of "Woodrow Wilson."

Materials

- "Woodrow Wilson," displayed on the whiteboard from the Resources CD
- Students' copies of the Building Prior Knowledge handout
- Students' notebooks
- Prior-knowledge notes from Lesson 1
- "Obstacles" concept map begun in Lesson 1
- Chart paper and markers

Teaching the Lesson

1. Invite students to talk with a partner to identify the genre characteristics of "Woodrow Wilson," a biography.

2. Circulate among students to listen to their conversations. Responses like those below indicate that students have identified characteristics of biography:

   It's about a past president, so he's an important person. Under the title it gives his birth and death date. It says under title that he was the leader of the U.S. in World War I. It starts when he was nine and goes to his death. Tells about his marriages and children. Gives information about his life. The title is a clue—his name.

   If students miss an important characteristic of the genre, take some time to point it out to them (see box on page 92 for a list of characteristics for biography). Be sure students understand that biographies reflect the point of view of the biographer and that students should read critically with this awareness.

3. Have students reread the prior-knowledge notes you took in Lesson 1. They might also wish to review the Building Prior Knowledge handout.

4. Ask pairs to set a purpose for listening to "Woodrow Wilson" a second time. Have them use the title, information from your notes, or the concept "obstacles" to set a purpose for listening to "Woodrow Wilson." If students have difficulty figuring out

Genre Characteristics: Biography

- Provides an account of a person's life, usually from early life through death
- Has subject who has usually done something to change the world; this person can be alive or dead
- Draws on primary and secondary sources
- Sets life story in historical context
- Often uses literary elements, such as dialogue
- Often includes maps, photos, or other historical documents
- Conveys the biographer's point of view and purpose for reporting on the person's life

a purpose for reading, show them that they can use the title to set a purpose: *My purpose is to find out more about Woodrow Wilson.*

5. Have students pair-share and discuss their purposes for listening, and then invite a few students to share different purposes.

6. Reread the selection aloud and have students follow along, keeping their purposes in mind. Explain that this is a second reading and that hearing the selection twice will deepen their comprehension and enable them to recall more details.

7. Ask students to identify details that relate to their purposes for listening. As you circulate, offer help to students as they recall relevant details, rereading the text from the whiteboard as necessary.

8. Return to the "obstacles" concept map. Invite students to pair-share and add more ideas to the map, encouraging them to add words and phrases based on the second reading. Make sure you ask them to connect their words and phrases to the concept, provide specific examples, and share their thinking with the entire class.

Wrap-Up

Point out the positive discussions students had and highlight the number of ideas they added to the concept map.

Making Inferences and Finding Central Ideas

In this lesson, you model how to use key details from the text to make logical inferences and find the central idea. Then pairs practice this skill as you listen in and provide support.

Materials

- "Woodrow Wilson," displayed on the whiteboard from the Resources CD
- Students' notebooks
- "Obstacles" concept map
- Chart paper and markers

Teaching the Lesson

1. Display "Woodrow Wilson" and tell students that today's focus is to use detail to infer and find central ideas.

2. Tell students that since this is a biography, you want to examine how the people and events in Wilson's life affected him. Think aloud about important details and what you can infer from them. Here's my thinking; adapt to your students' needs:

When we look closely at a person's life, we can learn how certain events and people affect the person, and we can learn from the choices the person makes. Today I'm going to look closely at the details Kathleen Krull presents about Wilson and see what I can infer about him. Since she identifies Wilson as "possibly dyslexic," I can infer that he struggled in school. Despite this challenge, he grew up to be a scholar and our most highly educated president, so I can infer that he wanted to learn and be successful, and that he worked very hard.

I find it interesting that Wilson firmly opposed women's right to vote, yet he was president when women started voting. Krull says that's because he found it politically useful to change his stance on the issue. I infer that he could sense the power of the women's movement and knew it was useless to oppose it any longer. Looking at his relationships with his wives and daughters, it's clear that he loved and valued the women in his life, so I also infer that his personal relationships with women led him to be more sympathetic to women's suffrage.

While he eventually accepted women's voting, apparently he did not believe in African Americans having the vote. Krull reports that he broke the promises for reform that he made to black voters, and he only met with African American leaders once. From these details, I can infer that he did not believe African Americans could exert political power as women had; I also infer that he was prejudiced against African Americans, perhaps because he did not know any personally, the way he had close relationships with his wives and daughters.

3. Read aloud the last two paragraphs of "Woodrow Wilson." Have students pair-share to discuss why Wilson didn't resign the presidency when he had a serious stroke. Here's what eighth graders suggested:

    • He gave in because she [Edith] was forceful, hid his condition, and ran the government well.

    • He let Edith make the decisions because he was too sick to argue. Also, he believed God ordained him to be president, so he should never resign.

4. Show students how your inferences point to the central idea. I say something like this:

    A central idea is a fundamental point the author tries to make. Everything in the text will somehow relate to this idea. In this short biography of Woodrow Wilson, one central idea is that Wilson changed his stand when it was politically advantageous. An example is his letting women have the vote but reversing his promise to desegregate government after he was elected, because at that time African Americans were not as powerful a political force as women.

5. I ask students to talk with their partners to see if they can identify another central idea. My eighth graders suggested that Wilson's dependence on women, especially Edith, his second wife, along with Wilson's belief that he was ordained by God to be president, allowed Wilson to let Edith run the government and hide his illness from others.

6. Return to the concept map and invite partners to generate words and phrases to add to the "obstacles" concept map. Have them make connections between words and phrases and the concept of obstacles and share these with the class.

Wrap-Up

Provide positive feedback on students' inferences and on discussing central ideas.

Close Reading and Finding the Author's Purpose

In this lesson, students practice close reading to make connections between events in "Woodrow Wilson." You will also show students how you determine the author's purpose and point of view.

Materials

- "Woodrow Wilson," displayed on the whiteboard from the Resources CD
- Students' notebooks
- Students' copies of Close Reading Guidelines (see page 262 and the Resources CD)

Teaching the Lesson

1. Have students retrieve their Close Reading Guidelines handout and review it with them.

2. Tell students that you are going to model how to close read to make connections between events and then determine what these connections reveal. This is what I say:

   Now I'm going to show you how I close read to find connections between events and see what these connections mean. The events in this short biography are in chronological order, reporting on Wilson's life from age nine to his death, which enables me to observe changes in Wilson's attitudes and personality as parts of his life unfold. The author says that Wilson was never robust which, when I close read, I figure out means strong and healthy. She says that Wilson had a "positive attitude" about his health. I connect this to his determination to succeed in school despite his challenges with reading—clearly he had a positive attitude about his intellect as well. This further connects to his belief that God had foreordained him to be president. I infer that the reason he felt positive about his abilities and health is that he believed God was taking care of him. This connects to his acceptance of death as well; he would not fear going to a God who had nurtured him his whole life.

   This idea about his positive belief in himself based on God connects to the central idea we discussed last time, about Wilson changing his stand when it was politically advantageous. Since he believed he was meant to president, he most likely felt he could do what was necessary to remain in power, even if it meant changing his position, or letting Edith run the country.

3. Invite students to talk with a partner and see if they can connect events in "Woodrow Wilson." Encourage them to close read to support making these connections. Here's what a pair of eighth graders said:

Wilson needed a woman by his side. His first wife ran the household and helped Wilson proofread his writing. Wilson married his second wife a little more than a year after his first wife died, showing his need to have a woman around. The second marriage took Wilson out of his depression; we close read and learned that he was no longer depressed because he whistled songs and danced while walking in public.

4. Invite students to pair-share to determine the author's purpose and point of view in "Woodrow Wilson." (Model this for students if you feel they need to continue to observe your thinking.)

A group of eighth graders agree that Kathleen Krull's purpose was to choose parts of Woodrow Wilson's life to show these points:

- He used his intelligence and hard work to overcome his disability.
- He was dependent on women and needed to be married.
- His actions with African Americans showed that Wilson was prejudiced.

This eighth-grade class believed that Krull's purpose was to show the human side of Woodrow Wilson, the leader of our country.

Wrap-Up

Point out students' good use of close reading to make connections between events and to figure out the author's purpose and point of view.

LESSON 5

Collaborative Discussions

In this lesson, you review how to make inferences; then students work in pairs to discuss text-specific questions—rereading, skimming, and close reading from the whiteboard as necessary to find evidence to support their ideas.

Materials

- "Woodrow Wilson," displayed on the whiteboard from the Resources CD
- Students' notebooks

- Copics of Discussion Prompts for "Woodrow Wilson" (see page 98 and the Resources CD), class set
- Students' copies of Close Reading Guidelines
- "Obstacles" concept map
- Chart paper and markers

Displaying the text in two-page view makes it easier for students to reread the text; see page 45.

Teaching the Lesson

1. Organize students into partners whose instructional reading levels are no more than one year apart. Students reading three or more years below grade level can work together with your support.

2. Have students take out their copy of the Close Reading Guidelines and briefly review them.

3. Explain to students that they're going to discuss some questions about "Woodrow Wilson" that ask them to infer and use close reading to comprehend the details in the text.

4. Ask students to pair-share and discuss everything they recall about making inferences and close reading. As you circulate among students, listen in and spotlight any responses that will help the class by asking partners to share their thinking.

5. Show students how you use the text to make an inference. Here's what I say:

   After reading the statement that the president and his wife, Edith, got a herd of sheep to munch on the lawn of the White House to save energy, I can infer that they were aware of the sacrifices Americans made, and they wanted to set an example of saving money for the war effort. Notice that the inference isn't stated in the text. I had to use the information and my own knowledge to infer.

6. Distribute the discussion prompts to students. Have partners discuss the prompts and find text evidence by rereading the parts that help contain the answer. Encourage students to use the Close Reading Guidelines for parts that confuse them and to make logical inferences from key details.

7. Give students about five to ten minutes to discuss the questions for "Woodrow Wilson." Encourage them to jot down notes and specific paragraph numbers that they used to find evidence. Circulate to listen, and extend or shorten the time as needed.

8. Invite partners to share their answers, and if they close read a part, explain how close reading helped them infer.

9. Return to the "obstacles" concept map. Have students add words and phrases

to the map and invite them to connect their ideas to the concept of "obstacles," sharing their ideas with the class.

DISCUSSION PROMPTS FOR "WOODROW WILSON"

1. Discuss and evaluate Wilson's attitude toward African Americans.

2. Find details that show that Wilson was both a forceful public figure and a shy man.

3. How did Wilson's first wife, Ellen, fit the role of a subservient woman?

4. How and why did Wilson's mood change after he married Edith?

5. Explain how during the war Wilson and Edith set an example for Americans.

6. Why was it ironic that Edith took over Wilson's duties when he had a stroke?

7. What do you learn about Edith when you read that she refused to let Wilson resign?

8. What is a central idea in "Woodrow Wilson"?

Wrap-Up

Provide feedback on the quality of students' discussions and on their ability to infer using text evidence.

LESSON 6

Assessment: Test-Taking Strategies

In this lesson, model how to strategically answer quiz items and find support in the text. Then have students complete the quiz with a partner.

Materials

- "Woodrow Wilson," displayed on the whiteboard from the Resources CD
- Prior-knowledge notes from Lesson 1
- Copies of the "Woodrow Wilson" quiz (see the Resources CD), class set
- Copies of Quiz Answer Sheet (see page 263 and the Resources CD), class set
- Quiz Answer Key for "Woodrow Wilson" (see page 267 and the Resources CD)

Teaching the Lesson

1. Distribute the "Woodrow Wilson" quiz. Reread aloud "Woodrow Wilson" and the quiz items at the end of the selection. Ask students to raise a hand if a part confuses them and they require a close reading; if so, model how to close read one section.

2. Review the Building Prior Knowledge notes.

3. Demonstrate how you answer the first quiz item. This model is thorough, so you can observe my thinking; adapt to the needs of your students. Here's my thinking:

I'll work through the first item that asks: Why did Wilson remarry little more than a year after Ellen died? *I'll think about the choices one at a time.*
A: He needed someone to proofread his writing. *Though Ellen helped Wilson with proofreading, the text does not give this as a reason for remarrying. In fact, Edith, his second wife, was his coworker, by Wilson's side at every public occasion. They did everything together (see paragraph 5).* B: He wanted his children to have a mother. *In the third paragraph the text says Wilson's three daughters worshipped him, but never mentions that he married Edith to provide them with a mother.* C: He needed a companion. *This choice seems reasonable. In the fourth paragraph we learn that at Ellen's funeral, Wilson "sobbed uncontrollably." He told an aide that he wished someone would assassinate him because he couldn't go on without Ellen. These details help me infer that Wilson was lonely, sad, and depressed without his wife. Once he became engaged to Edith, Wilson whistled vaudeville tunes and danced on and off the curbs of sidewalks. This further supports his need for a companion because with Edith in his life his sadness and depression left. He was no longer lonely because he had a companion to share his life.* D: He wanted someone to help him with his presidential duties. *In the sixth paragraph we learn that Edith did help Wilson with presidential duties, but only after he had a major stroke and could not complete his duties. Edith took over the duties so no one would know how sick Wilson was. This was not his reason for marrying a little more than a year after Ellen's death. I believe that C is the best choice—He needed a companion. For evidence, I'm using the details in paragraph 4.*

4. If you feel your students need extra support, you can model how you answer the second quiz item as well.

5. Give students the Quiz Answer Sheet. Tell them to write their name, the date, and the title of text at the top. Then have them record the answer(s) for the item(s) you modeled answering for them, writing the letter of the answer in the first column and the number(s) of the paragraph(s) containing the evidence they used in the second column. Note that they will *not* be writing a paragraph about one of their answers during this lesson because the focus is on helping students practice the test-taking strategies modeled.

6. Pair students with partners and have them complete

the remaining quiz items. If you have students who cannot read the text independently, work with them in a group, rereading passages for them so they can complete the quiz.

7.   When students finish, call out the answers as students self-check, or collect the quizzes to score later.

Wrap-Up

Acknowledge students for successfully reading and skimming "Woodrow Wilson" to locate the paragraphs that helped them find the best answer.

LESSON 7

Writing About Reading

This lesson lets you offer your students two options. The first is to plan and write a summary of "Woodrow Wilson," and the second is to plan and write an explanatory paragraph using text evidence from the biography. The summary is ideal for those developing readers who need to practice selecting information for summarizing. If you have enough class time and think that all students can benefit from both tasks, then invite students to complete both a summary and an explanatory paragraph. You might need two or three sessions for everyone to complete the plans and writing; set aside enough time for students to complete a first draft.

> Displaying the text in two-page view makes it easier for students to reread the text; see page 45.

Materials

- "Woodrow Wilson," displayed on the whiteboard from the Resources CD
- Students' notebooks
- Additional paper for writing a summary or paragraph
- Copies of Somebody-Wanted-But-So (SWBS) Organizer (see the Resources CD), for students writing summaries
- Copies of Guidelines for Writing a Summary (see page 266 and the Resources CD), for students writing summaries
- Copies of the Elements of a Paragraph handout (see page 265 and the Resources CD), for students writing explanatory paragraphs
- Copies of Rubric: Literature Summary and Rubric: Paragraph (see the Resources CD)
- Sticky notes

Teaching the Lesson

1. Determine which students will work on which assignment, either by assigning them a topic or allowing them to choose. In my seventh-grade class, I assigned writing the summary to my below-grade-level readers, and the explanatory paragraph to my on-grade-level students. To avoid confusion, make a list in your plan book or a notebook detailing who's writing a summary and who's writing an explanatory paragraph. Meet with each group separately, presenting the assignment as discussed below.

2. Gather students who will write a summary and distribute the Somebody-Wanted-But-So (SWBS) Organizer, the Guidelines for Writing a Summary handout, and the rubric. Note that the SWBS Organizer is used for narrative texts; it is a different planning form from the 5W's Organizer students used in the unit on informational texts and will require its own introduction. Introduce the assignment by saying something like this:

   Summarizing narratives is an important skill because it helps you select the most important elements from a story and put them together in a way that helps you remember them and identify the main points and themes the author is trying to convey. Writing a summary informs your reader about the text you have read.

   To help you plan and write a summary of narrative text, use the Somebody-Wanted-But-So graphic organizer, which guides you to identify the key details from the text: Somebody *is the protagonist;* Wanted *identifies the problem;* But *describes the obstacles or antagonistic forces; and* So *shows how the problems was resolved—without giving the ending away. Jot down important details from the text for each of these, and you'll be well on your way to writing a summary.*

   After you've filled out the organizer, use the Guidelines for Writing a Summary to draft your summary. You can use the rubric to revise your work. Let's review the directions, and then you can get to work.

   Walk students through the handouts. See page 102 for a sample summary.

3. Gather students who will write the explanatory paragraph and distribute the Elements of a Paragraph handout and the Rubric: Paragraph. Review the guidelines on pages 61–62 if necessary. Then invite students to respond to this statement about "Woodrow Wilson": *Wilson's two marriages revealed specific personality traits about this president.*

   They should write the statement in their notebook, collect evidence from the text to support it, then generate a topic sentence and write the paragraph.

4. As students write, circulate to observe students taking notes and then drafting a summary or paragraph.

5. Sit side by side with students who require extra support. Acknowledge any successes that students achieved. When possible, use questions rather than statements to

address areas that need more work. Questions honor and empower students. Write helpful suggestions on sticky notes and give the note to the student as a reminder of your conversation. Remind students to use the rubric to guide their revisions.

6. Gauge students' progress to determine how much time to allow for the writing.

If you feel students need additional modeling before moving on to the guided practice portion of the unit, work through Lessons 1-7 again using the excerpt from *Sir Francis Drake* as the read-aloud text (see the Resources CD).

Wrap-Up

Provide positive feedback on their detailed plans and their paragraphs.

Writing a Summary With the Somebody-Wanted-But-So Organizer

The Somebody-Wanted-But-So (SWBS) Organizer is the ideal tool for helping students plan and write a summary for biography and fiction. The framework helps students move from retelling to selecting key details. *Somebody* is the name of the protagonist, *Wanted* states a problem the protagonist faced; *But* names a force that worked against the protagonist; and *So* shows how the problem was resolved, without giving the ending away.

Once students have completed the organizer, they should generate a topic sentence that states the author's purpose and includes the title and author. Then students can turn notes into complete sentences. The handout Guidelines for Writing a Summary outlines the steps and provides a checklist for students to use to check their work.

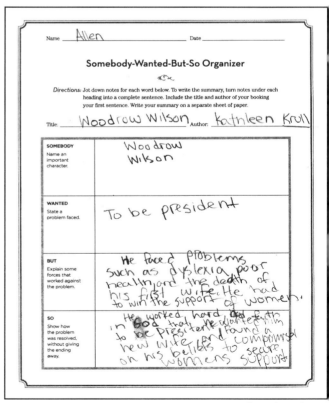

Sample notes

> In "Woodrow Wilson" Kathleen Krull chooses events from Wilson's life that show he wants to lead the country. Wilson prayed every morning and night that he believed in God wanted him to become president. He overcame trouble in school and poor health to become highly educated, the president of Princeton University, and the governor of New Jersey. He depended on his wife; Ellen took care of their home and proofread his work. When she died, he was very sad and did not know how he would continue. But less than a year when he married again. He went on the win the presidency by making promises to women and black citizens, promises he kept only when it was useful to him. He had a stroke while president but refused to give up power. He let his wife Edith take over his duties. He did not live long after presidency. He died two years after leaving the office.

Sample paragraph for "Woodrow Wilson"

Lessons 8 to 14

Guided Practice With a New Biography

In this next series of lessons, you start releasing responsibility to students, reviewing and coaching as they practice the skills and strategies you modeled with "Woodrow Wilson." Assign students a text based on their reading level; text complexity grids for each selection appear on page 104. Then work through the lessons at a pace that's reasonable for your students, allowing one to two weeks depending on students' needs.

Text Complexity Grids

Selection from *Idi Amin* by Steve Dougherty
Lexile®: 1040
Text Complexity: 1 = Accessible to 5 = Challenging

QUALITATIVE	1	2	3	4	5
Knowledge demands					X
Author's purpose				X	
Meaning				X	
Text structure				X	
Language/vocabulary				X	
Concepts				X	
Inferential thinking demands					X

Selection from *Napoleon Complex* by Karen Baicker
Lexile®: 970
Text Complexity: 1 = Accessible to 5 = Challenging

QUALITATIVE	1	2	3	4	5
Knowledge demands				X	
Author's purpose				X	
Meaning				X	
Text structure				X	
Language/vocabulary				X	
Concepts				X	
Inferential thinking demands					X

LESSON 8

Building Prior Knowledge and Setting Purposes

In this lesson, students receive a new passage; they preview and read for the gist with peer support. They also have the opportunity to add words to the concept map.

Materials

- Copies of excerpt from *Idi Amin* for students reading at or above grade level
- Copies of excerpt from *Napoleon Complex* for students reading below grade level
- Students' notebooks
- "Obstacles" concept map
- Chart paper and markers or interactive whiteboard

Teaching the Lesson

1. Review the method you modeled for building prior knowledge in Lesson 1. Distribute the copies of the texts to students. Have students suggest the number of paragraphs they need to read on the first page. Remind them to read the last paragraph and the quiz items.

   Your students might not know much about Idi Amin, and previewing the text might not provide enough background information. Set aside some time to familiarize students with Idi Amin. You can find detailed information on Wikipedia or other Web sites. Remember, when you enlarge students' background knowledge, you can improve their comprehension and recall.

2. Have students preview to build prior knowledge. Remind them to make a list in their notebooks of what they learn.

   - Read *Napoleon Complex* out loud to students who struggle with the text.
   - Follow directions for working with two groups by referring to Chapter 3, page 67.

3. Ask students to reread their lists and use the information to set purposes for reading. Remind them that to set purposes they can use the title, notes in their list of prior knowledge, or the concept of obstacles. Circulate and support students who need extra help.

4. Have students read the selection silently, using their prior knowledge to get the gist or general idea of the text.

5. Ask students who read the same passage to pair-share to discuss the gist of their selection and connect the content to "obstacles."

6. Circulate and listen to partner-talk to determine whether students have the gist. If some students seem confused, support them by helping them close read and/or reread.

7. Display the concept map and invite students to add words from their selection to the map, always connecting their ideas to the concept. Students share these words and phrases with the entire class.

Wrap-Up

Point out what students did well as they built their prior knowledge and set purposes. Give positive feedback on the words and phrases students added to the concept map.

LESSON 9

Review Close Reading, Inferring, and Central Idea

In this lesson, students will review the strategies of close reading, making inferences, and identifying central ideas.

Materials

- Students' copies of *Idi Amin*
- Students' copies of *Napoleon Complex*
- Students' copies of Close Reading Guidelines

Teaching the Lesson

1. Pair students with partners who are reading the same text.

2. Refresh students' recall of close reading; review the guideline sheet with them and discuss how the strategy can help them figure out the meaning of a difficult word or confusing passage. Remind students to use close reading when they come across a word or phrase they don't understand.

3. Have students reread their selection silently, keeping in mind the previous day's purpose for reading. Gather students who cannot read *Napoleon Complex* independently and read it aloud to them. Ask them to raise their hands when they hear a word or sentence(s) that confuses them, so you can model close reading. Otherwise, you can select words and sentences to close read.

4. Ask pairs to share how close reading helped them figure out a difficult word or a passage that confused them.

5. Invite pairs to discuss what they know about the central idea. Remind them of Lesson 3, in which you modeled finding a central idea for "Woodrow Wilson." Circulate and listen for comments such as: *It's like theme, but it's the important one. It's an idea that's connects to the whole thing. There can be more than one. It needs to come from inference because it's not said in the book.* Review the modeling you did with "Woodrow Wilson" for those students who can't explain central idea.

6. Ask partners to find a central idea for *Idi Amin* or *Napoleon Complex* and explain how the details in their piece helped them infer and pinpoint the central idea. Circulate and listen to partners discuss. Prompt students with questions such as: *What are the main events? What idea ties the main events together? What did the author want to show you? Can you connect the author's purpose to the central idea?*

7. Spotlight students who "get it" and have them explain to the class what helped them identify the central idea; this provides everyone with multiple models.

Wrap-Up

Acknowledge students for applying close reading and figuring out a central idea for *Idi Amin* or *Napoleon Complex*.

LESSON 10

Collaborative Discussions

In this lesson, partners work together to answer text-specific questions about the biography they read independently.

Materials

- Students' copies of *Idi Amin*
- Students' copies of *Napoleon Complex*
- Discussion Prompts for *Idi Amin* and *Napoleon Complex* (see page 108 and the Resources CD)
- Students' copies of Close Reading Guidelines

> **TEACHING TIP —**
> **SCAFFOLDING STUDENTS' READING**
>
> *Support students who can't read* Napoleon Complex *independently, by first pointing to the section in the text that answers the discussion question and then rereading that section for them.*

Teaching the Lesson

1. Pair students with partners who have read the same text. Gather students who can't read *Napoleon Complex* independently and work with them.

2. Display the discussion questions on a whiteboard or give a copy to each student. Invite partners to use the discussion prompts to discuss *Idi Amin* or *Napoleon Complex,* always showing where they found their answer in the text.

3. Have partners make connections between events and share ideas with other pairs who have read the same text.

4. Ask partners to share their inferences with the entire class. This provides all students with additional models of using details to infer.

Wrap-Up

Give students positive feedback for engaging in detailed discussions and for using text evidence to support their responses. Point out the connections students made between events in their text.

DISCUSSION PROMPTS FOR *IDI AMIN*

1. Discuss three things that Palestinian terrorists did to make their demands known to Israel and the world.

2. Why did Amin welcome the hijacked airplane to Uganda?

3. How did Israel spoil Amin's plans?

4. What did Amin do to the hostage Dora Bloch? Why do you think he did this? Explain why the author says this act was the beginning of the end for Idi Amin.

5. What is a *sham trial*? How did it affect Luwun and the Anglican bishops?

6. Why did church leaders around the world call Amin a "wicked man"?

7. What is a central idea in this biography? Use evidence from the text to support your thinking.

DISCUSSION PROMPTS FOR *NAPOLEON COMPLEX*

1. Why did Napoleon feel insecure when he was young?

2. What motivated Napoleon to abandon or give up the ideals of the Revolution—liberty, equality, fraternity?

3. Show that Napoleon was a brilliant military leader.

4. Why was the invasion of Austria in 1800 "the most daring the world has ever known"?

5. Name three obstacles Napoleon faced. How did he deal with each obstacle?

6. What is a central idea in *Napoleon Complex*? Use text evidence to support your thinking.

Assessment

In this lesson, students complete the quiz items that follow their text selection. Students have already read the items during their preview in Lesson 8 and should be familiar with them. In addition to answering the multiple-choice items and identifying paragraphs that support their answers, students will choose one item and defend their answer in a brief paragraph.

Materials

- Students' copies of *Idi Amin*
- Students' copies of *Napoleon Complex*
- Copies of the Quiz Answer Sheet (see page 263 and the Resources CD), class set
- Quiz Answer Keys for *Idi Amin* and *Napoleon Complex* (see page 267 and the Resources CD)

Teaching the Lesson

1. Give students the Quiz Answer Sheet. Go over the directions and encourage students to skim and reread parts of *Idi Amin* or *Napoleon Complex* so they can note the paragraph or paragraphs that contain evidence for their answer.

2. Have students complete the quiz independently. This includes choosing one answer that they'll defend in a short paragraph; remind them that they may not choose a vocabulary item to write about.

3. Support students who can't read *Napoleon Complex* or the quiz items independently. Reread the selection for students. Then read the quiz items one at a time and have students select the best answer.

4. When students finish, call out answers to the multiple-choice portion; have students self-correct and turn their papers in to you, or collect the papers and grade them yourself.

5. Separate the quizzes into two piles: students who scored a 4 or 5, and students who missed two or more multiple-choice statements.

6. Read the paragraphs students wrote to defend one of their answers. Check the response to make sure it has details from the text and follows the Guidelines for Planning a Paragraph on the Quiz Answer Sheet. Make note of students who have difficulty, and plan time to scaffold their learning.

Help students who struggled with the paragraph portion of the quiz by working with them in a small group. Show them how to take notes on evidence from the text and then write a brief paragraph that explains their thinking about a question, incorporating the answer from the quiz along with their own text evidence.

Wrap-Up

Give students positive feedback for returning to the text and skimming or rereading before selecting an answer and for defending one of their answers.

**TEACHING TIP —
SCAFFOLDING STUDENTS
AFTER THE QUIZ**

Work individually or with small groups of students who missed two or more questions. Do this as the rest of the class reads silently during the second half of your class period. Help students see how looking back in the text can support inferential thinking and recall of text details. These students might benefit from completing an additional practice selection that you choose, depending on how they do on the second-week assessment. See the Resources CD for additional selections.

LESSONS 12

Writing About Reading: Note Taking

Students collect evidence for an explanatory paragraph about their biography.

Materials

- Students' copies of *Idi Amin*
- Students' copies of *Napoleon Complex*
- Copies of the Note-Taking Guidelines for *Idi Amin* and *Napoleon Complex* (see page 111 and the Resources CD), class set
- Students' notebooks

Teaching the Lesson

1. Explain that today students will take notes on *Idi Amin* or *Napoleon Complex* in order to plan an explanatory paragraph. Distribute the Note-Taking Guidelines

for *Idi Amin* and *Napoleon Complex*; you may also want to display them on the chalkboard or project them onto a whiteboard.

2. As the students who are writing about *Idi Amin* work independently, taking notes on the quote from the text, support students who are working with *Napoleon Complex*. Because this group consists of developing readers and English language learners, I decided to let them choose a question the class had already discussed, so they would have background knowledge for the note-taking process.

3. Circulate as students work, supporting students who need help or have questions. Students may need help finding evidence or paraphrasing the text.

Wrap-Up

Provide positive feedback on students' use of the text to take detailed notes.

Note-Taking Guidelines for *Idi Amin*

"At long last, Idi Amin stood exposed to the world."

1. Write the quote in your notebook.

2. Skim and reread to find two to three key details that provide evidence for this quote. Write them in your own words in your notebook.

Note-Taking Guidelines for *Napoleon Complex*

1. Reread Discussion Prompts 2 and 3:
    *   What motivated Napoleon to abandon or give up the ideals of the Revolution—liberty, equality, fraternity?
    *   Show that Napoleon was a brilliant military leader.

2. Choose one prompt to address in a paragraph; write it in your notebook.

3. Find at least two key details from the text that provide evidence to support your point. Write the details in your notebook, using your own words.

Writing About Reading: Drafting

In this lesson, students write an explanatory paragraph about their text, drawing on the notes they took in the previous lesson and consulting the Elements of a Paragraph handout. Students will need more than 20 minutes to complete the writing; I suggest allowing 30 to 45 minutes for the task, either during one class period or two smaller chunks of time over two class periods.

Materials

- Students' copies of *Idi Amin*
- Students' copies of *Napoleon Complex*
- Students' copies of Elements of a Paragraph handout
- Students' copies of the Rubric: Paragraph
- Students' notebooks
- Additional paper for drafting a paragraph

Teaching the Lesson

1. Ask students to take out their Elements of a Paragraph handout and review the elements:

    - Title
    - Introductory sentence
    - Text-based evidence
    - Concluding sentence

2. Suggest to students who are writing about *Idi Amin* that they use the quote to develop an introductory sentence. Write the quote on the board for reference: "At long last, Idi Amin stood exposed to the world." Remind them that they can weave the quote into their introductory sentence.

3. Help the students writing about *Napoleon Complex* by asking them to restate the prompt they chose for their paragraph as a way to develop an introductory sentence. You can also encourage them to craft an original introductory sentence.

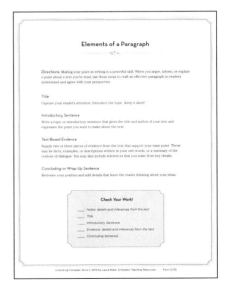

4. Instruct students to use their notes from the previous lesson to write a complete paragraph, following the guidelines on the handout.

5. Circulate and support students as necessary. Always begin by noting the positives a student has achieved, and remember to phrase suggestions as questions to honor and empower your students. Remind students to use the rubric to revise their writing.

6. Collect the paragraphs and assess them, using the rubric. You can note errors in spelling, usage, and punctuation and use this data for writing mini-lessons and in one-to-one conferences.

Wrap-Up

Provide positive feedback to students on using their notes to craft their paragraphs.

WRAPPING UP THE UNIT

Independent Practice and Assessment

In the last part of the unit, students work with a text independently, so you can assess their progress, scaffolding or extending their learning as appropriate.

Text Complexity Grid

"Cleopatra" by Kathleen Krull
Lexile®: 1090
Text Complexity: 1 = Accessible to 5 = Challenging

QUALITATIVE	1	2	3	4	5
Knowledge demands					X
Author's purpose			X		
Meaning				X	
Text structure			X		
Language/vocabulary				X	
Concepts					X
Inferential thinking demands				X	

Text Complexity Grid

Selection from *Ice Queen: Catherine the Great Seizes Power in Russia* by Louise Rozett

Lexile®: 840

Text Complexity: 1 = Accessible to 5 = Challenging

QUALITATIVE	1	2	3	4	5
Knowledge demands					X
Author's purpose				X	
Meaning				X	
Text structure				X	
Language/vocabulary				X	
Concepts					X
Inferential thinking demands				X	

ASSESSMENT

Reading a New Text Independently

Have students work on their own, as this is an assessment that will help you determine students' strengths and needs. They will build prior knowledge and read the text independently. For the assessment, you have three options: students can write a summary, compose an explanatory paragraph, or complete a Word Map about the unit's concept. I recommend that each student do at least one writing activity and complete the Word Map.

Set aside five or six consecutive days for the assessment. You will probably need two 30- to 45-minute classes for students to build prior knowledge, read for the gist, reread for deeper understanding, and complete the Word Map. Over the next three or four days, take about 35–45 minutes to have students complete the writing. If a few students need more time for taking notes and writing, give them the extra time.

Materials

- Copies of "Cleopatra" for students reading at or above grade level
- Copies of excerpt from *Ice Queen: Catherine the Great Seizes Power in Russia* for students reading below grade level
- Students' copies of Building Prior Knowledge handout

- Students' copies of Guidelines for Writing a Summary
- Copies of the SWBS Organizer (see the Resources CD), for student writing summaries
- Students' copies of the Elements of a Paragraph handout
- Copies of Writing Topics for each assessment text (see the Resources CD), for students writing paragraphs
- Copies of the Word Map (see the Resources CD), class set
- Students' copies of the Rubrics for Literature Summary and Paragraph
- Students' notebooks
- Additional notebook paper for writing summaries and/or paragraphs

Teaching the Lesson

1. Have students take out their copy of the Building Prior Knowledge handout while you distribute the assessment texts and copies of the Word Map.

2. Remind students to use the strategy they have practiced to build their prior knowledge and jot down a list of what they learned from their preview in their notebook. Tell them that on the first two days of the assessment, they should preview the text to build prior knowledge, then read for the gist. Encourage them to reread the text for deeper comprehension before they complete the Word Map.

3. Invite students to complete the Word Map, specifying how many characteristics and examples you want them to provide to demonstrate their understanding of the concept.

4. On the next day, ask those students who will be writing a summary to take out their Guidelines for Writing a Summary handout. Give them a SWBS Organizer and the rubric you will use to assess the summary.

5. Ask those students who will be writing a paragraph to take out their Elements of a Paragraph handout. Distribute the Writing Topics list and the rubric you will use to assess the paragraph.

6. Invite students to reread and take notes for their summaries

> ### TEACHING TIP —
> ### PEER ASSESSMENT
>
> *Have students give their plans and first drafts to a writing partner. Ask the partner to use the rubric and the Guidelines for Writing a Summary or Elements of a Paragraph handout to make sure all elements have been included. Partners give each other feedback that can improve their summaries or paragraphs. Have students write a second draft based on peer feedback. Collect and read the drafts.*

or paragraphs. Have them work through the writing process outlined on the Guidelines for Writing a Summary handout or the Elements of a Paragraph handout, consulting the corresponding rubric to check their work.

7. When students finish, have them turn in their work. Assess it using the rubric.

Interpreting Assessments

The paragraphs can show you whether students can make logical inferences and find specific text details from the selection. See the Scaffolding Suggestions chart on page 119 to help you support students with reading issues.

To scaffold students who require writing support, use the Scaffolding Suggestions for Helping Students Write Summaries and Paragraphs chart on the Resources CD.

Following Up the Assessment

Based on your assessment of students' writing, you can determine how many days to spend scaffolding and extending their learning. I recommend allowing at least one day for students to revise their writing based on your feedback; during that time, you can meet with your most struggling readers. Then you may choose to spend additional days working in small groups, scaffolding students who need it and extending the learning of those who are ready for more challenge.

Supporting Students Who Require Scaffolding

The chart on page 119 offers scaffolding suggestions based on students' writing, your observations as they read and discuss texts, and your conferences on independent and instructional reading. Support students with similar needs by working with groups of two or three. When students struggle and are unsuccessful with the assessment, work one-on-one with them.

At first, when you scaffold, you might do all or most of the modeling and thinking aloud. Follow-up conferences should gradually turn over to the student the responsibility for learning. You can do this gradual release by pairing the student with a peer, by continuing to confer with and observe the student's thinking, or by having the student work independently and then share her thinking with you. This can occur in two or three short conferences (see forms on the Resources CD). However, some students will need several conferences, and you might have to return to the skill as you move on to another unit.

Texts to Use for Scaffolding

Students can use the text read for their independent assessment or a biography you have selected. I've included two additional biographies on the Resources CD for this purpose as well.

Suggestions for Helping Students Think Across Texts

After students who were successful on the assessment revise their writing, you may want to follow up their learning by challenging them to think across the texts they have read during the unit; this task supports the Common Core State Standards 7 to 9 for reading informational texts. Once students have read, discussed, and analyzed each text in this unit, they will be able to find common themes and ideas among them. You can use the suggestions below to help students complete across-text thinking.

- Find one or two similar obstacles that two different people faced, and compare how each person dealt with the obstacle.
- Think about the obstacles two different people faced, and compare how the obstacles affected the course of their lives.
- Use two or more texts to compare what you learned about people from their decisions or from how they solved problems.
- Choose two people and explore which personality traits they had in common. Decide if these traits contributed to their ability to effect change or achieve their goals; give specific examples.
- Compare the central themes of two or more selections. Were they alike? Different? What caused the similarities or differences?

Ideas for Inquiry and Problem Solving Beyond the Text

If you have time to extend the unit, ask students to devise questions based on their reading, or use the questions below to spark an inquiry.

- How can reading biography help you better understand the past and deal with the present and future? Choose a historical figure, such as Idi Amin, and think about what his or her life tells us about why some leaders violate people's rights to life, liberty, and the pursuit of happiness.
- People can affect and change the course of history. Choose a person you read about and think about how that person affected and/or changed history. Identify a contemporary political, religious, or military leader, read about that person, and

use what you've learned to predict how the person might affect the present and future of his or her nation and the world.

- Based on your reading, list the positive personality traits you think are needed in leaders at school, or in your community, the nation, or the world. Collaborate with classmates to determine ways education and families can encourage these traits.

Students can use the texts they've read during the unit and/or research new texts to explore the issues raised by the questions, which are all connected to the theme of overcoming obstacles. Students can write a short paper to share their results, participate in a class discussion or debate, create posters displaying what they've learned—the possibilities are varied, and I find allowing students to choose their mode of presentation motivates and engages them.

TOP-NOTCH BIOGRAPHIES

On the Resources CD you will find a list of ten biographies to review for your class and/or school library.

CLOSING THOUGHTS AND QUESTIONS TO DISCUSS

You can continue professional study by discussing with a peer partner or a group of colleagues the parts of the lessons that worked and the parts that need refining. Here are some questions to guide your conversations:

- Why did some students have difficulty finding the central ideas in biography? What kinds of interventions helped them move forward?

- What details did students use to infer how the person in their biography changed over time? What strategies did you use to help them figure out these changes?

- Did understanding text structure or how the author organized information enable students to make connections between events and other people? What kinds of support did you offer students to help them make intertextual connections?

- How can studying students' notes and paragraphs help you better understand students' comprehension of the biography selections in this unit? Their ability to write a clear and compelling paragraph? What kinds of mini-lessons and support do you need to provide in the next unit?

Scaffolding Suggestions for Helping Students Read Biography

STUDENT'S NEED	POSSIBLE SCAFFOLD
Connect the biography to the concept of obstacles: Is unable to link the concept of obstacles to events, decisions, and problems a person faced	• Review the meaning of *obstacles* and how obstacles can affect people's lives. • Ask questions to help the student link the concept of obstacles to the biography he read: *What events in the person's life were obstacles? Was there a connection between the decisions the person made and the obstacles he or she faced? What people became obstacles? Explain why.*
Determine personality traits and how and why these changed over time: Has difficulty knowing what to look for in a text to figure out personality and changes	• Review personality traits and discuss how these differ from physical traits. • Model how you study what the person says and does to figure out personality traits. Then have the student think aloud and show you how he reasons. • Explain that events in a person's life and the people he or she interacts with can change personality traits. Think aloud and model this process again.
Learn about the person from others' point of view: Has trouble understanding how the people surrounding the protagonist can shed light on his or her personality traits	• With the student's help, list the other people in the biography. • Choose one of these people and show how you figure out how that person views the protagonist and what you can infer. • Choose another person, and help the student go through the process just as you did above.
Infer from the person's decisions: Needs support pinpointing decisions and then figuring out what these show about the person	• With the student's help, list key decisions the person made. • Model how you infer what the person is like based on his or her decisions. You can also infer how a decision affected others or an event. • Turn the process over to the student and give support when needed.
Infer from how the person solves problems: Needs supports analyzing how the person deals with problems and what this shows about the person's character	• With the student's help, list problems the person faced. • Model how you infer personality traits by analyzing how and why the person solved a problem. • Discuss the fact that some people avoid solving problems altogether. If you can identify such a situation, discuss it with the student and consider what inferences can be made.

CHAPTER 5

Reading Memoir

Memories. We all have them, and I find that middle-school students enjoy reading memoirs written by authors whose books they relish. My students give high marks to Betsy Byars's *The Moon and I*, Roald Dahl's *Boy: Tales of Childhood*, *Been to Yesterdays: Poems of a Life* by Lee Bennett Hopkins, *Looking Back: A Book of Memories* by Lois Lowry, and Jimmy Santiago Baca's *Stories From the Edge*. When I've asked students during conferences why they chose a memoir for independent reading, they've responded: "I wanted to learn more about the person." "I'm fascinated by the memories of others." "It helps me think about what I should write for my memoir." Memoir, a genre that has its roots in autobiography, can focus on one significant event in a person's life or recount and connect dozens of events.

The Common Core classifies memoir as literary nonfiction because memoir is usually an account of an event or time period in the author's life that he or she revisits, reflects on, and interprets within the context of his or her life. Memoir is personal, and as writers replay and interpret a significant and meaningful event or time in their lives, they can understand how they feel about it today and share lessons that they might not have understood as the event unfolded.

Memoirs contain narrative elements such as setting, real-life characters, dialogue, conflict, and a climax. Memoirs also contain specific details that breathe life into the event; they are written in first person, and the narrator is the author.

The memoirs in this chapter all relate to the concept of change. I want students to consider how the men and women who wrote these memoirs caused changes in their lives and dealt with changes caused by chance, by other people's decisions and actions, and by contemporary events. In this unit, I will use the memoir "The Opening of a New World" by Malcolm X as an anchor text to model strategies that help students meet the CCSS by

- recalling key details and making logical inferences
- finding themes
- understanding the genre and text structure
- locating words and phrases that create mood or tone
- identifying author's purpose and point of view
- participating in collaborative discussions

Here are lessons you can easily combine. These are only suggestions. Combine those lessons that you believe will best support your students.

- Lessons 1 and 2
- Lessons 3 and 4
- Lessons 13 and 14

Lessons 1 to 8

Model How to Read Memoirs

In this set of lessons, you will use an anchor text to model key skills and strategies that readers use when tackling memoirs. As you model, students will deepen their understanding of important skills, such as making logical inferences, identifying themes, understanding text structure, finding evidence to answer text-specific questions, determining the author's purpose and point of view, and identifying mood or tone by selecting words from specific passages.

Text Complexity Grid

"The Opening of a New World" by Malcolm X

Lexile®: 960

Text Complexity: 1 = Accessible to 5 = Challenging

QUALITATIVE	1	2	3	4	5
Knowledge demands					X
Author's purpose				X	
Meaning				X	
Text structure				X	
Language/vocabulary				X	
Concepts					X
Inferential thinking demands				X	

LESSON 1

Getting Ready to Read

In this first lesson, you use the protocol on the Building Prior Knowledge handout to generate knowledge about a topic by strategically previewing the text. You also begin a "change" concept map, which you'll add to throughout the unit.

Materials

- "The Opening of a New World," displayed on the whiteboard from the Resources CD
- Students' notebooks
- Students' copies of Building Prior Knowledge handout (see page 261 and the Resources CD)
- Chart paper and markers for taking notes and generating the "change" concept map

TEACHING TIP — STRATEGY FOR STUDENTS

Your students might not know much about Malcolm X, and simply previewing the text will not give them enough background information. Set aside enough time to enlarge students' background knowledge of Malcolm X. To do this you might first visit the official Malcolm X Web site to familiarize yourself or refresh your memory about the facts of Malcolm X's life (http://www.malcolmx.com/). You can also get a good overview on Wikipedia. Then share this information with the class. By building students' prior knowledge, you enable them to deepen their comprehension of the memoir "The Opening of a New World," which is about Malcolm X's years in prison.

Teaching the Lesson

1. Have students take out their Building Prior Knowledge handout and display "The Opening of a New World."

Displaying the text in two-page view makes it easier for students to reread the text; see page 45.

2. Show students how they can build prior knowledge independently using "The Opening of a New World." I say something like this:

   In this unit we'll be reading several memoirs and thinking about the concept of change in people's lives. A memoir is a first-person narrative in which the author recounts a significant event or time period from his or her life. As always, it's helpful to build our knowledge of a text before diving into it, so I'm going to preview our first memoir, "The Opening of a New World" by Malcolm X, by reading the first two paragraphs, the last paragraph, and the five quiz items at the end of the text. Then I will list what I have learned from my reading. Follow along as I read these parts out loud.

3. Read the paragraphs and quiz items aloud and ask students to follow along. Then name all the details you recall from the preview and explain to students that talking about details they remember lets them determine whether they can recall enough details or need to reread to gather more.

4. Write on chart paper what you learned from your preview. Here's my list:
   - Malcolm X learned to read in prison.
   - He wanted to be like Bimbi, a fellow prisoner who knew a lot.
   - He tried to read, but couldn't understand most of the words; he just went through the motions—pretended to read.
   - In Norfolk Prison Colony, Malcolm X still pretended to read.
   - He became motivated to learn to read in Norfolk Prison Colony.

5. Ask students to add any other ideas to the list. Here's what some eighth-grade students added:
   - Spent night reading. Faked sleep when the guard passed by every hour.
   - Read until three or four in the morning.

6. Tell students that today the class will start a concept map by thinking about the concept of "change" in "The Opening of a New World," and they'll revisit the map as they read other memoirs in the coming weeks.

7. Write the word *change* on chart paper. Tell students that change can take place both within and outside of a person—our own feelings and thoughts can change, and other people, decisions, and events can change us. Then ask students to turn to a partner and take two or three minutes to discuss the idea of change, generating words and phrases that relate to this concept. Make sure students connect their idea to change.

8. Ask students to share the words they came up with; accept any word or phrase students offer as long as students can link it to "change." Record responses on the concept map. Eighth-grade students offered these three suggestions: *your friends, moving, losing a pet.*

9. Read "The Opening of a New World" aloud, asking students to listen for the gist or general idea of the memoir.

10. Ask students to pair-share and discuss the gist of "The Opening of a New World." Then invite partners to share their ideas with the class.

Wrap-Up

Provide positive feedback on students' listening skills and their contributions to the concept map.

LESSON 2

Identifying Genre Characteristics and Setting Purposes

In this lesson, students explore characteristics of memoirs and set a purpose for the second reading of " The Opening of a New World."

Materials
- "The Opening of a New World," displayed on the whiteboard from the Resources CD
- Students' notebooks
- Prior-knowledge notes from Lesson 1
- "Change" concept map begun in Lesson 1
- Chart paper and markers

Teaching the Lesson

1. Invite students to work in pairs to identify the characteristics of "The Opening of a New World" that make it a memoir.

2. Circulate among students to listen to their brief conversations. Responses like those below indicate that students are tuning in to the key characteristics of the genre: *It's written in the first person. In the first paragraph, he tells about himself and says "my prison duties." It says "by Malcolm X"—so it's a memoir.* If students miss an important characteristic of the genre, take some time to point it out to them (see box at right for a list of characteristics of memoir).

> ### Genre Characteristics: Memoir
>
> - Written in first person; author is the narrator
> - Recounts and reflects on a significant event or time period in the author's life
> - Is nonfiction
> - Often uses literary elements, such as dialogue

3. Have students reread the prior-knowledge notes you compiled in the previous lesson.

4. Ask pairs to set a purpose for listening to "The Opening of a New World" a second time. Remind pairs to use the title, information from the prior-knowledge notes, or the concept of change to set a purpose for listening to the passage again. If students have difficulty figuring out a purpose for listening, show them that they can use the title to create a purpose: *My purpose is to find what new world was opened for Malcolm X.* Ask students to jot down in their notebooks their purpose for reading under the heading: Purpose for Reading: "The Opening of a New World."

5. Have students pair-share and discuss their purposes for listening. Then invite a few students to share different purposes.

6. Read the selection aloud and have students follow along, keeping their purposes in mind. Explain that hearing the selection a second time will deepen their comprehension and enable them to recall more details.

7. Return to the "change" concept map and invite students to pair-share and add more ideas to the map based on the second reading. Make sure you ask them to connect their words and phrases to the concept and provide specific examples so that the entire class benefits from each student's thinking.

Wrap-Up

Point out the positive discussions students had and compliment them on the number of ideas they added to the concept map.

Making Inferences and Finding Themes

In this lesson, you model how to use key details from the text to make logical inferences and find themes. Afterward pairs practice this skill as you listen in and provide support.

Materials

- "The Opening of a New World," displayed on the whiteboard from the Resources CD
- Students' notebooks

Teaching the Lesson

1. Display "The Opening of a New World" and tell students that today's focus is to use text details to infer and find themes. Ask them to follow along as you reread the third, fourth, and fifth paragraphs of "The Opening of a New World," beginning with "I saw that the best thing I could do . . ." and ending with "... I read my own handwriting."

2. Present a think-aloud to show how you use specific text details to infer and find themes. Here's what I say:

   I can infer that having a dictionary changed Malcolm X's life. Up until that point he was barely literate. I can infer that Malcolm X was determined to learn to read and improve his handwriting when he copied and reread page after page in the dictionary. I can also infer that his engaging in the tedious work of copying words he didn't always understand showed that the task absorbed him and that he enjoyed it.

   The details in these paragraphs and the inferences I made from them led me to a theme: when you find your own motivation to work hard, that motivation can sustain you through the hard work more than if you're doing the work just because you want to be like someone else. In the passage we read, the desire to know a lot like Bimbi didn't cause Malcolm X to work hard; he just went through the motions of reading. But when he discovered a method that engaged and interested him, he continued to use it.

3. Read aloud the sixth paragraph. Invite students to pair-share and use the information in this paragraph to make one logical inference and find one theme.

> You can use the passages from "The Opening of a New World" that I suggest in the lesson, or you can select your own passages.

Here's what sixth graders offered:

- One pair inferred that copying was helping Malcolm X's memory, because he says that the next morning he woke up thinking about the words he copied.

- Another pair inferred that Malcolm X was amazed at writing words he never knew existed. He also saw the he had a great memory—he says he could recall the words' meanings "with little effort," which encouraged him to continue to copy, reread, and remember.

- A theme offered by one pair was that if you experience success when you work hard, the success motivates you to keep on working. For support, students pointed out that once Malcolm X experienced pleasure in copying words and remembering what each one meant, and when he experienced progress, he wanted to continue to work hard.

4. Reread the rest of "The Opening of a New World" and ask pairs to infer and find themes. Then invite students to discuss their inferences and themes with the entire class to show how key details supported finding themes.

Wrap-Up

Give students positive feedback on their ability to use text details to infer and find themes in "The Opening of a New World."

LESSON 4

Interpreting Language and Discussing Text Structure

In this lesson, students focus on the language of the text, exploring how it relates to the concept of change and the themes and inferences discussed in the previous lesson. In addition, you will model how to identify text structure and discuss why understanding a text's structure can help readers comprehend a text more deeply.

Materials
- "The Opening of a New World," displayed on the whiteboard from the Resources CD
- Students' notebooks
- "Change" concept map begun in Lesson 1
- Key words from the passage, written on chart paper (see Step 2 on page 128)
- Chart paper and markers

Teaching the Lesson

1. Display the "change" concept map and invite students to add words and phrases from the passage that relate to the concept of change. Ask them to connect their ideas with specific details from the text and/or their own experiences.

2. Choose 10 to 20 words from passage that relate to the themes and inferences that you and students identified. Before the lesson, I write these words on chart paper:

   prison studies, dictionary, tablets, pencils, copying, painstaking, ragged handwriting, proud, words, remember, miniature encyclopedia, new world, reading, truly free, prison library's shelves, rehabilitation, read and understand, reading in that glow

   Ask students to reread the words and pair-share to connect the language to themes and logical inferences in the text. My students linked the words and phrases to the inference that learning to read opened Malcolm X to learning, thinking about information, connecting ideas, and seeing the world through educated eyes. One sixth-grade girl explained that the words themselves shouted books, learning, motivated reading, and changing your life through education.

3. Explain to students that it's also important to understand the organization and structure of this passage. Ask students to turn to their partner and discuss how Malcolm X organized his memoir. Here are the points sixth-grade students made:

   - It's in time order (sequence)—the order that his learning to read happened. But it starts with a flashback.

   - I think he started in Charlestown Prison to show that wanting to read out of envy for Bimbi wasn't a good reason. He uses cause and effect too when he shows the results of trying to be like Bimbi with reading.

   - He takes you through decisions in the order he made them: getting a dictionary, pencil, and tablet; copying and rereading; remembering words and their meanings; wanting to read more. This is kind of like problem and solution. He wanted to read and couldn't [problem]; the solution was getting a dictionary and copying it into his notebook.

   - He uses description to tell about the prison library and the prisoners who debated and teachers from Harvard. I can infer he wanted me to know how smart many prisoners were and that they wanted to learn.

   - He ends with how he figured out how to read after lights out—this is problem-solution. He wanted you to know that reading and learning were his life. He says learning made him free.

Wrap-Up

Give students positive feedback for listening and discussing how knowing structure helps them navigate and comprehend texts.

Close Reading and Finding Author's Purpose

In this lesson, you will demonstrate the strategies of close reading and finding the author's purpose. Students will practice after you model. Then students will add words and phrases to the concept map.

Materials

- "The Opening of a New World," displayed on the whiteboard from the Resources CD
- Students' notebooks
- Students' copies of Close Reading Guidelines (see page 263 and the Resources CD)
- "Change" concept map from previous lessons
- Chart paper and markers

Teaching the Lesson

1. Ask students to retrieve their copies of Close Reading Guidelines and display "The Opening of a New World." Review the close reading handout and then model the strategy. Tell students that if they come upon a new word and can't figure out its meaning, or encounter a sentence or short passage that confuses them, a close reading can help them use context clues to determine meaning and "unconfuse" a confusing passage. Following is an example of what you might say:

    I'm unsure what the word riffling *means in the fourth paragraph. I slow down my reading and look for clues in the sentence: "I spent two days just riffling uncertainly through the dictionary's pages."*

        I know Malcolm X is turning pages when it says "through the dictionary's pages." I know uncertainly *means "unsure." So he's looking through the dictionary, not sure of what to do. So* riffling *probably means just turning pages but not reading.*

2. Have partners practice close reading to figure out the meaning of *inevitable* in the eighth paragraph: "I suppose it was *inevitable* that as my word-base broadened, I could for the first time pick up a book and read and now begin to understand

what the book was saying." Circulate among the students to offer support. One pair explained that they figured out *inevitable* from clues in the sentence: "*Broadened* means that he got lots more words. Knowing more words helped him understand what he read. This understanding was *inevitable*—that means it happened because he had lots of words he knew."

3. Invite partners to discuss Malcolm X's purpose for writing this memoir and his point of view. I remind students that the thinking they did for understanding the text's structure will support them with pinpointing the author's purpose.

    Every eighth-grade student agreed that Malcolm X's purpose for writing this memoir was to show that although he was in prison, learning to read made him a free and educated man. Malcolm X's point of view, students said, was that reading can change your life and break a bad cycle because he went from living on the streets to being on television and speaking. He became a famous African-American leader.

4. Return to the concept map and invite students to pair-share and add words and phrases related to the concept of change. Remind students, as they share with the class, to clearly connect their ideas to the concept.

Wrap-Up

Point out how well students applied the close reading strategy as they figured out difficult words. Let them know how pleased you are that they readily understood author's purpose and point of view.

LESSON 6

Collaborative Discussions

In this lesson, you review how to make inferences. Then, students work in pairs to discuss text-specific questions, rereading, skimming, and close reading from the whiteboard as necessary to find evidence to support their ideas.

Materials
- "The Opening of a New World," displayed on the whiteboard from the Resources CD
- Students' notebooks
- Copies of Discussion Prompts for "The Opening of a New World" (see page 132 and the Resources CD), class set
- Students' copies of Close Reading Guidelines

Teaching the Lesson

1. Organize students into pairs of readers whose instructional reading levels are no more than one year apart. Students who cannot read the text independently can work together with your support.

2. Have students take out their copy of Close Reading Guidelines.

3. Explain to students that they're going to answer some questions today about "The Opening of a New World" that ask them to infer and use close reading to comprehend the details in the text.

4. Ask students to pair-share and discuss everything they recall about making inferences and close reading. As you circulate among students, listen in and spotlight any responses that will help the class by asking select partners to share their thinking. If necessary, show students how you use a passage to infer. Here's what I say:

   I can infer what the phrase "opening a new world" means in the title. Learning to read allowed Malcolm X to read books that introduced him to new ideas and new people. So he entered a new world beyond the streets, where his only goal had been to survive. His ability to read and his exposure to new ideas led to a new life as well, one where he became a leader and a popular speaker and appeared on television. These new experiences were a new world to him as well—all made possible by learning to read.

5. Give the discussion prompts to students. Have partners discuss the prompts and find text evidence by rereading the passage or passages that lend support to the answer. Encourage students to use the Close Reading Guidelines for words or passages that are challenging.

6. Give students five to ten minutes to discuss the prompts for "The Opening of a New World." Encourage them to jot down notes and to note which paragraphs they used to find evidence. Circulate to listen, and extend or shorten the discussion time as needed.

7. Invite partners to share their answers, and if they used close reading to clarify anything, have them explain how close reading helped them infer.

Wrap-Up

Point out what worked during discussions. Compliment students on their recall and their use of inferring and close reading.

LESSON 7

Assessment: Test-Taking Strategies

In this lesson, model how to strategically answer quiz items and find support in the text. Then have students complete the quiz with a partner.

Materials

- "The Opening of a New World," displayed on the whiteboard from the Resources CD
- Copies of "The Opening of New World" quiz (see the Resources CD), class set
- Copies of the Quiz Answer Sheet (see page 263 and the Resources CD), class set
- Quiz Answer Key for "The Opening of a New World" (see page 267 and the Resources CD)

Teaching the Lesson

1. Distribute the quiz. Reread "The Opening of a New World" aloud to the class. Ask students to raise a hand if there's any part that confuses them and would thus be a candidate for close reading. If so, model close reading of a sample section.

2. Show students how you answer the first quiz item. The model is thorough, so you can see my thinking; adapt for the needs of your students. Here's my thinking:

    I'll work through the first item, which reads: A theme of this memoir is that . . . *First I'm going to think about the prompt. A theme is an important idea that comes from details in the text; it's important, but it doesn't have to relate to the entire text the way a central idea does. So it should be an important idea from the text details. Okay, now I'll read the answer choices.* A: prison is the best place to learn. *Well, I can cross that one right out; certainly prison isn't the best place to learn!* B: Bimbi told Malcolm X to get with it and learn. *Well, Bimbi was a model for Malcolm X, but that's not really a theme of the text, so I'm going to cross it off as well.* C: hard work can help you achieve your goals. *That statement is true; I remember many details from the text about that, so C could be the answer.* D: just talk to people who can read and you'll know a lot. *I know that's not true! And it's not supported by any details from the text. So C is the strongest answer.*

Now I'm going to go back to the text and locate evidence that supports it. In the second paragraph, we read that in Charleston Prison Malcolm X tried to emulate Bimbi by reading to get knowledge, so that's where his desire started. Then, in paragraph three, Malcolm says that when he went to Norfolk Prison Colony, he requested a dictionary and some tablets so he could learn words, since not knowing words is what stopped him from reading the books. The next several paragraphs describe his learning, Then, in paragraph eight, he describes how he spent every free moment reading. So while there are details throughout the memoir, I'll write down paragraphs two, three, and eight because I found specific evidence there. It's possible that you might find evidence other places, and that's fine too, as long as you can explain how the evidence supports your answer.

3. If you feel your students need extra support, you can model how you answer the second quiz item as well.

4. Give students the Quiz Answer Sheet. Instruct them to write their name, the date, and the title of the text at the top. Then have them record the answer(s) for the item(s) you modeled, writing the letter of the answer in the first column and the number(s) of the paragraph(s) where the evidence was found in the second column. Note that they will *not* be writing a paragraph about one of their answers during this lesson because the focus is on helping students practice the test-taking strategies modeled.

5. Pair students with partners and have them complete the last three or four questions of the quiz. If you have students who cannot read the text independently, work with them in a group, rereading passages for them so they can complete the quiz.

6. When students finish, call out the answers as students self-check, or collect the quizzes to score later.

Wrap-Up

Acknowledge students for successfully rereading and skimming "The Opening of a New World" to locate the paragraphs that helped them find the best answers.

Writing About Reading

This lesson lets you offer your students two options. The first is to plan and write a summary of "The Opening of a New World, " and the second is to plan and write a paragraph supporting a thesis statement using text evidence from the memoir. The summary is ideal for those developing readers who need to practice selecting information for summarizing. Your on-grade-level and above-level readers can complete the argument paragraph. If you have enough class time and feel that all students can benefit from both tasks, invite students to complete both a summary and an argument paragraph. You might need two or three classes for everyone to complete the plans and writing; set aside enough time for students to complete a first draft.

Materials

- "The Opening of a New World," displayed on the whiteboard from the Resources CD
- Students' notebooks
- Additional paper for writing a summary or paragraph
- Copies of Somebody-Wanted-But-So (SWBS) Organizer (see the Resources CD), for students writing summaries
- Students' copies of the Rubric: Literature Summary (see the Resources CD)
- Students' copies of Guidelines for Writing a Summary (see page 266 and the Resources CD)
- Students' copies of Elements of a Paragraph handout (see page 265 and the Resources CD)
- Students' copies of the Rubric: Paragraph (see the Resources CD)
- Sticky notes

Teaching the Lesson

1. Determine which students will work on which assignment, either by assigning them a topic or allowing them to choose. For my eighth-grade class, I assigned writing a summary to my below-grade-level readers, and an argument paragraph to my students who were at and above grade level. To avoid confusion, in your plan book or a notebook, make a list of who's doing which activity.

2. Introduce the writing about reading task, explaining how the lesson will work. I say something like this:

   Today we're going to be writing about the text we've been working with. There are two types of writing assignments. One group will write a summary of the text, and a second group will write a paragraph that argues in support of Malcolm X's belief that learning to read can change a person's life. I've divided you into groups. I'll meet with the summary group first to go over the assignment; the rest of you may read independently until I finish.

3. Gather students who will write a summary and distribute the SWBS planner (see guidelines on page 102). Review the purpose of writing a summary and then have students jot down notes on the planner as you circulate and offer support. Provide a sample topic sentence for students to use as their introductory sentence: *In the memoir "Opening of a New World," Malcolm X shows how learning to read in prison changed his life.* Students can also craft their own sentence; just remind them to include the title and author of the text. Invite students to use their notes on the planner to write a summary on a separate sheet of paper.

> Displaying the text in two-page view makes it easier for students to reread the text; see page 45.

4. Gather students who will write an argument paragraph, distribute the Elements of a Paragraph handout, and review the guidelines. Invite students to write a paragraph that argues for this statement based on "The Opening of a New World:" *Learning to read and write can change a person's life.* Have students find three or four pieces of evidence from the passage that support the thesis statement and record them in their notebooks. Remind students to use the Elements of a Paragraph handout to guide their first draft.

5. As students work, circulate to observe them as they take notes and then begin drafting their summary or argument. Remind them to use their rubric to revise their writing.

6. Sit side by side with students who require extra support. Acknowledge any successes that students achieve. When possible, use questions rather than statements to address areas that need more work. Questions honor and empower students. Write helpful suggestions for students on sticky notes and give the note to the student as a reminder of your conversation.

> If you feel students need additional modeling before moving on to the guided practice portion of the unit, work through Lessons 1–8 again using "The Day I Walked and Walked" as the read-aloud text (see the Resources CD).

7. Gauge students' progress to determine how much time to allow for the writing and whether it will be completed during the next class.

Wrap-Up

Provide positive feedback on students' detailed notes and how well they focused on writing summaries and/or argument paragraphs.

Guided Practice With a New Memoir

In this next series of lessons, you start releasing responsibility to students, reviewing and coaching as they practice the skills and strategies you modeled with "The Opening of a New World." Assign students a text based on their reading level; text complexity grids for each selection appear below. Then work through the lessons at a pace that's reasonable for your students, allowing one to two weeks, depending on students' needs.

Text Complexity Grids

"Helen Keller and Anne Sullivan" by Helen Keller
Lexile®: 1040
Text Complexity: 1 = Accessible to 5 = Challenging

QUALITATIVE	1	2	3	4	5
Knowledge demands				X	
Author's purpose			X		
Meaning			X		
Text structure			X		
Language/vocabulary				X	
Concepts				X	
Inferential thinking demands				X	

"Tickling a Trout" by Joseph Bruchac
Lexile®: 880
Text Complexity: 1 = Accessible to 5 = Challenging

QUALITATIVE	1	2	3	4	5
Knowledge demands					X
Author's purpose			X		
Meaning			X		
Text structure				X	
Language/vocabulary				X	
Concepts				X	
Inferential thinking demands				X	

Building Prior Knowledge and Setting Purposes

In this lesson, students receive a new passage; they preview and read for the gist or general idea with peer support. They also have the opportunity to add words to the concept map.

Materials

- Copies of "Helen Keller and Anne Sullivan" for students reading at or above grade level
- Copies of "Tickling a Trout" for students reading below grade level
- Students' notebooks
- "Change" concept map from previous lessons
- Chart paper and markers or interactive whiteboard

> Read "Tickling a Trout" aloud to students who struggle with reading the text. Follow the directions for working with two groups provided in Chapter 3, page 67.

1. Review the method you modeled for building prior knowledge that you modeled in Lesson 1. Distribute the copies of the passages to students. Ask students to suggest the number of paragraphs they need to read on the first page. Remind them that in addition to reading the first paragraph or two on page 1, they should read the title, the final paragraph, and the statements on the quiz.

2. Have students preview their text to build prior knowledge and then turn to a partner who's reading the same text and share the details they can recall. Remind students to make a list in their notebooks of everything they learned.

3. Ask students to reread their lists and use the information to set purposes for reading. Remind them that to set purposes they can use the title, their notes from Step 2, or the concept of change. Circulate and support students who need extra help.

4. Have students read the selection silently, using their prior knowledge to get the gist or general idea of the selection.

5. Ask students who read the same passage to pair-share to discuss the gist of their selection and connect the content to the concept of change.

6. Circulate and listen to partner discussions to determine whether students have

the general idea of their passage. If some students seem confused, support them by helping them close read and/or reread.

7. Display the "change" concept map and invite students to add words from their selection to the map. Always ask students to connect their word or phrase to the idea of change, so the entire class benefits from their thinking.

Wrap-Up

Point out what students did well as they built their prior knowledge and set purposes. Acknowledge the words and phrases students added to the concept map.

LESSON 10

Exploring Text Structure, Mood, Tone, and Author's Purpose

In this lesson, students will analyze the text structure of their memoir, select words to determine mood and tone, and pinpoint the author's purpose for writing the memoir.

Materials

- Students' copies of "Helen Keller and Anne Sullivan"
- Students' copies of "Tickling a Trout"
- Students' notebooks

Teaching the Lesson

1. Have students take out their memoir selection and tell them they are now going to reread it to determine its text structure and identify the author's purpose. Remind them of the excellent thinking they did about text structure and author's purpose with "The Opening of a New World" in Lessons 4 and 5 (see pages 128–130).

2. Pair students with partners who have read the same text. Have students reread the memoir, jotting down in their notebooks notes about text structure and author's purpose. Gather students who could not read "Tickling a Trout" independently and reread the text to them.

3. Invite pairs to discuss the text structure of their piece, considering how the organization contributes to the meaning and conveys the author's purpose. Discuss the text structure and author's perspective with your small group.

4. Use these prompts to help students think about structure if they need more support: *How did the writer organize information from beginning to end? Did the writer give background information? At what point in the text did you encounter this information? Why was background information helpful? Did the writer include real people? Were there narrative elements such as dialogue, inner thoughts, conflicts, or problems to be solved? Why are details so important to this memoir?*

My sixth-grade students recognized the flashback as a structural device in "Tickling a Trout." Partners said that the phrase "I remember when Grampa Jesse showed me how to tickle a trout," and the asterisks that separate the paragraphs that described present events and past memories also helped them follow the story. In the last part of the piece, the author returns to the present, when the family is on the mountain. Students felt that the flashback let the author show that in sixth grade he was a "nerd" and a flop at casting a spinner and catching trout. Students pointed out that being a flop at casting set up a problem-solution scenario, and that the author used descriptive details throughout the memoir.

Bruchac's purpose, students pointed out, was to show how much he learned from Grampa, how these experiences built his confidence, and how they're still helping him as an adult.

Students who read "Helen Keller and Anne Sullivan" said that the author's purpose was to tell about the most important event in her life—how she learned about language from her teacher, Anne Sullivan.

Students agreed that Keller used chronological order to describe the events of her teacher arriving at her home and trying to teach her. In the third paragraph, she breaks from that organization to make a comparison with a ship to help readers understand how she felt when she didn't understand language. She then returns to using chronological order, and students noted that she slowed down the action when she described the day she realized that words represented objects. They also pointed out that Keller contrasts how she was before the event with how she felt after the event.

Partners' choices of words and phrases from "Helen Keller and Anne Sullivan" and "Tickling a Trout" will differ, and this is okay as long as students can link the words to the author's purpose and/or to a mood, tone, or emotion the author creates.

5. Invite students to skim their text and choose 10 to 20 words and phrases from a few paragraphs that connect to the author's purpose and/or that set a mood or tone.

6. Circulate and listen in as pairs select and discuss their word and phrase choices from "Helen Keller and Anne Sullivan" and "Tickling a Trout." Support students who have difficulty getting started by thinking aloud to show how you select words that relate to a mood or the author's purpose.

7. Invite partners from each group to share with the entire class their word choices, along with the connections they made to the mood and/or author's purpose.

Wrap-Up

Give students positive feedback for their efforts to understand text structure and the author's purpose and for connecting the memoir's language to its mood or purpose.

LESSON 11

Collaborative Discussions

In this lesson, partners work together to answer text-specific questions about the memoir they read independently.

Materials

- Students' copies of "Helen Keller and Anne Sullivan"
- Students' copies of "Tickling a Trout"
- Discussion Prompts for "Helen Keller and Anne Sullivan" and "Tickling a Trout" (see pages 141 and 142 and the Resources CD)
- Students' copies of Close Reading Guidelines
- T-chart template (see the Resources CD)
- "Change" concept map from previous lessons
- Chart paper and markers or interactive whiteboard

Teaching the Lesson

1. Pair students with partners who have read the same text.

2. Display the discussion questions on a whiteboard or give a copy to each

student. Invite partners to use the discussion questions to discuss "Helen Keller and Anne Sullivan" or "Tickling a Trout."

3. Have partners use the questions and their discussions to make two logical inferences. Ask students to write inferences and the text evidence that supports them in their notebooks by making a T-chart. Display a model on a whiteboard or post one on chart paper and share examples such as the ones below. (See page 70 for more on T-charts.)

> ### TEACHING TIP — SCAFFOLDING STUDENTS' READING
>
> *Support students who cannot read "Tickling a Trout" independently by first pointing to the section in the text that answers the question and then having them reread that section. If students are unable to read it themselves, read it aloud to them.*

4. Ask partners to share their inferences and text evidence with the entire class; doing this provides additional models for all students.

5. Return to the concept map, Have partners pair-share for words and phrases related to "change." As their share their words, write them on the map. Make sure students clearly connect their words and phrases to the concept of change.

Wrap-Up

Give positive feedback on students' lively discussions and their ability to use text evidence to infer.

DISCUSSION PROMPTS FOR "HELEN KELLER AND ANNE SULLIVAN"

1. How did Helen Keller lose her sight and hearing?
2. Why does Keller describe a ship in the third paragraph?
3. Describe how Anne Sullivan tried to teach Keller language.
4. What is the significance of the doll?
5. What finally caused the breakthrough for Keller? Why do you think it worked?
6. How did Keller change from the beginning to the end of the memoir?
7. What can you infer about Anne Sullivan from the text?
8. What are some themes of this memoir?

LESSON 12

Assessment

In this lesson, students complete the quiz that follows their text selection. In addition to answering the multiple-choice items and identifying paragraphs that support their answers, students will choose one of their answers and defend it in a brief paragraph.

Materials

- Students' copies of "Helen Keller and Anne Sullivan"
- Students' copies of "Tickling a Trout"
- Copies of the Quiz Answer Sheet (see page 263 and the Resources CD), class set
- Quiz Answer Keys for "Helen Keller and Anne Sullivan" and "Tickling a Trout" (see page 267 and the Resources CD)

Teaching the Lesson

1. Give students the Quiz Answer Sheet and review the quiz directions. Encourage them to skim and reread parts of their memoir so they can note the paragraph or paragraphs they use to select an answer.

2. Have students complete the quiz independently. This includes choosing one answer to defend in a short paragraph; remind them that they may not choose a vocabulary item.

3. Support students who can't read "Tickling a Trout" or the accompanying quiz

items by reading the selection and quiz items to them. Read the quiz items one at a time and have students select the best answer.

4. When students finish, call out answers to the multiple-choice portion; have students self-correct and turn their papers in to you, or collect the papers and grade them yourself.

5. Separate the quizzes into two piles: students who scored a 4 or 5, and students who missed two or more multiple-choice items.

6. Read the paragraph students wrote to defend one of their answers. Check to make sure it contains details from the text. Make note of students who have difficulty, and plan time to scaffold their learning.

Help students who struggled with the paragraph portion of the quiz by working with them in a small group. Show them how to take notes on evidence from the text and then write a brief paragraph that explains their thinking about a question, incorporating the answer from the quiz along with their own text evidence.

Wrap-Up

Give students positive feedback for returning to the text and skimming or rereading before selecting an answer and for defending one of their answers.

LESSON 13

Writing About Reading: Note Taking

In this lesson, students will take notes for a suggested topic that relates to "Helen Keller and Anne Sullivan" or "Tickling a Trout" and record their notes in their notebooks.

Materials

- Students' copies of "Helen Keller and Anne Sullivan"
- Students' copies of "Tickling a Trout"
- Copies of the Note-Taking Guidelines for "Helen Keller and Anne Sullivan" and "Tickling a Trout" (see page 144 and the Resources CD)
- Students' notebooks

Teaching the Lesson

1. Explain that today students will take notes on "Helen Keller and Anne Sullivan" or on "Tickling a Trout" to plan an explanatory paragraph. Distribute the Note-Taking Guidelines for each text; you may also want to display them on the chalkboard or project them onto a whiteboard.

2. Ask students who are writing about "Helen Keller and Anne Sullivan" to work independently, finding evidence from the text to support the selected quotation, while you work with students taking notes about "Tickling a Trout." Because this second group consists of developing readers, I scaffold them by using a prompt based on one of the discussion questions they explored (see page 142), so that they have some background knowledge.

3. Circulate as students work, supporting students who need help or have questions. Students may need help finding evidence or paraphrasing the text.

Wrap-Up

Give students positive feedback on their use of the text to take detailed notes.

Note-Taking Guidelines for "Helen Keller and Anne Sullivan"

1. Think about how the "light" of language changed Helen Keller's life. Jot down in your notebook the ideas you have.
2. Skim "Helen Keller and Anne Sullivan" to find three pieces of evidence that support your point of view about how the "light" of language changed her life. Evidence can be facts and/or inferences you made based on text details.
3. Write the notes in your own words in your notebook.

Note-Taking Guidelines for "Tickling a Trout"

1. Think about the life lessons Joseph learned when his grandfather taught him how to tickle a trout. Jot down in your notebook the ideas you have.
2. Skim "Tickling a Trout" to find one important life lesson that Joseph learned from his grandfather and then clearly show how Joseph used this lesson later in his life. You may find details that support one of your ideas from Step 1, and you may choose an additional lesson.
3. Record in your notebook the specific evidence that shows the lesson(s) Joseph learned, using your own words. Your evidence may be a fact or an inference based on a specific detail.

Writing About Reading: Drafting

In this lesson, students write an explanatory paragraph about their text, drawing on the notes they took in the previous lesson and consulting the Elements of a Paragraph handout. Students will need more than 20 minutes to complete the writing; I suggest allowing 30 to 45 minutes for the task.

Materials

- Students' copies of "Helen Keller and Anne Sullivan"
- Students' copies of "Tickling a Trout"
- Students' copies of Elements of a Paragraph handout
- Students' copies of the Rubric: Paragraph
- Students' notebooks
- Additional notebook paper for drafting a paragraph

Teaching the Lesson

1. Have students take out their copies of the Elements of a Paragraph handout and review.

2. For the introductory sentence, students writing about "Helen Keller and Anne Sullivan" can compose a statement that reflects their point of view, or they may use this sample: *In her memoir, Helen Keller explains how the "light" of language changed her life and made her eager for each new day.* Offer students writing about "Tickling a Trout" a model introductory sentence that they can use or adapt: *In the memoir "Tickling a Trout," Grampa Jesse teaches Joseph life lessons that he remembers and uses throughout his life.*

3. Instruct students to use their notes from the previous lesson to write a complete paragraph, following the guidelines on the handout.

4. Circulate and support students as necessary. Always begin by noting the positives a student has achieved, and remember to phrase suggestions as questions to honor and empower your students. Remind them to use the rubric to revise their work.

5. Collect the paragraphs and assess them using the rubric. You can note errors in spelling, usage, and punctuation and use this data for writing mini-lessons and in one-to-one conferences.

Wrap-Up

Provide positive feedback to students for using their notes to craft their paragraphs.

Independent Practice and Assessment

In the last part of the unit, students work independently with a new memoir, so you can assess their progress, scaffolding or extending their learning as appropriate.

Text Complexity Grids

Excerpt from "Narrative of the Life of Frederick Douglass" by Frederick Douglass
Lexile®: 1040
Text Complexity: 1 = Accessible to 5 = Challenging

QUALITATIVE	1	2	3	4	5
Knowledge demands				X	
Author's purpose				X	
Meaning				X	
Text structure				X	
Language/vocabulary					X
Concepts				X	
Inferential thinking demands					X

Excerpt from *Geronimo's Story of His Life* taken down and edited by S. M. Barrett
Lexile®: 980
Text Complexity: 1 = Accessible to 5 = Challenging

QUALITATIVE	1	2	3	4	5
Knowledge demands					X
Author's purpose				X	
Meaning				X	
Text structure				X	
Language/vocabulary					X
Concepts				X	
Inferential thinking demands				X	

Reading a New Text Independently

Have students work on their own, as this is an assessment that will help you determine students' strengths and needs. They will build prior knowledge and read the text independently. For the assessment, you have three options: students can write a summary, compose an explanatory paragraph, or complete a Word Map about the unit's concept. I recommend that each student do at least one writing activity and complete the Word Map.

Set aside five or six consecutive days for the assessment. You will probably need two 30- to 45-minute classes for students to build prior knowledge, read for the gist, reread for deeper understanding, and complete the Word Map. Over the next three or four days, take about 35–45 minutes to have students complete the writing. If a few students need more time for taking notes and writing, give them the extra time.

Materials

- Copies of excerpt from *Narrative of the Life of Frederick Douglass* (see the Resources CD), for students reading at or above grade level
- Copies of excerpt from *Geronimo's Story of His Life* (see the Resources CD), for students reading below grade level
- Students' copies of the Building Prior Knowledge handout
- Students' copies of Guidelines for Writing a Summary
- Copies of the SWBS Organizer (see the Resources CD), for student writing summaries
- Students' copies of the Elements of a Paragraph handout
- Copies of Writing Topics for each assessment text (see the Resources CD), for students writing paragraphs
- Copies of the Word Map (see the Resources CD), class set
- Students' copies of the Rubrics for Literature Summary and Paragraph
- Students' notebooks
- Additional notebook paper for writing summaries and/or paragraphs

Teaching the Lesson

1. Have students take out their copy of the Building Prior Knowledge handout while you distribute the assessment texts and copies of the Word Map.

2. Remind students to use the strategy they have practiced to build their prior knowledge and jot down a list of what they learned from their preview in their notebook. Tell them that on the first two days of the assessment, they should preview the text to build prior knowledge, then read for the gist. Encourage them to reread the text for deeper comprehension before they complete the Word Map.

3. Invite students to complete the Word Map, specifying how many characteristics and examples you want them to provide to demonstrate their understanding of the concept.

4. On the next day, ask those students who will be writing a summary to take out their Guidelines for Writing a Summary handout. Give them a SWBS Organizer and the rubric you will use to assess the summary.

> **TEACHING TIP —**
> **PEER ASSESSMENT**
>
> *Have students give their plans and first drafts to a writing partner. Ask the partner to use the rubric and the Guidelines for Writing a Summary or Elements of a Paragraph handout to make sure all elements have been included. Partners give each other feedback that can improve their summaries or paragraphs. Have students write a second draft based on peer feedback. Collect and read the drafts.*

5. Ask those students who will be writing a paragraph to take out their Elements of a Paragraph handout. Distribute the Writing Topics list and the rubric you will use to assess the paragraph.

6. Invite students to reread and take notes for their summaries or paragraphs. Have them work through the writing process outlined on the Guidelines for Writing a Summary handout or the Elements of a Paragraph handout, consulting the corresponding rubric to check their work.

7. When students finish, have them turn in their work. Assess it using the rubric.

Interpreting Assessments

The paragraphs can show you whether students can make logical inferences and find specific text details from the selection. See the Scaffolding Suggestions chart on pages 151–152 to help you support students with reading issues.

To scaffold students who require writing support, use the Scaffolding Suggestions for Helping Students Write Summaries and Paragraphs chart on the Resources CD.

Following Up the Assessment

Based on your assessment of students' writing, you can determine how many days to spend scaffolding and extending their learning. I recommend allowing at least one day for students to revise their writing based on your feedback; during that time, you can meet with your most struggling readers. Then you may choose to spend additional days working in small groups scaffolding students who need it and extending the learning of those who are ready for more challenge.

Supporting Students Who Require Scaffolding

The chart on pages 151–152 offers scaffolding suggestions based on students' writing, your observations as they read and discuss texts, and your conferences on independent and instructional reading. Support students with similar needs by working with groups of two or three. When students struggle and are unsuccessful with the assessment, work one-on-one with them.

At first, when you scaffold, you might do all or most of the modeling and thinking aloud. Follow-up conferences should gradually turn over to the student the responsibility for learning. You can do this gradual release by pairing the student with a peer, by continuing to confer with and observe the student's thinking, or by having the student work independently and then share her thinking with you. This can occur in two or three short conferences (see forms on the Resources CD). However, some students will need several conferences, and you might have to return to the skill as you move on to another unit.

Texts to Use for Scaffolding

Students can use the text they read for their independent assessment (see page 146) or a text you have selected. I also include an additional memoir on the Resources CD.

Suggestions for Helping Students Think Across Texts

After students who were successful on the assessment revise their writing, you may want to follow up their learning by challenging them to think across the texts they have read during the unit; this task supports the Common Core State Standards 7 to 9 for reading. Once students have read, discussed, and analyzed each text in this unit, they will be able to find common themes and ideas among them. You can use the suggestions below to help students complete across-text thinking.

- Use two or more memoirs from this unit to compare and contrast how people dealt with change and problems.
- In "The Opening of a New World" and "Helen Keller and Anne Sullivan," Malcolm X and Helen Keller learned important life lessons. Explain what they learned and the conditions that motivated them.
- Choose two people and list their personality traits, which you inferred from reading their memoirs. Discuss personality traits common to both and explain how these traits can foster change.
- A memoir should be about significant events in a person's life. Choose two memoirs from this unit and do the following for each:
  - Explain why the memory was significant.
  - Show how the memory changed and/or transformed the person's life.

Ideas for Inquiry and Problem Solving Beyond the Text

If you have time to extend the unit, ask students to devise questions based on their reading, or use the prompts below to spark an inquiry.

- The people in these memoirs made changes in their lives based on the experiences they recount. Use a person studied in history, science, mathematics, or the fine arts, research his or her life, and explain how that person created change and what events and/or people caused the change.
- If you could create change at school, or in your family or community, what would these changes be? How would you foster the changes? Who would you involve to help you and what would these people do?
- Write an editorial for your school or local newspaper that recommends a much-needed change at school or in your community. Give reasons for the change and show how making the change will benefit others.
- How can memories, life experiences, reading, and conversations develop someone's ability to deal with bullying and ostracizing?

Students can use the texts they've read during the unit and/or research new texts to explore the issues raised by the questions, which are all connected to the theme of change. Students can write a short paper to share their results, participate in a class discussion or debate, create posters displaying what they've learned—the possibilities are many, and I find allowing students to choose their mode of presentation motivates and engages them.

> **TOP-NOTCH MEMOIRS**
>
> On the Resources CD you'll find a list of ten memoirs to review for your class and/or school library.

CLOSING THOUGHTS AND QUESTIONS TO DISCUSS

You can continue professional study by discussing with a peer or a group of colleagues the parts of the lessons that worked and the parts that need refining. Here are some questions to guide your conversations:

- How did you support students who had difficulty finding themes and making logical inferences in the memoirs they read?

- Which students could explain the text structure of the memoir they read? Why were they able to do this? Was it the questions you posed? A particular strategy? How did you scaffold students who had difficulty thinking about text structure? Share your ideas with team or department members.

- How did students react to selecting words and phrases from a memoir to determine mood or tone or to connect to the author's purpose? What strategies did you use to help partners choose words and then think with them?

- How can studying students' notes and paragraphs help you better understand their comprehension of the memoir selections in this unit? Their ability to write a clear and compelling paragraph? What kinds of mini-lessons and support do you need to provide in the next unit?

Scaffolding Suggestions for Helping Students Read Memoirs

STUDENT'S NEED	POSSIBLE SCAFFOLD
Analyze how individuals, ideas, and events develop and interact in the memoir: Needs support with connecting these elements to one another and to themes	• Use questions to help the student make these connections: • *How does what the people say and do connect to a theme or the author's purpose?* • *Why do you think the author chose to recount this memory?* • *How does a theme connect to the author's purpose and point of view?*

STUDENT'S NEED	POSSIBLE SCAFFOLD
Writing craft and structure: Needs help figuring out the structure, narrative elements, mood and tone, and specific techniques such as foreshadowing and flashback	• Make sure the student understands what a flashback is and why authors use the technique. • Ask the student to point to the place in the memoir where the flashback starts. *How does this use of flashback affect the memory?* • Review the meaning and purpose of foreshadowing. Have the student find an example of foreshadowing in the text and explain how it prepares the reader for events and themes to come. • Review the text structure of any memoir that the student had difficulty understanding and sorting through. Review narrative elements and ask the student to point out some that appear in the memoir and to explain how they support what the author is saying. • Review narrative elements: events, rising action, conflicts, climax, people (major and minor), dialogue, inner thoughts
Author's purpose and point of view and how these shape the memoir: Needs support in determining the purpose for writing about the memory and the significance of the memoir	• Use these questions to help the student figure out the significance of a specific memoir and the author's purpose for writing it: *Why is this memoir significant to the author? To others in the text? Why did the author write about this memory? What was he/she trying to show readers?*
Integrating themes and author's purpose across texts: Needs help finding common threads among memoirs	• Have the student list the themes from two or three memoirs. Then have him circle those that are common to two or all three. • Help the student identify common writing techniques, tones, or author's purposes, by inviting him to consider two memoirs by different authors. • Help the student compare two people from two memoirs and look at their problem solving and decision making to see if they are similar.

CHAPTER 6

Reading Myths

For more than two thousand years, myths and ancient history have held a fascination for readers. Every culture has its myths, and while we may be most familiar with those from ancient Greece and Rome, we're wise to recognize the rich mythological heritage of cultures and countries across the globe. It's important for students to have a deep knowledge of mythology and ancient history, because poems and novels frequently have references to these old stories and their historical settings. *The Hunger Games* by Suzanne Collins, a favorite among middle-school readers, gains depth if students know about gladiators and their fights with wild beasts in front of huge crowds in Rome's Colosseum. In ancient Rome and in *The Hunger Games*, death became a form of entertainment for the masses.

Myths are narrative stories that often explain natural phenomena or how human beings, animals, and the environment came into being. Myths can also be interpreted as allegories, presenting symbols of philosophical ideas and exploring how they play out in the world—think of Athena symbolizing wise judgment and righteous warfare.

The main characters in myths are the gods from a specific culture, heroes with great powers, and human beings. The gods in this unit on myths are anthropomorphic: they have godly powers but also act like human beings. Anthropomorphic gods can be angry, jealous, show favoritism, mete out unfair punishments, and make unfair decisions.

The myths in this chapter all relate to the concept of decisions. By reading the myths, students can consider what motivates the gods and humans to make decisions and how decisions affect our lives and the lives of others.

In this unit, I will use the myth "Helios" from *D'Aulaires' Book of Greek Myths* as an anchor text to model how to apply the following Common Core Reading Standards:

- identify the central idea and how it develops
- infer why and how a character changes over time
- make connections between events in the myth
- identify author's purpose and point of view
- recall details, make logical inferences, and identify themes

Here are lessons you can easily combine. These are only suggestions. Combine those lessons that you believe will best support your students.

- Lessons 1 and 2
- Lessons 5 and 6
- Lessons 7 and 8

Narrative Elements and Myths

Myths follow narrative text structure and contain a protagonist, antagonistic forces, settings, plot, and a climax. You can approach the myths using these narrative elements, which you will examine closely in Chapter 8, Teaching the Short Story. On the Resources CD you will find a list of these narrative elements along with definitions and examples from the short-story anchor text, "Through the Tunnel" by Doris Lessing. In this lesson, I emphasize the CCSS anchor strategies noted above.

Model How to Read a Myth

In this set of lessons, you will use an anchor text to model key skills and strategies that readers use when reading literary texts such as myths. As you model, students will deepen their understanding of important skills, such as identifying the central idea and how it develops, explaining how and why a character changes over time, making connections between events, and discerning the author's purpose.

Text Complexity Grid

"Helios" from *D'Aulaires' Book of Greek Myths*
Lexile®: 1040
Text Complexity: 1 = Accessible to 5 = Challenging

QUALITATIVE	1	2	3	4	5
Knowledge demands				X	
Author's purpose				X	
Meaning			X		
Text structure			X		
Language/vocabulary				X	
Concepts				X	
Inferential thinking demands					X

LESSON 1

Getting Ready to Read

Materials

- "Helios," displayed on the whiteboard from the Resources CD
- Students' notebooks
- Students' copies of Building Prior Knowledge handout (see page 261 and the Resources CD)

- Chart paper and markers for taking notes and generating the concept map

Teaching the Lesson

1. Have students take out their Building Prior Knowledge handout and display "Helios."

2. Show students how they can build prior knowledge independently using "Helios." I say something like this:

   We're beginning a new unit on myths today. I'm sure you've encountered myths before, so you have some ideas about what they're like. But it's always a good idea to build our prior knowledge before reading a new text, so let's walk through our procedure for previewing a text. Note that since this is a narrative text, we won't read the last paragraph because that would give away the ending. Follow along as I read the first two paragraphs and the quiz items out loud.

3. Read the paragraphs and quiz items aloud, and then retell the details you recall. Remind students that talking about the details they remember helps them determine whether they can recall enough details or need to reread the preview part to gather more.

4. Write down what you learned from your preview on a sheet of chart paper. Here's my list:

   - The god Helios rides his chariot to make the sun rise.
   - Helios was so bright that only gods could look at him without going blind.
   - Helios's horses were wild but he had the strength to guide them along the narrow path.
   - The horses wanted to reach the evening palace and ran quickly downhill to reach their stables.
   - Helios passed a herd of white cows and a herd of sheep on his way to the evening palace.

5. Ask students to add any other ideas to the list. Here's what my eighth-grade students added:

   - The chariot glowed like fire.
   - Helios had a white cow for every day of the year.
   - He had a sheep for each night of the year.

6. Tell students that today the class will start a concept map by thinking about the concept of decisions. Write the word *decisions* on chart paper and say something like this:

   Decisions are made by the characters in myths. All sorts of conditions, both internal and external, can lead characters to make decisions. Forces outside the characters' control—such as nature or the actions of others— can also necessitate a decision. Turn to your partner and take two or three minutes to discuss what you know about decisions; try to find words and phrases that relate to this concept. It's okay if no ideas come to mind. We'll revisit the concept map several times during this unit of study.

7. Accept any word or phrase students offer as long as they can link it to the concept of decisions. My eighth-grade students offered three suggestions. I asked them to directly connect these ideas to "decisions" and then wrote them on the map: *a response to a dare, an accident, while driving a car.*

8. Read "Helios" out loud, telling students to listen for the gist or general idea.

9. Ask students to pair-share and discuss the gist of "Helios." Then invite partners to share their ideas with the class.

Wrap-Up

Provide positive feedback on students' listening skills and their contributions to the concept map.

LESSON 2

Identifying Genre Characteristics and Setting Purposes

In this lesson, students explore characteristics of myths and set a purpose for the second reading of "Helios."

Materials

- "Helios," displayed on the whiteboard from the Resources CD
- Students' notebooks
- Prior-knowledge notes from Lesson 1
- "Decisions" concept map begun in Lesson 1
- Chart paper and markers

Teaching the Lesson

1. Invite students to pair-share to identify the characteristics of "Helios" that make it a myth.

2. Circulate among students and listen in on their brief conversations. Responses like those below indicate that students are identifying the characteristics of myths: *It has gods in it. I know that Zeus is a Greek god and is in myths. Zeus is in this myth. The sun rises and sets because Helios drives his chariot—that's myth stuff.; Zeus changes the sisters into poplar trees—that's in a lot of myths—it explains natural things.* If students miss an important characteristic of the genre, take some time to point it out to them (see box below for a list of characteristics for myths).

Genre Characteristics: Mythology

- Uses narrative structure and elements; fictional.
- Characters include gods and goddesses, humans, and other nonhuman creatures.
- May explain a natural phenomenon or historical event.
- May tell story of creation of a people or the world.
- Is associated with a culture.
- Has universal themes.
- Often contains magical or supernatural events.
- Gods and goddesses are often disguised.
- Classical myths occur in the distant past.

---

3. Have students reread the building-prior-knowledge notes you compiled in Lesson 1.

4. Ask pairs to set a purpose for listening to "Helios" a second time. Ask them to use the title, information from the prior-knowledge notes, or the unit theme "decisions" to set a purpose for listening to "Helios" again. If students have difficulty figuring out a purpose for listening, show them that they can use the concept of decisions to form a purpose: *My purpose is to find out how the concept of decisions connects to "Helios."*

5. Reread the selection aloud and have students follow along, keeping their purposes in mind. Explain that hearing the selection a second time will deepen their comprehension and enable them to recall more details.

6. Have students pair-share and discuss their purpose for listening to "Helios," and then invite a few students to share their purposes. Next, ask students to identify details that relate to their purposes for listening. As you circulate, offer help by pointing to sections that can help them find details that relate to their purpose for listening to "Helios."

7. Return to the "decisions" concept map and invite students to pair-share and add more ideas to the map.. Have students add words and phrases based on the second reading. Make sure you ask them to connect their words and phrases to the concept and provide specific examples.

Wrap-Up

Point out the positive discussions students had and compliment them on the number of ideas they added to the concept map.

LESSON 3

Exploring Character Changes and Finding Central Ideas

In this lesson, students will study events, decisions, and a character's interactions with other characters to determine how and why a character changes. In addition, they will also identify the central idea of "Helios."

Materials

- "Helios," displayed on the whiteboard from the Resources CD
- Students' notebooks
- Prior-knowledge notes from Lesson 1
- "Decisions" concept map
- Chart paper and markers

Teaching the Lesson

1. Present a think-aloud to demonstrate how you use events, other characters, and Helios's decisions to determine how he changed in this myth. Here's my thinking:

   Today we're going to look closely at the events in "Helios" to examine how Helios changed. The first part of the myth describes a strong and proud Helios firmly guiding the chariot across the heavens. Then Phaëthon, Helios's mortal son, asks his father to grant him "his dearest wish." Without

Unlocking Complex Texts © 2013 by Laura Robb, Scholastic Teaching Resources 〜 **159** *hesitation, Helios swears on the River Styx to grant it. This action shows us how much he loves his son and wants to please him. It was also a rash act—Helios did not think through the possible consequences. When he hears the wish, he sorely regrets his vow. Helios knows Phaëthon cannot control the chariot and fears for his life. He tries to warn Phaëthon and begs him to change his mind, to no avail. Phaëthon insists on driving the chariot, and Helios prepares him as best he can, but "sadly"—he knows it will be of no use. The strength and confidence we saw early in the myth has evaporated. Helios is powerless to stop his son, bound by his rash oath. So we can trace the change in Helios to Phaëthon's request and Helios's own rash oath, along with Phaëthon's unwise insistence on having his way. These things changed Helios from a powerful god to a powerless father doomed to watch his son perish because of his own poor decision.*

2. Read aloud the last paragraph. Have students pair-share to explore another change and the decision that causes the change. Here's what some of my seventh-grade students said:

   Phaëthon's sisters could not stop crying for their brother. So Zeus pitied them and decided to turn them into poplar trees.

   Zeus also turned their tears into drops of amber. He decided to do this because they could not stop crying over Phaëthon's death.

3. Show students how you use information in Steps 1 and 2 to pinpoint the central idea. Remind students that a central idea is a fundamental point the author tries to make; it relates to the entire story. One central idea of "Helios" is that people shouldn't make blind promises; they should know what it is they're being asked to do. Another central idea is that a mortal should not strive to do what immortals can do because the results can be dangerous, even deadly.

4. Ask students to pair-share to see if they can find another central idea. My seventh graders suggested that another central idea in "Helios" is that when you make a decision, you should consider how the decision affects your life and the lives of others. For support

EXPLAIN THE GREEK CONCEPT OF HUBRIS TO STUDENTS

The Greek term for having excessive pride or self-confidence, for thinking that as a mortal you are equal to or even better than the gods, is *hubris*. Phaëthon's failure was brought on by hubris, for he believed that he could drive Helios's chariot even though his father, Helios, warned Phaëthon that a mortal could not do this task. Invite students to look for hubris in other myths they read.

from the myth, students said that Phaëthon never thought that he might not be able to drive the chariot. He never considered that his demand would result in his death and the transformation of his sisters into poplar trees.

5. Return to the "decision" concept map and invite students to pair-share to find words and phrases to add to the map. Have them make explicit connections between the words and phrases and the concept of decisions.

Wrap-Up

Compliment students on their discussions of decisions and on their understanding of the central idea.

Connecting Events to Find Themes and Identify Author's Purpose

In this lesson, students will use close reading to study the events in "Helios." They'll make connections between events and analyze these connections. They'll also identify the author's purpose.

Materials

- "Helios," displayed on the whiteboard from the Resources CD
- Students' notebooks
- Students' copies of Close Reading Guidelines (see page 262 and the Resources CD)

Teaching the Lesson

1. Ask students to retrieve their copies of Close Reading Guidelines and review the handout with them.

2. Demonstrate how to close read to find connections between events. This close-reading model is thorough so you can observe my thinking; adapt for the needs of your students. Here's my thinking:

    I'm going to close read the fifth paragraph, which is important because it's where Phaëthon is introduced and makes his wish. In the second sentence we learn he is "mortal" and "very proud of his radiant father." So Helios is a god but his son is not. The son looks up to the father. The next sentence says, "Phaëthon came to him and begged him to grant his dearest wish." So he didn't come right out and ask to drive the chariot; instead, he begged for a wish to be granted, and not just any wish—"his dearest wish." I'm thinking that he knew his father wouldn't grant his request if he knew what it was, so he felt he had to hide it. Then the next sentence says, "Helios, who was very fond of his handsome son, rashly swore by the River Styx to give him any wish he might have, but when he heard Phaëthon's wish, he sorely regretted his oath." Hmmm. So we learn Helios loves his son and that he swears to grant his wish. Now, Helios didn't have to do that. He could have asked what the wish was first. I'm thinking that he hated to see his son beg and wanted to make him happy at any cost. He wasn't thinking, though, that the wish could be dangerous; the text says, "rashly swore," so I think that's a point the author is trying to make really clear for us. We know right away that Helios "sorely regretted his oath," so we know it's going to be something bad. And the next line tells us: "He tried in vain to make his son change his mind, for what Phaëthon wanted was to drive the sun chariot for one day, and Helios knew that no one but himself could handle the spirited steeds." So Helios tried to reason with Phaëthon, but "in vain"; it was no use. The text tells us the wish, and that Helios is aware that no one else can "handle the spirited steeds." We saw their power in the first two paragraphs, so we have a sense of how hard they are to control.

Okay, so this close reading helps me make a few connections. Phaëthon knows his father isn't going to want to grant his wish, so he "begs" him to grant "his dearest wish" without saying what it is. Helios loves his son and wants to please him—so much so that he makes the foolish decision to promise to fulfill the wish without knowing what it is. When Phaëthon reveals the wish, Helios is distraught because he knows Phaëthon cannot control the chariot. He tries to change Phaëthon's mind, but Phaëthon refuses to listen to reason. The central idea we discussed last time is so clear in this paragraph—you definitely should not promise to do something without knowing the details first! But there are two other ideas at work in this section: People can sometimes manipulate their loved ones to get what they want. Phaëthon knew he was going to have to work on his father to get his wish, so he approached him right before he was leaving and begged him; I can picture it so clearly! He knew his father would want to appease him, and he planned this carefully. Related to this idea is another one: Parents will do anything for their children.

3.   Invite students to pair-share and see if they can connect other events in "Helios." Encourage them to close read to support making these connections. Here's what some of my seventh graders said:

When Zeus sees that Phaëthon can't control the horses and that he almost freezes and burns Earth because the chariot brings the sun too close and then too far from Earth, he knows he has to take over to save Earth.

Phaëthon couldn't think his way out. I inferred that because he did not try to do anything when the chariot was out of control. He was thrown halfway out of the chariot, then grew dizzy—but he didn't take any action.

4. Invite students to pair-share to determine the author's purpose in "Helios." Steer students to recalling your modeling and their suggestions for connecting events and finding themes in "Helios," Steps 2 and 3. (Continue to model this for students if you feel they need to observe more of your thinking.) Here's what my seventh-grade students said:

The author wanted to show what happens to a mortal like Phaëthon who has too much pride and wants to be like his father, the god Helios. The author is showing how important it is to listen to the advice of a person with experience and not to be blinded by your own wishes.

Once seventh-grade students understood the concept of hubris, they agreed that the author's main purpose was to show the result of hubris in a mortal like Phaëthon.

Wrap-Up

Acknowledge students' use of close reading to make connections between events and to figure out the author's purpose.

LESSON 5

Collaborative Discussions

In this lesson, you review how to make inferences; then students work in pairs to discuss text-specific questions—rereading, skimming, and close reading from the whiteboard as necessary to find evidence to support their ideas.

Materials

- "Helios," displayed on the whiteboard from the Resources CD
- Students' notebooks
- Copies of Discussion Prompts (see page 165 and the Resources CD), class set
- Students' copies of Close Reading Guidelines

- "Decisions" concept map from previous lessons
- Chart paper and markers

Displaying the text in two-page view makes it easier for students to reread the text; see page 45.

Teaching the Lesson

1. Organize students into pairs of readers whose instructional reading levels are no more than one year apart. Students reading three or more years below grade level can work together with your support.

2. Have students take out their copy of the Close Reading Guidelines.

3. Explain to students that they're going to answer some questions today about "Helios" that ask them to infer and use close reading to help them comprehend the details in the text.

4. Ask students to pair-share and discuss everything they recall about making inferences and close reading. Circulate among students and spotlight responses that will help the class by asking partners to share their thinking.

5. Show students how you make an inference in "Helios." Here's what I say:

   Based on the text, I can infer that Helios loves and values his children. The text says that every day Helios visits with his five daughters, the Heliades, and talks to them about everything he saw on that day's journey. Because he loves his son Phaëthon so much, he makes a rash promise that he is forced to keep.

6. Distribute copies of the discussion prompts to students. Have partners discuss the questions and find text evidence by rereading the paragraph or paragraphs that contain support for the answer. Encourage students to use the Close Reading Guidelines for parts that confuse them.

7. Give students five to ten minutes to discuss the questions for "Helios." Remind them to jot down notes and to note which paragraphs they used to find evidence. Circulate to listen, and extend or shorten the discussion time as needed.

8. Invite partners to share their answers, and if they used close reading to clarify anything, have them explain how close reading helped them infer.

9. Return to the "decisions" concept map and have students add words and phrases, inviting them to explicitly connect their ideas to the concept of decisions.

Wrap-Up

Provide positive feedback on students' discussions.

LESSON 6

Assessment: Test-Taking Strategies

In this lesson, you model how to strategically answer quiz items and find support in the text. Then students complete the quiz with a partner.

Materials

- "Helios," displayed on the whiteboard from the Resources CD
- Copies of "Helios" quiz (see the Resources CD), class set
- Copies of the Quiz Answer Sheet (see page 263 and the Resources CD), class set
- Quiz Answer Key for "Helios" (see page 267 and the Resources CD)

Teaching the Lesson

1. Distribute the quiz. Reread aloud "Helios" and the quiz items. Ask students to raise a hand if there's any part that confuses them and would thus be a candidate for close reading. If so, model close reading of a sample section.

2. Show students how you answer the first quiz item. The model is thorough, so you can observe my thinking. Adapt to the needs of your students. Here is my thinking:

   I'll work through the first quiz item, which reads: When Helios grants Phaëthon a wish before knowing what the wish is, you can infer that Helios . . . *Before I read the answers, I'll think about that. I can tell that Helios wants to please his son and must love him very much. Now I'll read the possible answers.* A: didn't want to listen to his son whine and complain. *Well, maybe that's true, although I didn't get that feeling when I was reading. But I'll keep it for now.* B: loves Phaëthon and never thought his son's wish would be unreasonable. *That's true, too. I'm sure Helios wouldn't have granted the wish if it had ever occurred to him it might be dangerous.* C: feels he can go back on his promise. *I know that is not true; if he had felt that way, Phaëthon never would have driven the chariot. So I can cross that one off.* D: thought that letting Phaëthon drive the chariot would make him immortal. *I know that's not true, so I'll just cross it off. So A and B are my possibilities; I'll go back and check the text to see which one is the better answer. I'm skimming . . . Yes, here in paragraph 5 is where we meet Phaëthon. It does say Phaëthon begged for his wish; I know I hate it when my kids beg. But I don't see any evidence that it annoyed Helios at the time; it actually says Helios was very fond of his son and rashly swore to grant his wish. He didn't have to do that; he could have asked what it was first. So A is not a good choice after all. That leaves B: loves Phaëthon and never thought his son's wish would be unreasonable. That sounds to me like the answer, after rereading. He wouldn't swear to keep the promise if he thought it would be unreasonable; I think he did that because he wanted to please Phaëthon because he loved him. So B is the answer, and the evidence is in paragraph 5.*

3. If you feel your students need extra support, you can model how you answer the second quiz item as well.

4. Give students the Quiz Answer Sheet. Tell them to write their name, the date, and the title of the text at the top. Then have them record the answer(s) for the item(s) you modeled, writing the letter of the answer in the first column and the number(s) of the paragraph(s) where the evidence was found in the second column. Note that they will *not* be writing a paragraph about one of their answers during this lesson because the focus is on helping them practice the test-taking strategies modeled.

5. Pair students with partners and have them complete the last three or four questions of the quiz. If you have students who cannot read the text independently, work with them in a group, rereading paragraphs for them so they can complete the quiz.

6. When students finish, call out the answers as students self-check, or collect the quizzes to score later.

Wrap-Up

Acknowledge students for successfully rereading and skimming "Helios" to locate the paragraphs that helped them find the best answers.

Writing About Reading

This lesson offers two options. The first is to plan and write a summary of "Helios," and the second is to plan and write an argumentative paragraph using text evidence from this myth. The summary is ideal for those developing readers who need to practice selecting information for summarizing. Students reading at or above grade level can complete the argumentative paragraph. You might need two or three classes for everyone to complete their plans and writing; set aside enough time for students to complete a first draft. If you have enough class time and feel that all students can benefit from both writing tasks, then invite students to complete a summary and argumentative paragraph.

Materials

- "Helios," displayed on the whiteboard from the Resources CD
- Students' notebooks
- Additional paper for writing a summary or paragraph
- Copies of Somebody-Wanted-But-So (SWBS) Organizer (see the Resources CD), for students writing summaries
- Students' copies of the Guidelines for Writing a Summary (see page 266 and the Resources CD)
- Students' copies of Elements of a Paragraph handout (see page 265 and the Resources CD)
- Students' copies of Rubrics for Literature Summary and Paragraph (see the Resources CD)
- Sticky notes

Displaying the text in two-page view makes it easier for students to reread the text; see page 45.

Teaching the Lesson

1. Determine which students will work on which assignment, either by assigning them a topic or allowing them to choose. For my seventh-grade class, I assigned writing a summary to my below-grade-level readers, and an argumentative paragraph to my students who were reading at and above grade level. To avoid confusion, in your plan book or a notebook, make a list of who is doing which activity. Introduce the writing about reading task, explaining how the lesson will work. I say something like this:

    Today we're going to be writing about the text we've been working with. There are two types of writing assignments we'll work on. One group will write a summary, and a second group will write an argumentative paragraph that takes a stand on Zeus's motivation for destroying the chariot. I've divided you into groups. I'll meet with the summary group first to go over the assignment; the rest of you may read independently until I finish.

2. Gather students who will write a summary and distribute the SWBS planner, the Guidelines for Writing a Summary handout, and Rubric: Literature Summary. Review the guidelines and the sections of the planner; then have students fill in the planner. Circulate among students to offer support.

3. Ask students to generate a topic sentence that includes the title of the selection. On the board or chart paper, write this sample topic sentence and tell students that they can use it or compose their own: "In 'Helios,' Phaëthon's dearest wish is granted, only to end in disaster." Students should write their summary on a separate sheet of paper when they finish their planning; remind them to use complete sentences. When everyone understands the task and is ready to work, send them off to complete the writing independently.

4. Gather students who will write an argumentative paragraph. Distribute the Elements of a Paragraph handout and the paragraph rubric; review the guidelines. Invite students to write a paragraph that argues for or against this statement: *Zeus acted out of concern for the people of Earth, even though it cost the life of Phaëthon.* Students should collect three or four pieces of evidence from "Helios" that support their point of view and write them in their notebooks. Then they'll turn the notes into an argumentative paragraph complete with a concluding sentence that sums up the evidence and restates how it all supports the thesis statement.

5. Circulate to observe students taking notes and drafting a summary or argumentative paragraph. Remind them to use their rubrics to revise their writing.

6. Sit side by side with students who require extra support. Acknowledge any successes that students achieved. When possible, use questions rather than statements to address areas that need more work. Questions honor and empower students. Write helpful suggestions on sticky notes and give the note to the student as a reminder of your conversation. Make sure to point out the positives a student has achieved, and remember to phrase suggestions as questions to honor and empower your students.

If you feel students need additional modeling before moving on to the guided practice portion of the unit, work through Lessons 1-6 again using "Orpheus" as the read-aloud text (see the Resources CD).

7. Gauge students' progress to determine how much time to allow for the writing and whether it will be completed during the next class.

Wrap-Up

Compliment students on their detailed plans and their use of the text to gather evidence.

Lessons 8 to 13

Guided Practice With a New Myth

In this next series of lessons, you start releasing responsibility to students, reviewing and coaching as they practice the skills and strategies you modeled with "Helios." Assign students a text based on their reading level; text complexity grids for each selection appear below. Then work through the lessons at a pace that's reasonable for your students, allowing one to two weeks depending on students' needs.

Text Complexity Grids

"Twin Titans and the Creation of Man" retold by Mallery Blake
Lexile®: 1120
Text Complexity: 1 = Accessible to 5 = Challenging

QUALITATIVE	1	2	3	4	5
Knowledge demands				X	
Author's purpose				X	
Meaning				X	
Text structure				X	
Language/vocabulary				X	
Concepts					X
Inferential thinking demands					X

"Athena and Arachne" retold by Allen Brownell
Lexile®: 900
Text Complexity: 1 = Accessible to 5 = Challenging

QUALITATIVE	1	2	3	4	5
Knowledge demands					X
Author's purpose				X	
Meaning				X	
Text structure				X	
Language/vocabulary				X	
Concepts				X	
Inferential thinking demands					X

Building Prior Knowledge and Setting Purposes

In this lesson, students receive a new passage; they preview and read for the gist with peer support.

Materials

- Copies of "Twin Titans and the Creation of Man" for students reading at or above grade level
- Copies of "Athena and Arachne" for students reading below grade level
- Students' notebooks
- "Decisions" concept map from previous lessons
- Chart paper and markers or interactive whiteboard

> Read "Athena and Arachne" aloud to students who are struggling with the text. For guidelines on working with two groups see Chapter 3, page 67.

Teaching the Lesson

1. Review the method you modeled in Lesson 1 for building prior knowledge. Distribute the copies of the passages to students. Ask students to suggest the number of paragraphs they need to read on the first page. Remind them that in addition to reading the first paragraph or two on page 1, they should read the title, and the statements on the assessment quiz.

2. Have students preview the selections to build prior knowledge and then turn to a partner who's reading the same text and share the details they can recall. Remind students to make a list in their notebooks of everything they learned.

3. Ask students to reread their lists and use the information to set purposes for reading. Remind them that to set purposes they can use the title, their notes from Step 2, or the unit theme of decisions. Circulate and support students who need extra help

> Encourage students to read the selection two times to deepen their recall and comprehension.

4. Have students read the selection silently, using their prior knowledge and purpose for reading to get the gist or general idea of the selection.

5. Ask students to pair-share to discuss the gist of their selection and connect the content to the concept of decisions.

6. Circulate and listen to partner discussions to determine whether students have

the general idea of their passage. If some students seem confused, support them by helping them close read and/or reread.

7. Display the "decisions" concept map and invite students to add words from their selection, always showing how their ideas link to the concept.

Wrap-Up

Point out what students did well as they built their prior knowledge and set purposes. Acknowledge the words and phrases students added to the concept map.

LESSON 9

Review Close Reading to Make Inferences, Find Central Ideas, and Identify Author's Purpose

In this lesson, students can use close reading to review and practice making inferences, finding central ideas, and identifying the author's purpose.

Materials

- Students' copies of "Twin Titans and the Creation of Man"
- Students' copies of "Athena and Arachne"
- Students' copies of Close Reading Guidelines
- Students' notebooks

Teaching the Lesson

1. Pair students with partners who have read the same myth, and have them take out their texts. Refresh students' recall of close reading; review the guideline sheet with them and discuss how the strategy can help them figure out the meaning of a difficult word or confusing passage. Remind students to use close reading when they come across a word or phrase they don't understand.

2. Have students reread the selection silently, keeping in mind the purpose for reading that they set in the previous lesson. Read "Athena and Arachne" aloud to students who cannot read it independently. Ask them to raise their hands when they hear a word or sentence that confuses them, so you can model close reading. If no one raises a hand, you can select some challenging words and sentences to close read.

3. Ask pairs to share how close reading helped them figure out a difficult word or a passage that confused them.

4. Invite pairs to discuss what they know about the central idea. Remind them of Lesson 3 where you discussed central ideas for "Helios." As you circulate, listen in on discussions. You may hear comments like these: *It's like theme, but it's the important one. It's an idea that connects to the whole thing. There can be more than one. It needs to come from inference because it's not said in the text. The big central idea is the author's purpose.* Review the modeling you did using "Helios" for all or for some students who can't explain central idea (see page 160).

5. Ask partners to find a central idea for "Twin Titans and the Creation of Man" or "Athena and Arachne," jot down the idea in their notebooks, and explain how the details in their piece helped them infer and pinpoint the central idea. Circulate and listen to partners discuss. Prompt students with questions such as: *What are the main events? What idea ties the main events together? What did the author want to show you? Can you connect the author's purpose to the central idea? Are purpose and central idea the same?*

6. Spotlight students who "get it" and have them explain what helped them identify the central idea; when students share, they provides the class with additional models.

Wrap-Up

Acknowledge students for applying close reading and figuring out central ideas for "Twin Titans and the Creation of Man" and "Athena and Arachne."

LESSON 10

Collaborative Discussions

In this lesson, partners work together to answer text-specific questions about the myth they read independently. They will use the evidence they find to make logical inferences and analyze and connect events in the myth.

Materials

- Students' copies of "Twin Titans and the Creation of Man"
- Students' copies of "Athena and Arachne"

- Discussion Prompts for "Twin Titans and the
  Creation of Man" and "Athena and Arachne"
  (see below and page 174 and the Resources CD)

Teaching the Lesson

**TEACHING TIP —
SCAFFOLDING
STUDENTS' READING**

*Support students who
struggle to read "Athena and
Arachne" by first pointing to
the section in the text that
answers the question and
then having them reread
that section. If students are
unable to read it themselves,
read it aloud to them.*

1. Pair students with partners who have read the
   same text and have them take out their myths.
   Gather students who can't read "Athena and
   Arachne" independently and work with them.

2. Display the discussion prompts for each text
   on a whiteboard or give a copy to each student.
   Invite partners to use the discussion prompts
   to discuss their myth, citing text evidence to
   support answers.

3. Ask pairs to review the events in "Twin Titans and the Creation of Man" or in
   "Athena and Arachne" and make connections between different events to infer
   a character trait or analyze why a trait changes, identify a change in outlook or
   emotions, or discuss how others view Prometheus, Epimetheus, or Athena.

4. Circulate among students and help them make connections between events. Have
   pairs share their connections with other pairs who have read the same text.

Wrap-Up

Acknowledge students' detailed discussions and their use of text evidence to support
their responses. Point out the excellent connections students made between events in
their text.

DISCUSSION PROMPTS FOR "TWIN TITANS AND THE CREATION OF MAN"

1. Compare and contrast Epimetheus and Prometheus.

2. Why does Prometheus steal fire from the gods?

3. Evaluate the punishment Zeus gives Prometheus. Do you think it is just or unjust?
   Explain why.

4. Evaluate the punishment Zeus gives man. Do you think it is fair? Why or why not?

5. Why did Zeus put hope in Pandora's box?

6. What is a theme in this myth? Support your response.

1. Why does Zeus swallow his wife, Metis?

2. Explain why Athena had to burst out of Zeus's head.

3. Why does Athena win the contest with Arachne?

4. Evaluate the punishment Athena gives Arachne. Is it fair? Why or why not?

5. Use evidence from the text to describe three personality traits of Athena and three of Arachne.

6. Compare and contrast Arachne and Phaëthon from "Helios."

LESSON 11

Assessment

In this lesson, students complete the quiz that follows their text selection. In addition to answering the multiple-choice items and identifying paragraphs that support their answers, students will choose one of their answers and defend it in a brief paragraph.

Materials

- Students' copies of "Twin Titans and the Creation of Man"
- Students' copies of "Athena and Arachne"
- Copies of the Quiz Answer Sheet (see page 263 and the Resources CD), class set
- Quiz Answer Keys for "Twin Titans and the Creation of Man" and "Athena and Arachne" (see page 267 and the Resources CD)

Teaching the Lesson

1. Give students the Quiz Answer Sheet and review the quiz directions. Encourage them to skim and reread parts of their myth so they can note the paragraph or paragraphs they use to choose an answer.

2. Have students complete the quiz independently. This includes choosing one answer to defend in a short paragraph, following the guidelines on the Quiz Answer Sheet. Remind them that they may not choose a vocabulary item to write about.

3. Support students who can't read "Athena and Arachne" or the accompanying quiz items by reading the selection and quiz items to them. Read the quiz questions one at a time and have students select the best answer.

4. When students finish, call out answers to the multiple-choice portion; have students self-correct and turn their papers in to you, or collect the papers and grade them yourself.

5. Separate the quizzes into two piles: students who scored a 4 or 5, and students who missed two or more multiple-choice statements.

6. Read the paragraphs students wrote to defend one of their answers. Check to make sure it contains details from the text. Make note of students who had difficulty and plan time to scaffold their learning.

Work in a small group to help students who struggled with the paragraph portion of the quiz. Show them how to take notes on evidence from the text and then write a brief paragraph that explains their thinking about a question, incorporating the answer from the quiz along with their own text evidence.

Wrap-Up

Give students positive feedback for returning to the text and skimming or rereading before selecting an answer and for writing a defense of one of their answers.

LESSON 12

Writing About Reading: Note Taking

In this lesson, students take notes for a suggested topic that relates to "Twin Titans and the Creation of Man" or "Athena and Arachne" and record their notes in their notebooks.

Materials

- Students' copies of "Twin Titans and the Creation of Man"
- Students' copies of "Athena and Arachne"

- Copies of the Note-Taking Guidelines for "Twin Titans and the Creation of Man" and "Athena and Arachne" (see page 176 and the Resources CD)
- Students' notebooks

Teaching the Lesson

1. Explain that students will be taking notes on "Twin Titans and the Creation of Man" and "Athena and Arachne" to plan an explanatory paragraph. Distribute the Note-Taking Guidelines for each myth.

2. As students who are writing about "Twin Titans and the Creation of Man" work independently—taking notes from the text on the selected quote—support students taking notes on "Athena and Arachne." Because this group consists of developing readers, I have provided a scaffold for the writing by asking them to revisit discussion question 3 (see page 174), so that they have some background knowledge.

3. Circulate as students work, supporting students who need help or have questions. Students may need help finding evidence or paraphrasing the text.

Note-Taking Guidelines for "Twin Titans and the Creation of Man"

Prometheus risks Zeus's wrath when he steals fire from the gods and gives it to man.

1. Copy the statement into your notebook.

2. Reread "Twin Titans and the Creation of Man" to find two or three pieces of text evidence in support of the statement. Jot down specific details in your own words.

Note-Taking Guidelines for "Athena and Arachne"

Why does Athena win the contest with Arachne?

1. Copy the question into your notebook; it's one of the discussion prompts from Lesson 10.

2. Reread "Athena and Arachne" to find two pieces of text evidence that support your answer to the question; jot down notes in your notebook.

Wrap-Up

Provide positive feedback on students' use of the text to take detailed notes.

Writing About Reading: Drafting

In this lesson, students write an explanatory paragraph about their text, drawing on the notes they took in the previous lesson and consulting the Elements of a Paragraph handout. Students will need more than 20 minutes to complete the writing; I suggest allowing 30 to 45 minutes for the task over two days.

Materials

- Students' copies of "Twin Titans and the Creation of Man"
- Students' copies of "Athena and Arachne"
- Students' copies of the Rubric: Paragraph
- Students' notebooks
- Additional paper for drafting a paragraph
- Students' copies of the Elements of a Paragraph handout

Teaching the Lesson

1. Have students take out their copies of the Elements of a Paragraph handout. Review the guidelines together. Remind students that the introductory sentence must include the title of the myth.

2. Students writing about "Twin Titans and the Creation of Man" can use the statement from the Note-Taking Guidelines (in the previous lesson) as their introductory sentence, or create one of their own. Copy the sentence onto the board for easy reference: *In "Twin Titans and the Creation of Man," Prometheus risks Zeus's wrath when he steals fire from the gods and gives it to man.*

3. Students writing about "Athena and Arachne" can turn the question from the Note-Taking Guidelines and turn it into an introductory sentence, or craft one of their own. Offer them a model if they need one: *In "Athena and Arachne," Athena wins the contest because she is a goddess.*

4. Instruct students to use their notes from the previous lesson to write a complete paragraph, following the guidelines on the Elements of a Paragraph handout. Remind them to use the rubric to revise their writing.

5. Circulate and support students as necessary. Always begin by noting the positives a student has achieved, and remember to phrase suggestions as questions, to honor and empower your students.

6. Collect the paragraphs and assess them using the rubric. You can note errors in

spelling, usage, and punctuation and use this data for writing mini-lessons and in one-on-one conferences.

Wrap-Up

Compliment students on using their notes to craft their paragraphs.

WRAPPING UP THE UNIT

Independent Practice and Assessment

In the last part of the unit, students work with a text independently, so you can assess their progress, scaffolding or extending their learning as appropriate.

Text Complexity Grids

"Peace, Not Revenge" retold by Kendall Conboy

Lexile®: 1180

Text Complexity: 1 = Accessible to 5 = Challenging

QUALITATIVE	1	2	3	4	5
Knowledge demands				X	
Author's purpose				X	
Meaning				X	
Text structure			X		
Language/vocabulary				X	
Concepts					X
Inferential thinking demands				X	

"Manco Capac and the Rod of Gold" retold by Lulu Delacre

Lexile®: 970

Text Complexity: 1 = Accessible to 5 = Challenging

QUALITATIVE	1	2	3	4	5
Knowledge demands				X	
Author's purpose			X		
Meaning				X	
Text structure			X		
Language/vocabulary				X	
Concepts				X	
Inferential thinking demands				X	

Reading a New Text Independently

Have students work on their own, as this is an assessment that will help you determine students' strengths and needs. They will build prior knowledge and read the text independently. For the assessment, you have three options: students can write a summary, compose an explanatory paragraph, or complete a Word Map about the unit's concept. I recommend that each student do at least one writing activity and complete the Word Map.

Set aside five or six consecutive days for the assessment. You will probably need two 30- to 45-minute classes for students to build prior knowledge, read for the gist, reread for deeper understanding, and complete the Word Map. Over the next three or four days, take about 35–45 minutes to have students complete the writing. If a few students need more time for taking notes and writing, give them the extra time.

Materials

- Copies of "Peace, Not Revenge" (see Resources CD), for students reading at or above grade level
- Copies of "Manco Capac and the Rod of Gold" (see Resources CD), for students reading below grade level
- Students' copies of the Building Background Knowledge handout
- Students' copies of Guidelines for Writing a Summary
- Copies of the SWBS Organizer (see the Resources CD), for student writing summaries
- Students' copies of the Elements of a Paragraph handout
- Copies of Writing Topics for each assessment text (see the Resources CD), for students writing paragraphs
- Copies of the Word Map (see the Resources CD), class set
- Students' copies of the Rubrics for Literature Summary and Paragraph
- Students' notebooks
- Additional notebook paper for writing summaries and/or paragraphs

Teaching the Lesson

1. Have students take out their copy of the Building Prior Knowledge handout while you distribute the assessment texts and copies of the Word Map.
2. Remind students to use the strategy they have practiced to build their prior knowledge and jot down a list of what they learned from their preview in their notebook. Tell them

that on the first two days of the assessment, they should preview the text to build prior knowledge, then read for the gist. Encourage them to reread the text for deeper comprehension before they complete the Word Map.

TEACHING TIP —
PEER ASSESSMENT

Have students give their plans and first drafts to a writing partner. Ask the partner to use the rubric and the Guidelines for Writing a Summary or Elements of a Paragraph handout to make sure all elements have been included. Partners give each other feedback that can improve their summaries or paragraphs. Have students write a second draft based on peer feedback. Collect and read the drafts.

3. Invite students to complete the Word Map, specifying how many characteristics and examples you want them to provide to demonstrate their understanding of the concept.

4. On the next day, ask those students who will be writing a summary to take out their Guidelines for Writing a Summary handout. Give them a SWBS Organizer and the rubric you will use to assess the summary.

5. Ask those students who will be writing a paragraph to take out their Elements of a Paragraph handout. Distribute the Writing Topics list and the rubric you will use to assess the paragraph.

6. Invite students to reread and take notes for their summaries or paragraphs. Have them work through the writing process outlined on the Guidelines for Writing a Summary handout or the Elements of a Paragraph handout, consulting the corresponding rubric to check their work.

7. When students finish, have them turn in their work. Assess it using the rubric.

Interpreting Assessments

The paragraphs can show you whether students can make logical inferences and find specific text details from the selection. See the Scaffolding Suggestions chart on page 183 to help you support students with reading issues.

To scaffold students who require writing support, use the Scaffolding Suggestions for Helping Students Write Summaries and Paragraphs chart on the Resources CD.

Following Up the Assessment

Based on your assessment of students' writing, you can determine how many days to spend scaffolding and extending their learning. I recommend allowing at least one day for students to revise their writing based on your feedback; during that time, you can meet with your most struggling readers. Then you may choose to spend additional days working in small groups scaffolding students who need it and extending the learning of those who are ready for more challenge.

Supporting Students Who Require Scaffolding

The chart on page 183 offers scaffolding suggestions based on students' writing, your observations as they read and discuss texts, and your conferences on independent and instructional reading. Support students with similar needs by working with groups of two or three. When students struggle and are unsuccessful with the assessment, work one-on-one with them.

At first, when you scaffold, you might do all or most of the modeling and thinking aloud. Follow-up conferences should gradually turn over to the student the responsibility for learning. You can do this gradual release by pairing the student with a peer, by continuing to confer with and observe the student's thinking, or by having the student work independently and then share her thinking with you. This can occur in two or three short conferences (see forms on the Resources CD). However, some students will need several conferences, and you might have to return to the skill as you move on to another unit.

Texts to Use for Scaffolding

Students can use the myth read for their independent assessment or one you have selected. I also include two additional texts on the Resources CD.

Suggestions for Helping Students Think Across Texts

After students who were successful on the assessment revise their writing, you may want to follow up their learning by challenging them to think across the texts they have read during the unit; this task supports the Common Core State Standards 7 to 9 for reading. Once students have read, discussed, and analyzed each text in this unit, they will be able to find common themes and ideas among them. You can use the suggestions below to help students complete across-text thinking.

- Compare the personality of two different gods, giving specific examples of their actions and words and the reactions and words of people.
- Compare what angers and what pleases the gods in two different myths.
- Compare the decisions that gods make and decisions that humans make in two different myths.
- Discuss and try to find reasons for why these cultures believed in gods that were so much like human beings. You can do some research on the Internet by going to these sites:

—*http://en.wikipedia.org/wiki/Anthropomorphism*

—*http://www.newworldencyclopedia.org/entry/Anthropomorphism*

Ideas for Inquiry and Problem Solving Beyond the Text

If you have time to extend the unit, ask students to devise questions based on their reading, or use the questions below to spark an inquiry.

- Why do we read Greek myths today? Can you find relevance in these stories to your life? To your community?

- Read stories about ancient Greek superheroes—for example, Theseus, Hercules, or Perseus—and connect what you learn to twenty-first-century superheroes such as Spider-Man, Superman, the Green Hornet, and so on.

- The Greeks considered hubris—humans thinking they were equal to or better than the gods—a sin, and punished hubris among human beings such as Arachne and Phaëthon with severity. Search newspapers, magazines, and the Internet for modern-day examples of hubris and explore whether our society's punishments are similar to those of ancient Greece.

Students can use the texts they've read during the unit and/or research new texts to explore the issues raised by the questions, which are all connected to the theme of decisions. Students can write a short paper to share their results, participate in a class discussion or debate, create posters displaying what they've learned—the possibilities are many, and I find allowing students to choose their mode of presentation motivates and engages them.

> **TOP-NOTCH MYTHOLOGY TEXTS**
>
> On the Resources CD you will find a list of ten mythology texts to review for your class and/or school library.

CLOSING THOUGHTS AND QUESTIONS TO DISCUSS

You can continue professional study by discussing with a peer or a group of colleagues the parts of the lessons that worked and the parts that need refining. Here are some prompts to guide your conversations:

- Share with colleagues how students found relevance to their lives and the world with the study of Greek myths.

- How can you use one of these myths as a mentor text for having students compose a modern-day myth? What in nature, technology, aeronautics, space travel, or science could the myth explain?
- The myth about Athena is an allegory about the goddess and the girl who challenged her to a weaving contest. What problems in our society can be addressed in an allegory? Some to consider are poverty, hunger, terrorism, random shootings, and so on. How might you teach this to your students?

Scaffolding Suggestions for Helping Students Read Mythology

STUDENT'S NEED	POSSIBLE SCAFFOLD
Understanding allegory and applying it to the myths: Has difficulty explaining what the myth symbolizes	• Review the definition of allegory and show the student how you apply the concept to "Helios." • Using a different myth, offer these questions that can help the student figure out what the myth symbolizes: *What does the god do for or to people? What are the actions and reactions of the gods and/or human beings? How do these actions help you figure out the allegory?*
Finding anthropomorphic traits the gods display: Needs support in separating divine and human traits	• Review with the student the meaning of *anthropomorphic*. • Make a list of human traits that Helios displays in that myth. • Using another myth, have the student study the god's reactions to situations, people, and words spoken and pinpoint the traits she notices.
Understanding lessons and themes in the myths: Has difficulty figuring out the themes and purposes of the myths	• Ask the student to think about the main purposes or point of the myth. *What is it trying to teach us about nature? About people? About justice? About vanity? About the place of human beings?*
Comparing gods from Greek, Norse, and Inca cultures: Needs help grasping similar themes, purposes, and divine and human traits	• Work with two myths from different cultures and review their themes—what each myth represents or is trying to teach. Help students see whether the purposes of the two different myths are to explain the natural world or to illustrate what the gods represent to the people. • Repeat this exercise, this time looking at the divine traits the gods exhibit and the human traits they show. • Model and think aloud as much as you have to in order for students to observe your process and internalize it so that they can make similar comparisons.

CHAPTER 7

Reading Short Stories

Felicia was a seventh grader intensely interested in short stories. "I have read ten short stories this week," she told me during a conference. "I see myself in so many of them," she said. "I'm reading and reading as many as I can to learn more about the short story's structure, and then I'll write my own." Like Felicia, many middle-school students I teach love short stories—partly because they are short and accessible, but also because many of them deal with growing up, a subject middle schoolers are keenly interested in. The three short stories in this unit include three diverse protagonists and show how events, personal decisions, and other characters contribute to their maturing process.

Because each of these stories is long relative to the reading selections in other units, I've included only two: "Through the Tunnel" by Doris Lessing serves as the anchor text; "The Circuit" by Francisco Jiménez is for the guided practice portion of the unit.

For independent practice and assessment, I recommend using short stories from your own curriculum.

The lessons in this unit model some of the Common Core State Standards for reading literature. I also discuss how to analyze a story using literary elements such as protagonist, antagonistic forces, and setting. For each short story in the unit, I offer text-specific, high-level questions for students to discuss, along with suggestions for assessment, but there is no quiz. On the Resources CD, you'll find a framework for writing an analytical essay as well as project ideas that call for collaboration and independent thinking; these are excellent ways to augment student learning during the unit.

The short stories in this chapter all relate to the concept of "growing up," this unit's theme. I want students to consider what protagonists live through and the kinds of decisions they make that move them forward on their journey to adulthood. By reading and thinking deeply about themes in short stories, by understanding the short story's structure and connecting the concept of growing up to each one, by gaining insights into what causes characters to grow and change, and by inferring the personality traits of a character, students will develop a knowledge base that will enable them to read and understand literature on a deeper level.

In this unit, I model how to apply the strategies that enable students to meet the following CCSS for reading literature:

- understand literary elements
- make logical inferences about setting, characters, and plot
- study the reasons for a character changing from the beginning to the end of a story
- identify the central idea and how it developed
- cull words and phrases that create mood or tone, and connect these to inferences and/or central ideas
- engage in collaborative discussion
- recall details, make logical inferences, and identify themes

Lessons 1 to 8

Model How to Read a Short Story

In this first set of lessons, you will use an anchor text to model the skills and strategies that readers use when tackling a short story. You will model how to think about a short story using narrative literary elements, such as protagonist and setting. You'll also model how to make logical inferences, identify the central idea and show how this idea developed, gather words to determine mood or tone, and link these words to inferences and/or the central idea.

Text Complexity Grid

"Through the Tunnel" by Doris Lessing
Lexile®: 880
Text Complexity: 1 = Accessible to 5 = Challenging

QUALITATIVE	1	2	3	4	5
Knowledge demands			X		
Author's purpose			X		
Meaning			X		
Text structure			X		
Language/vocabulary			X		
Concepts				X	
Inferential thinking demands				X	

LESSON 1

Getting Ready to Read

In this lesson, you'll review how to build prior knowledge for a short story and begin a concept map for the concept of growing up.

Materials

- "Through the Tunnel," displayed on the whiteboard from the Resources CD
- Students' notebooks
- Chart paper and markers for taking notes and generating the concept map

Teaching the Lesson

1. Display "Through the Tunnel" on the whiteboard.

2. Show students how they can build prior knowledge with a short story. The procedure is a little different from what they've done with other genres. Since it is a story, they should not read the ending, so they can wonder about and predict what will happen. In addition, they should focus on identifying the characters, setting, and problem, to get a handle on the story. To introduce the modified building-prior-knowledge routine for short stories, I say something like this:

   This is a short story, so we approach it a little differently—but we still take time to build our prior knowledge. First, read the title and think about what it might mean. Then, read the first six or eight paragraphs and ask yourself questions that can help you wrap your head around the story by thinking about the characters you are introduced to, what the problem might be, and where the story takes place: Who are the characters? Can I identify the protagonist? Can I identify a problem the protagonist is facing or will face? What is the setting? What might the title mean, given the setting? What can I tell about relationships between characters?

3. Read aloud the first six paragraphs of "Through the Tunnel," then say out loud all the details you recall from this preview, reminding students that talking about a text can help them tell whether they remember enough from the preview of the story or if they should reread it.

4. Write on a sheet of chart paper a list of what you learned in the preview. Here's my list:

   - Jerry, an English boy, goes to the beach with his mom.
   - His mother senses that Jerry would like to be alone at the beach: ". . . would you rather not come with me?"
   - First, Jerry doesn't want to go to a different beach. He changes his mind and asks to go to the rocks.

5. Invite students to pair-share and add to the list. Here's what my sixth-grade students said:

   - The mother shows trust when she tells Jerry to come back to the big beach or to the villa.
   - Jerry is an only child; his dad died; his mom is a widow.
   - His mother doesn't want to be possessive, but she worries.

6. Invite students to pair-share and discuss what they have learned about the characters, problem, and setting in "Through the Tunnel." Circulate and listen to their conversations. Prompt them with questions that send them back to the text, such as: *Who do you think is the main character? Why? What is the setting? Have any problems surfaced? What conflicts between Jerry and his mom might arise?*

7. Write down what students share on chart paper. These are hunches based on a small amount of text, and it's helpful for students to know that they will probably make some adjustments while reading the story.

   - *Main Character or Protagonist:* Jerry—it's his story, as his mom stays at another beach. The conflict is here—Jerry feels torn between pleasing his mom by being with her and going off on his own.
   - *Setting:* a big beach and a small one with rocks
   - *Problem:* One might be between Jerry and his mom; she worries that something may happen to him when he's off on his own, but Jerry wants independence.

8. Tell students that today the class will begin creating a concept map by thinking about the concept of growing up in "Through the Tunnel." Write "growing up" on a sheet of chart paper. Discuss the concept by saying something like this:

   Growing up is an interior process; it happens within a person. Evidence that a person is growing up can be seen in his or her decisions, actions, and interactions. Turn to your partner and take two or three minutes to discuss the concept of growing up and try to share ideas and examples that relate to this concept, from your own experience or from the text.

9. Accept any suggestions the students offer as long as they can link their ideas to the concept of growing up. My sixth graders offered three suggestions, which I asked them to explicitly connect to growing up and wrote on the map: *being responsible for school work and chores; valuing advice from adults; being able to babysit younger siblings.*

10. Read aloud "Through the Tunnel."

Wrap-Up

Give students positive feedback on their listening skills and their contributions to the concept map.

Understanding Literary Elements

To navigate fictional texts, it's helpful for students to know the definitions of literary terms such as *plot* and *climax*, but it's also important for students to see these elements at work in a short story. In this lesson, you'll introduce or review these literary elements, model how to identify some of them in "Through the Tunnel," and ask students to set a purpose for reading the story.

Materials

- "Through the Tunnel," displayed on the whiteboard from the Resources CD
- Students' notebooks
- Copies of Literary Elements handout (see the Resources CD), class set
- "Growing up" concept map, begun in Lesson 1
- Chart paper and markers

Teaching the Lesson

1. Distribute the Literary Elements handout and review these terms with your students: *protagonist, antagonist, setting, plot, climax, denouement, conflict, problem, resolution,* and *theme*. If any terms are new to students, take a moment to define them and discuss examples from other texts you've read, and be sure to discuss them in "Through the Tunnel."

> **TEACHING TIP ‿**
>
> *You will need two class periods for this lesson (about 45 minutes each).*

2. Tell students that identifying the literary elements of a story can help them better remember and comprehend the story. Remind them of the previous lesson where they identified character, setting, and problem—three key literary elements that helped them get ready to read and predict what might happen in the story. If students can identify the conflict, recognize the resolution, understand the denouement, and trace the plot, it will be easier for them to recall and discuss the text.

3. Have students reread the building-prior-knowledge notes that you compiled in Lesson 1. Ask students to set a purpose for their second listening of "Through the Tunnel." Remind them that they can turn the title into a question to form

a purpose—*Why did the author name this story "Through the Tunnel?"* Students can also use the concept map to set a purpose—*What does the story have to do with growing up?* Yet another possibility is to use the information from the preview—*Why is the story set by the sea?* Have students pair-share and discuss their purpose for listening to "Through the Tunnel" and then invite a few students to share their purposes.

4. Read the text aloud to students. Explain that hearing the story a second time will deepen their comprehension and enable them to recall more details. Remind them to think about literary elements as they read and see if they can identify them in the story.

5. When you finish reading, invite students to pair-share and discuss examples from "Through the Tunnel" for each literary element on the handout. Next, ask pairs to share their ideas with the class. Here is a summary of three literary elements that my sixth graders identified:

- *Protagonist and Problems:* Jerry is the protagonist; the story is all about him. His problem is to show himself and his mother that he is responsible and does not have to be with her all the time. Jerry wants to separate from his mother and that's part of growing up. Jerry challenges himself to go through the tunnel, trains himself to hold his breath, and makes it through. At the end, when his mom tells him she doesn't think he should swim again that day, he doesn't argue. We inferred that he's reached his goal and has grown up and he doesn't have the need to argue with her.

- *Antagonistic forces:* Jerry's mom is an antagonistic force. He feels she doesn't want to give him the independence he craves—even though she lets him go to the small beach by himself. The boys are antagonistic forces and they work against Jerry by not including him in the group and also by showing him the tunnel. Jerry's desire to make it through the tunnel is an antagonistic force that propels Jerry to figure out how to meet this challenge. He uses a large rock to sink quickly to the tunnel's opening and practices holding his breath so he can make it through.

TEACHING TIP ⁓

If students are unfamiliar with literary elements, go over the Literary Elements handout with them. Discuss the examples from "Through the Tunnel" and other narrative texts students have read to deepen students' understanding.

- *Climax:* The climax is when Jerry makes it through the tunnel. This is near the end, which is where the climax comes. The denouement, or return to normalcy, is when he returns home and feels no need to argue with his mom or return to the bay.

6. Return to the "growing up" concept map and have students pair-share and add words and phrases to the map based on the text. Make sure you ask them to explicitly connect their words and phrases to the concept of growing up.

Wrap-Up

Point out the positive discussions students had and their ability to use story details to show their understanding of literary elements, and compliment them on the number of ideas they added to the concept map.

LESSON 3

Making Inferences About Characters and Finding Themes

In this lesson, you will show students how you use details from "Through the Tunnel" to make logical inferences about the characters and to pinpoint themes. Students will have the opportunity to practice what you model.

Materials
- "Through the Tunnel," displayed on the whiteboard from the Resources CD
- Students' notebooks

Teaching the Lesson

1. Tell students that, in this lesson, they will find key details and make inferences about characters based on the details. Then, students will consider what themes the details and inferences suggest. Remind students that a theme comes from the text but can be generalized and applied to life outside the story, for instance, *when children grow up, they want to separate from their parents* is one theme readers can draw from "Through the Tunnel," based on Jerry's experience at the beach.

2. Reread aloud paragraph nine of "Through the Tunnel," beginning with "When he was so far . . ." and ending with ". . . but all at once very lonely."

3. Present a think-aloud to show how you use specific text details to infer and find themes. Here's what I say:

Jerry is floating far out, far enough so that he can see the beach where his mother is. When he can see the beach, he looks for his mother. This detail tells me he cares about her and wants to know where she is and that she's all right. She is far away—"a speck of yellow" that "looked like a slice of orange peel." In the next sentence, we read that he is relieved to have seen her, yet lonely too. I can infer Jerry is happy and proud to have separated from his mother but still wants to be connected to her. The words relieved *and* lonely *suggest the theme that separating from your mother is part of growing up, but growing up can be lonely because you do it on your own.*

4. Pair up students and invite them to infer and find a theme from a passage of "Through the Tunnel" that you read out loud. I read aloud paragraph 13, beginning with "Jerry dived, shot past the school . . ." and ending with ". . . water like a foolish dog." You can select any passage from the story for students to discuss. Here's what my sixth graders said about paragraph 13:

We inferred that Jerry feels insecure because he has not made it through the tunnel—the detail that supports this is "in a panic of failure." Jerry wants these boys to accept him, even be friends with him. When he acts like a "foolish dog" to get the boys' attention and speaks in English, a language they don't understand, the author shows how much Jerry wants to be part of their group. A theme is that if you're desperate for friendship and acceptance, acting goofy is not a way to get it. In paragraph 15 the boys ignore him and dive to go through the tunnel again, reinforcing the idea that acting goofy doesn't help you make friends.

5. Continue having pairs infer and find other themes until you feel students understand the importance of using text evidence to support inferences and themes. Circulate among students and help those who are struggling with the process.

Wrap-Up

Provide positive feedback on students' ability to use text details to infer and find themes in "Through the Tunnel."

Exploring Themes and Mood and Finding Central Ideas

In this lesson, students closely examine language from the story, exploring how words and phrases connect to themes and create a mood. Students then consider the central idea of the story and relate the themes to it.

Materials

- "Through the Tunnel," displayed on the whiteboard from the Resources CD
- Students' notebooks
- Key words from the story, written on chart paper
- "Growing up" concept map begun in Lesson 1
- Chart paper and markers

Teaching the Lesson

1. Choose words and phrases from "Through the Tunnel" that relate to the themes and inferences that you and students identified in the previous lesson. Before the lesson, write the words on chart paper. These are words I have used: *control his breathing, big stone, movement of blood, chest hurting, nose bled badly, weak and dizzy, limp.*

2. Ask pairs to reread the words and phrases and to consider the mood they evoke. My sixth graders responded with "fear" and "danger." They also noted that the words referred to the physical signs of how hard it is for Jerry to separate from his mom and prove he can be like the big kids and go through the tunnel on his own. Students linked the words and phrases to the inference they had made previously that Jerry wants to show the boys that he can go through the tunnel, that he is as grown up and independent as the boys. One pair contrasted the bright red of the nose bleeds, which they felt symbolizes the pain of living and growing up, with the darkness of the tunnel, which symbolizes the dangerous journey Jerry takes to prove his independence.

3. Ask students to think about their insights—their inferences and themes, their thoughts about the story's language and mood—and identify a central idea that these all point to. Remind students that a central idea relates to the entire story; all elements in the story should relate to the central idea. The sixth graders

agreed that a central idea in "Through the Tunnel" is that to grow up can be difficult and can involve danger and pain.

4. Now invite students to pair-share and find more themes in the story. Themes often relate to the central idea of a story. A story can have several themes because a theme relates to one or a small set of events, while the central idea grows out of the entire story. Reread aloud these paragraphs: 20, 21, 30, 31, 34, 44–48; they contain support for an important theme and show how the author develops it. By returning to these paragraphs, you're inviting students to use close reading to find text evidence to support a theme. My sixth graders identified the following theme: Determination and persistence are necessary to achieve goals. They explained their thinking this way:

Jerry wants to swim through the tunnel, but he knows he can't. So he decides to train himself. When he first tries to find the opening to the tunnel, the salt water stings his eyes. He knows he needs goggles to solve that problem, so he asks his mother for them and pesters her until she buys them. Then he immediately goes back to the rock and dives into the water. The seal around the goggles breaks, so Jerry knows he needs another way to get into the water, and he figures one out. Then he carefully explores the rock surface, searching for the opening. He finds it, but knows before he attempts it he must learn to control his breathing. He works on this skill for days, suffering discomfort and pain, including bloody noses and a frustrating delay when his mom insists he accompany her to the big beach. Even when he is able to hold his breath for the amount of time the big boys took to swim through the tunnel, he waits: "Probably now, if he tried, he could get through that long tunnel, but he was not going to try yet. A curious, most unchildlike persistence, a controlled impatience, made him wait." It's clear that Jerry would never have been successful going through the tunnel if he hadn't had the determination and persistence to make the necessary preparations.

5. Ask partners to connect a theme they identified to the central idea of "Through the Tunnel." My students noted that determination and perseverance are qualities people can develop as they face the challenges of growing up.

6. Encourage partners to find more details that support other themes in the story and have students link each one to the central idea. Tell students that as long as they can support a suggested theme with text evidence, it is valid.

7. Display the "growing up" concept map and invite students to pair-share and find words and phrases from the story that connect to the concept of growing up. Make sure that you ask students to make their connections explicit.

Wrap-Up

Compliment students on their ability to use text evidence to identify the story's themes and a central idea.

LESSON 5

Collaborative Discussions

In this lesson, students will review and practice making inferences as they discuss text-specific questions and find text evidence to support their answers.

Materials

- "Through the Tunnel," displayed on the whiteboard from the Resources CD
- Students' notebooks
- Discussion Prompts for "Through the Tunnel" (see page 196 and the Resources CD), class set
- Students' copies of Close Reading Guidelines

Teaching the Lesson

1. Pair students with partners whose instructional levels are no more than one year apart. Gather in a small group students who cannot read the text independently; they will work with you.

2. Have students retrieve their copy of the Close Reading Guidelines handout.

3. Explain to students that they're going to discuss some questions about "Through the Tunnel" that will require them to close read and make inferences.

4. Ask students to pair-share and discuss everything they recall about making inferences and close reading. Circulate among the students and spotlight responses that will help the class by asking partners to share their thinking.

5. Distribute the discussion prompts to students. Encourage students to use the Close Reading Guidelines for words or passages that confuse them.

6. Show students how you close read and make inferences from a passage in the story. Here's what I say about the paragraph 38 (shown on page 196):

   The phrase "counting wildly" and repeating the numbers help me infer that Jerry is panicked but also aware of his state of mind because he remembers that he's said the same number earlier. Even though victory is near, Jerry can't control the fear and anxiety that sweep through him.

7. Review and explain the terms *symbol* and *symbolize* by asking students to explain what the American flag is a symbol of (patriotism, love of and respect for country, the United States of America, and so on). Help students understand that a symbol is something that can also stand for something else, and that they will need this information to discuss one of the prompts.

8. Give students about five to ten minutes to discuss the prompts for "Through the Tunnel." Encourage them to jot down notes and specific paragraph numbers that they used to find evidence. Circulate to listen in on discussions, and extend or shorten the time as needed.

9. Invite partners to share their answers with the class and, if they close read a part, to explain how close reading helped them infer.

> *"A hundred, a hundred one . . . the water paled. Victory filled him. His lungs were beginning to hurt. A few more strokes and he would be out. He was counting wildly; he said a hundred and fifteen, and then, a long time later, a hundred and fifteen again."*

Wrap-Up

Point out what worked well during the discussions. Compliment students on their recall and application of inferring and close reading.

DISCUSSION PROMPTS FOR "THROUGH THE TUNNEL"

1. Why does Jerry make the decision to swim through the tunnel?

2. Why doesn't Jerry tell his mother about his plans to prepare for swimming through the tunnel?

3. Why is it no longer important for Jerry to go to the bay after he's made it through the tunnel?

4. Identify three personality traits that Jerry displays. Use text evidence to support your answer.

5. How does Jerry change from the beginning to the end of "Through the Tunnel"? What has caused these changes?

6. Compare the way Jerry views his mother with the way you view her.

7. How does "Through the Tunnel" connect to the concept of growing up?

8. What do the tunnel and the bay symbolize?

Assessment: Writing About Reading

In this lesson, you have three assessment options to choose from: students can write a summary or an explanatory paragraph, or they can define a set of literary elements and provide examples from "Through the Tunnel." For your advanced thinkers and writers, I include directions on the Resources CD for planning and writing an analytical essay.

Displaying the text in two-page view makes it easier for students to reread the text; see page 45.

I recommend that you set aside three class periods for students to think, plan, draft, edit, and revise their writing, which will serve as an assessment of their comprehension.

Materials

- "Through the Tunnel," displayed on the whiteboard from the Resources CD
- Students' notebooks
- Additional paper for writing a summary or paragraph
- Copies of Somebody-Wanted-But-So (SWBS) Organizer (see the Resources CD), for students writing summaries
- Students' copies of Guidelines for Writing a Summary (see page 266 and the Resources CD)
- Students' copies of Elements of a Paragraph, for students writing explanatory paragraphs (see page 265 and the Resources CD)
- Students' copies of Rubric: Literature Summary
- Students' copies of Rubric: Paragraph
- Copies of Literary Elements Assessment, for students defining literary elements (see the Resources CD)

Teaching the Lesson

1. Determine which students will work on which writing assignment, and split the class into groups.
2. Meet with each group in turn, introducing the assignments as described below.
3. As students work, circulate and offer assistance as necessary.

4. Sit side by side with students who require extra support. Acknowledge any successes that students achieved. When possible, use questions rather than statements to address areas that need more work. Questions honor and empower students. Write helpful suggestions on sticky notes and give the note to the student as a reminder of your conversation.

Wrap-Up

Point out how well students worked on their summaries, paragraphs, and definitions.

Planning and Writing a Summary of "Through the Tunnel"

1. Give students copies of the Somebody-Wanted-But-So Organizer and have them take out their Guidelines for Writing a Summary and their Rubric: Literature Summary.

2. Review the elements of a summary and how to use the SWBS organizer. Remind students of the importance of an introductory sentence, and offer one if students need the support: *In "Through the Tunnel," Doris Lessing shows that Jerry wants to grow up and make decisions independently from his mother.*

3. Have students take notes on the form to outline their summary.

4. Ask students to complete the summary on a separate sheet of paper by using their notes and the model introductory sentence.

5. Have students use the rubric to check and revise their work.

Planning and Writing an Explanatory Paragraph

1. Have students take out their Elements of a Paragraph handout, their Rubric: Paragraph, and the discussion prompts from Lesson 5; post or distribute the following quotes from "Through the Tunnel."

- "He swam back to shore, relieved at being sure she was there, but all at once very lonely."

- "To be with them, of them, was a craving that filled his whole body."

- "But now, now, now. He must have them this minute, and no other time."

continued on next page

---

continued . . .

- "All night, the boy dreamed of the water-filled cave in the rock, and as soon as breakfast was over he went to the bay."

2. Ask students to select either a discussion prompt from Lesson 5 or one of the quotes to explain in a paragraph. Students may select their own quote from the text; just be sure they show it to you so you can approve it.

3. Have students write their selected quote or prompt in their notebooks, along with a preliminary topic sentence that states their point. They may explain how the line they've chosen relates to a theme or central idea of the story, or they may explain their response to a prompt.

4. Tell students to revisit the text to find at least three pieces of evidence in the story to help explain their point. Encourage students to jot down specific details in their own words.

5. When students believe they have enough evidence, have them show you their notes before they begin drafting. When they are ready, have them follow the guidelines on the Elements of a Paragraph handout to draft their explanatory paragraph. Remind them to use the Rubric: Paragraph to check and revise their work.

Writing Analytical Essays

Analytical writing—making a claim or developing a thesis based on a text and then supporting the claim or thesis with details and inferences from the text— is one type of argumentative writing. The Common Core State Standards say on page 24 of the appendix: ". . . the Standards put particular emphasis on students' ability to write sound arguments on substantive topics and issues, as this ability is critical to college and career readiness."

On the Resources CD, I include a section on teaching students to write analytical essays. The lessons include developing a claim or thesis; using criteria to set writing standards for content, craft and technique, and writing conventions; completing a writing plan and first draft; and having students use criteria to self-revise and edit and/or peer-revise and edit. Though I urge teachers to support students as they plan and complete a first draft, I recommend that for grading purposes, teachers read second drafts, after students have had a chance to revise and edit and improve the essay.

Before testing students on literary terms, make sure they have a solid understanding of the terms by asking them to write a definition of each one and provide examples using "Through the Tunnel" or another story you select. If students' assessments reveal misunderstandings or confusions about the terms, be sure to reteach and provide examples from "Through the Tunnel" and other stories the class has read. Once you determine that students have a thorough understanding of the terms, you may test students on the elements by administering the same assessment but having students provide examples from "The Circuit" or a text of your choosing.

Literary Elements Assessment

1. Select five or more terms from the Literary Elements handout for which you want to assess students' knowledge and understanding.

2. Either write the name of the terms you are assessing on the Literary Elements Assessment sheet and make copies for students, or hand out the sheet and have students fill in the elements by copying them from the board.

3. Tell students they should do two things for each literary element:
   - Define the term in a complete sentence.
   - Demonstrate understanding of the term by providing examples from the short story they read.

4. Give students enough time to write their definitions and examples. Collect the assessments and grade, assigning fewer points to the definition and more points to the connections students make to the text.

If you feel students need additional modeling before moving on to the guided practice portion of the unit, work through Lessons 1–6 again using "La Bamba" as the read-aloud text (see the Resources CD).

Guided Practice With a New Short Story

In this next series of lessons, you start releasing responsibility to students, reviewing and coaching as they practice the skills and strategies you modeled with "Through the Tunnel." Work through the lessons at a pace that's reasonable for your students, allowing one to two weeks, depending on students' needs.

Text Complexity Grid

"The Circuit" by Francisco Jiménez
Lexile®: 730
Text Complexity: 1 = Accessible to 5 = Challenging

QUALITATIVE	1	2	3	4	5
Knowledge demands					X
Author's purpose			X		
Meaning			X		
Text structure			X		
Language/vocabulary				X	
Concepts				X	
Inferential thinking demands					X

LESSON 7

Building Prior Knowledge and Setting Purposes

In this lesson, students have the opportunity to build prior knowledge and set purposes for reading, with the support of a partner. To complete this lesson, you'll need two 30- to 40-minute classes.

Materials

- Copies of "The Circuit" (see the Resources CD), class set
- Students' notebooks

- Students' copies of the Literary Elements handout
- "Growing up" concept map from previous lessons
- Chart paper and markers or interactive whiteboard

"The Circuit" is from Francisco Jiménez's award-winning collection of autobiographical short stories: *The Circuit: Stories From The Life of a Migrant Child*. I highly recommend this book for all middle-school classrooms.

Teaching the Lesson

1. Distribute the short story.

2. Review the method you modeled for building prior knowledge in Lesson 1 (pages 187–188). Ask students to suggest the number of paragraphs they need to read to preview the story. My sixth graders said they would preview the first eight paragraphs. Remind them to read and think about the title.

3. Have students preview to build prior knowledge and then turn to a partner and share the details they can recall. Remind students to make a list in their notebooks of everything they learn.

TEACHING TIP —

Read the story aloud to students who can't read it independently. Follow directions for working with two groups provided in Chapter 3, page 67.

4. Ask students to reread their lists and use the information to set purposes for reading. Remind them that to set purposes they can refer to the title, their prior-knowledge notes, or the concept of growing up. Circulate and support students who need extra help.

5. Have students read the story silently. Gather students who can't read "The Circuit" independently and read the story aloud as they follow along.

6. Ask students to pair-share to discuss the gist of the story and connect the content to the idea of growing up.

7. Circulate and listen to partner discussions to determine whether students have the gist of the story. If some students seem confused, support them by helping them close read and/or reread.

8. Ask students to reread the story to deepen their recall and comprehension, reminding them to pay attention to the story elements such as antagonistic forces, settings, and so on.

9. Display the "growing up" concept map and invite students to add words and phrases from the story that relate to the concept of growing up. Always ask students to explicitly connect their words or phrases to the concept.

Wrap-Up

Point out what students did well as they built their prior knowledge and set purposes for reading. Give positive feedback on the words and phrases students added to the concept map.

LESSON 8

Understanding Literary Elements

In this lesson, students will develop an understanding of literary elements. Pairs will discuss the definitions of the elements, connect each element to the story, and write connections made in their notebooks. You will need about two class periods (30 minutes each) or one longer block to complete this lesson.

Materials

- Students' copies of "The Circuit"
- Students' notebooks
- Students' copies of the Literary Elements handout
- "Growing up" concept map from previous lessons
- Chart paper and markers or interactive whiteboard

Teaching the Lesson

1. Have students reread their building-prior-knowledge notes and the purposes they set for reading their story.

2. Ask students to retrieve and review the Literary Elements handout; encourage students to ask questions to clarify their understanding of the literary terms.

3. Invite students to pair-share and discuss examples of each of the elements in the story, jotting notes in their notebooks. Circulate among students and provide support for those who need it.

4. Ask pairs to share their ideas with the class. Here is a summary that a pair of sixth graders wrote about the antagonistic forces in "The Circuit."

   - *Antagonistic forces in "The Circuit":* These are forces that work against the protagonist and cause conflicts and problems. In "The Circuit," always moving to find work in the fields—the life of a migrant working family—

causes the narrator to be sad because he loses friends each time the family moves. Going to school and making friends with the teacher, Mr. Lema, is an antagonistic force because the narrator wants to become a better reader and learn to play the trumpet. Mr. Lema promises that, during lunch, he will help the narrator play the trumpet. The narrator's excitement over music lessons turns to sadness and quiet acceptance when he sees that the car is packed and ready to move to another spot. He never cries or complains but continues on "the circuit."

5. Return to the "growing up" concept map and ask students to pair-share and add more ideas to the map that relate to the concept of growing up. Make sure you ask them to connect their words and phrases to the concept and provide specific examples.

Wrap-Up

Acknowledge students for participating in their discussions. Give them positive feedback on their ability to use story details to show their understanding of literary elements, and on their additions to the concept map.

LESSON 9

Making Inferences and Finding Themes

In this lesson, students infer the personality traits of the characters in the story and use plot events to find themes, always citing text evidence to support their thinking. Set aside about two blocks of 20 minutes each, as deep thinking takes time.

Materials

- Students' copies of "The Circuit"
- Students' notebooks
- T-Chart: Making Logical Inferences About a Character Trait (see the Resources CD)

Teaching the Lesson

1. Have students turn to their partner and pair-share everything they remember about making inferences. Remind students of the work they did in Lesson 3 with "Through the Tunnel."

2. Ask students to pair-share to make inferences about the role of the setting in the story. To support students, ask questions such as: *How did the setting affect the protagonist? Was the setting an antagonistic force? Why or why not? How did the setting change the protagonist? How did it affect the protagonist's decisions?* You might want to project these questions onto a whiteboard or jot them down on chart paper. Point out that the setting can have a big influence on the characters and plot events, so it's always a good idea to consider the role of setting in a story.

3. Have partners study the protagonist in the story. First, ask students to study what the protagonist says, thinks, does, and decides, as well as his interactions with other characters, in order to infer the personality traits of the narrator of "The Circuit." Show students how to organize their inferences into a T-chart. What follows are parts of the T-charts my sixth graders developed for the story.

Protagonist: Narrator **Personality Trait**	**Story:** "The Circuit" **Text Evidence**
1. uncommunicative	1. Hated moving to Fresno; disliked working in fields all day—never told this to his parents.
2. anxious, lacking self-confidence	2. Feels nervous when the bus takes him to school; worries that he's behind; fears reading in front of the class; feels odd hearing English.

4. Ask partners to study the plot events in the story and use them to infer a theme in the story. Circulate among students and support them with these and other questions, which you can project onto a whiteboard or write on chart paper: *How did one key plot event help you infer a theme? Show how you used several plot events to infer a theme. How did the title help you find a theme? How did your purpose for reading support finding a theme?*

5. My students offered these themes:

   - *A theme from "The Circuit":* The constant travel of a migrant family can be disappointing to a child wanting friends and an education.
   - *Text evidence:* The narrator loses a friend when the family moves to Fresno. Mr. Lema, the narrator's teacher, becomes a friend who helps the narrator catch up with reading and offers to give the narrator music

lessons. But the family moves again and there will be no trumpet lessons for the narrator.

6. Continue having pairs infer and find other themes until you feel students understand the importance of using text evidence to support inferences and themes. Circulate among students and help those who are struggling with the process.

Wrap-Up

Compliment students on their ability to use text details to infer and find themes in "The Circuit."

LESSON 10

Exploring Themes and Mood and Finding a Central Idea

In this lesson, students choose five to ten words and connect these to the mood and themes in the short story. In addition, they will identify a central idea and find text evidence that supports their choice. Returning to the concept map, students will add words related to the concept of growing up.

Materials

- Students' copies of "The Circuit"
- Students' notebooks
- Chart paper and markers or interactive whiteboard

Teaching the Lesson

1. Have students find words and phrases that relate in some way to one of the themes they identified in Lesson 9; tell them to record the words in their notebooks.

2. Have partners identify the mood or tone the words create and record it in their notebooks. Invite students to share their thinking with the class.

3. Have students think about the plot of the story, the sequence of events that unfolded. Ask partners to discuss the events of the story and identify a central idea. Remind students that a central idea relates to and grows out of the story as a whole, whereas a theme might only be related to a section of the story. Make sure students can support their choice of a central idea with evidence throughout the text that shows how the author developed the idea. Here's what two of my sixth graders shared:

- *Central idea for "The Circuit":* Your parents' lifestyle can support or destroy your hopes and dreams.

  Text evidence: The author shows what life on the circuit for the narrator is like: moving and leaving a new friend, leaving a shack that became home, working long hours in the fields to earn money for the family, and having the hopes of getting an education and learning to play the trumpet dashed when the family moves once again.

4. Tell students that short stories can have more than one central idea and that the examples shared in the previous step are not the only possibilities. The criterion for a central idea should be that there is text evidence that clearly supports an idea threaded through the story.

Wrap-Up

Compliment students on their ability to use text evidence to identify a central idea and show how the author developed it.

LESSON 11

Collaborative Discussions

In this lesson, students review making inferences and discuss text-specific questions, using text evidence to support their answers.

Materials

- Students' copies of "The Circuit"
- Students' notebooks
- Copies of Discussion Prompts for "The Circuit" (see page 208 and the Resources CD)
- Students' copies of Close Reading Guidelines

Teaching the Lesson

1. Pair students with partners whose instructional levels are no more than one year apart. Gather students who cannot read the text independently; you will work with this group.
2. Have students take out their copies of the Close Reading Guidelines handout.
3. Explain to students that they're going to answer some questions about the story

that ask them to infer and use close reading to help them comprehend the details in this text.

4. If your students need a brief review, ask them to pair-share and discuss everything they recall about making inferences and close reading. Circulate among students and spotlight responses that will help the class by asking partners to share their thinking.

5. Display the discussion prompts on the whiteboard or pass out copies to students. Have partners discuss the questions and find text evidence by rereading the passage or passages that contain the answer. Encourage students to use the Close Reading Guidelines when they encounter words or passages that confuse them. If students need a refresher on close reading, choose one passage from the story and model how to close read.

6. Give students about five to ten minutes to discuss the questions. Encourage them to jot down notes and specific paragraph numbers that they used to find evidence. Circulate to listen in on their discussions, and extend or shorten the time as needed.

7. Support students who struggle with reading the text independently by working with them in a small group, reading the text to them.

8. Invite partners to share their answers with their group. If they close read a section, have them explain to the group how close reading helped them infer.

Wrap-Up

Point out what worked well during discussions. Compliment students on their recall and their application of close reading and inferring.

DISCUSSION PROMPTS FOR "THE CIRCUIT"

1. Why is this story called "The Circuit"?
2. How does being a child in a migrant family affect the narrator?
3. Why is Papa proud of his car?
4. Why doesn't the narrator share his feelings, hopes, and dreams with his parents?
5. Use the plot to evaluate the kind of work in the fields that adults and children do.
6. Why does the narrator want to tell his family about learning to play the trumpet?
7. Does the narrator grow up and change in this story? Cite text evidence.
8. What does the circuit symbolize?

Assessment: Writing About Reading

In this lesson, I present three options for assessing students' comprehension; they are the same ones introduced in Lesson 6, and they can be used with any short story or literary text students read. You will need two or more class periods to complete the assessments. Respond to students' needs and extend the time as needed.

Materials

- Students' copies of "The Circuit"
- Students' notebooks
- Additional paper for writing a summary or paragraph or defining literary elements
- Copies of Somebody-Wanted-But-So (SWBS) Organizer (see the Resources CD), for students writing summaries
- Copies of Guidelines for Writing a Summary (see page 266 and the Resources CD)
- Copies of Elements of a Paragraph handout for students writing explanatory paragraphs (see page 265 and the Resources CD)
- Copies of Rubric: Literature Summary (see the Resources CD), for students writing a summary
- Copies of Rubric: Paragraph (see the Resources CD), for students writing a paragraph
- Copies of Literary Elements Assessment for students defining literary elements (see the Resources CD)

Teaching the Lesson

1. Determine which students will work on which writing assignment, and split the class into groups.

2. Meet with each group in turn, introducing the assignment as described below.

3. As students work, circulate and offer assistance as necessary.

4. Sit side by side with students who require extra support. Acknowledge any successes that students achieve. When possible, use questions rather than statements to address areas that need more work. Questions honor and empower students. Write helpful suggestions on sticky notes and give the note to the student as a reminder of your conversation.

Planning and Writing a Summary

1. Give students copies of the Somebody-Wanted-But-So Organizer, Guidelines for Writing a Summary, and the Rubric: Literature Summary.

2. Review the elements of a summary and how to use the SWBS form. Remind students of the importance of an introductory sentence, and offer a model if students need one: In "The Circuit," Francisco Jiménez shows the hardships of being a child in an immigrant family.

3. Have students take notes on the form to plan their summary.

4. Ask students to complete the summary on a separate sheet of paper by using the Guidelines for Writing a Summary.

5. Have students use the rubric to check and revise their work.

Planning and Writing an Explanatory Paragraph

1. Give students the Elements of a Paragraph handout and the Rubric: Paragraph; have them take out the discussion prompts from Lesson 11.

2. Ask students to either select a discussion prompt or find a brief quote from the text that they will explain in a paragraph.

3. Have students write their selected quote or prompt in their notebooks, along with a preliminary topic sentence that states their point. They may explain how a quote relates to a theme or central idea of the story, or they may explain their response to a prompt.

4. Tell students to revisit the text to find at least three pieces of evidence from the short story to help explain their point. Encourage them to jot down specific details in their own words.

5. When students believe they have enough evidence, have them show you their notes before they begin drafting. When they are ready, have them follow the guidelines on the Elements of a Paragraph handout to draft their explanatory paragraph. Remind them to use the rubric to check and revise their work.

Literary Elements Assessment

1. Select the same terms you assessed in Lesson 6 (see page 197).

2. Either write the name of the terms you are assessing on the Literary Elements Assessment sheet and make copies for students, or hand out the sheet and have students fill in the elements as you call them out.

3. Tell students they should do two things for each literary element:
   - Define the term in a complete sentence.
   - Demonstrate understanding of the term by providing examples from the short story they read.

4. Give students enough time to write their definitions and examples. Collect the assessments and grade them.

Wrap-Up

Point out how well students worked on their summaries, paragraphs, and definitions.

Interpreting the Assessments

When evaluating each assessment, be sure to point out what students did well as well as addressing their needs. I have listed suggestions for grading each type of assessment below.

- *Summaries and Paragraphs:* Use the rubrics to evaluate the writing.

- *Literary Elements Assessment or Test:* Assign points to the definition and to the text examples that show students' understanding of the definition and the ability to apply it to a text. I suggest you weight the example greater than the definition. If each literary element is worth 15 points, I would assign 5 points to the definition and 10 points to the example.

Following Up the Assessment

After you've evaluated the assessments, organize students into pairs. Have them help each other revise and edit their summaries and/or paragraphs, as well as improve their definitions of and examples of the literary elements.

Work with students whose written work shows that they need your support. Refer to the Scaffolding Suggestions chart on pages 215–216 to plan interventions that meet students' specific needs. Then you may choose to spend additional days working in small groups scaffolding students who need it and extending the learning of those who are ready for more challenge.

Supporting Students Who Require Scaffolding

The chart on pages 215–216 offers scaffolding suggestions based on students' writing, your observations as they read and discuss texts, and your conferences on independent and instructional reading. Consult the Scaffolding Suggestions for Helping Students Write Summaries and Paragraphs on the Resources CD if students need help with their writing. Support students with similar needs by working with groups of two or three. When students struggle and are unsuccessful with the assessment, work one-on-one with them.

At first, when you scaffold, you might do all or most of the modeling and thinking aloud. Follow-up conferences should gradually turn over to the student the responsibility for learning. You can do this gradual release by pairing the student with a peer, by continuing to confer with and observe the student's thinking, or by having the student work independently and then share her thinking with you. This can occur in two or three short conferences (see forms on the Resources CD). However, some students will need several conferences, and you might have to return to the skill as you move on to another unit.

Suggestions for Helping Students Think Across Texts

Once students have read, discussed, and analyzed the stories in this unit, they will be able to find common themes and ideas between them. You can use the suggestions below to help students complete across-text thinking.

- Use the short stories from this unit to discuss the kinds of experiences that enable young adults to grow up. Evaluate the path each protagonist took and then choose the one you prefer and explain why you prefer it.

- Part of growing up is coping with difficult and challenging situations. Identify the challenging situations the protagonist in each story dealt with and how doing this contributed to his growing up.

- Choose two characters and list the personality traits you inferred from their actions, decisions, and words. Discuss personality traits that can foster change and growing up.

- Each protagonist in the short stories in this chapter separated from something or someone as part of the growing-up process. Plan an oral presentation that discusses what the protagonist separated from, why that was a logical choice for him, and how the separation contributed to his growing up.

Ideas for Inquiry and Problem Solving Beyond the Text

If you have time to extend the unit, ask students to devise questions based on their reading, or use the questions below to spark an inquiry.

- Use the short stories in this unit and your own personal experiences to write a guide to growing up for middle-school students. Include these topics: making decisions, relationships with peers, relationships with adults, developing friendships, responsibility at school and at home, and independence. You can create this guide with a partner or on your own.

- Create a blog where you write about the benefits and downsides of taking on a challenge as risky as the one Jerry took on in "Through the Tunnel." Invite peers and teachers to respond to the blog.

Students can use the texts they've read during the unit and/or research new texts to explore the issues raised by the questions, which are all connected to the theme of growing up. Students can write a short paper to share their results, participate in a class discussion or debate, create posters displaying what they've learned—there are many possibilities, and I find allowing students to choose their mode of presentation motivates and engages them.

CLOSING THOUGHTS AND QUESTIONS TO DISCUSS

You can continue professional study by discussing with a peer or a group of colleagues the parts of the lessons that worked and the parts that need refining. Here are some questions to guide your conversations:

- How did you support students who had difficulty using examples from a short story to show their understanding of literary elements?

- Discuss the lessons for writing an analytical essay. How much time did students need? How did having criteria help students plan, draft, revise, and edit? Share and discuss with colleagues the entire process of how you coached students through the writing of an analytical essay. Share with the group the work of a student who struggled, so you can gather feedback in order to better support the student.

- Which scaffolding suggestions from the chart on pages 215–216 did you find most helpful for your students? Share these with colleagues. Were there any scaffolds you tried that weren't listed on the chart? Discuss them with colleagues, and explain why these were helpful to students.
- How can studying students' notes and paragraphs help you better understand their comprehension of the short-story selections in this unit? Their ability to write a clear and compelling paragraph? What kinds of mini-lessons and support do you need to provide in the next unit?

TOP-NOTCH SHORT STORY COLLECTIONS

On the Resources CD you will find a list of ten short story collections to review for your class and/or school library.

Scaffolding Suggestions for Helping Students Read Short Stories

The scaffolding suggestions in the following chart focus on literary elements, some of which have not been addressed explicitly in the lessons in this chapter. However, you will no doubt teach these elements as students study short stories and other literature, so I've included scaffolding suggestions for them.

STUDENT'S NEED	POSSIBLE SCAFFOLD
Identifying the protagonist: Needs support figuring out which is the main character; has trouble identifying the key problem the protagonist faces	• Ask the student which character plays the important role throughout the story. Or ask, "Who is the story about?" • Ask, "Which character has the big problem to solve?"
Pinpointing the problem the protagonist faces: Needs help separating the big problem from smaller ones or understanding what problems are	• Help the student understand that the protagonist in a short story has a key problem to solve and often smaller, related problems. • Make sure the student understands what a problem is. Start with problems students deal with in their own lives, such as not completing homework, falling and breaking an arm or leg, wanting to become part of the popular group at school. • Once the student understands what problems are and that we all have them, ask her or him to identify the big problem the protagonist must try to resolve.

STUDENT'S NEED	POSSIBLE SCAFFOLD
Understanding antagonistic forces: Has difficulty showing how a force works against the protagonist; needs help to expand knowledge of what these forces can be: emotions, inner thoughts, nature, setting, and so on	• Help the student understand that antagonistic forces can work against the protagonist and cause conflict or tension. Antagonistic forces can be inside a person—such as emotions or thoughts. Antagonistic forces can also be nature (storms), the setting of a story, other characters, or decisions. • Offer the student an example and discuss it. Try using Jerry in "Through the Tunnel" and explain that the desire to swim through the tunnel worked against Jerry until he figured out how to do it. • To guide the student, ask: "What people, situations, or settings worked against the protagonist? How did the protagonist deal with these?"
Inferring from the setting: Needs help understanding that an inference is unstated in the text; has difficulty pinpointing more than one setting	• First, make sure that the student understands the term *setting*—where and when the story takes place. Stories can have more than one setting. For an example point out that "Through the Tunnel" was set on the big beach, the bay, the tunnel, and inside the villa. • Have the student identify the settings in his or her short story. Then ask the student to think about how the setting affected the protagonist, how the setting brought about a specific decision, or how the setting changed the course of the plot of the story. • Think aloud and model, gradually turning over to the student the thinking about setting.
Using the plot to find the central idea: Has difficulty explaining the difference between central idea and theme; needs help figuring out the plot events	• Review the meaning of central idea: explain that for the idea to be central, it has to relate to and grow out of most of the plot. • Show the student how you used the plot in "Through the Tunnel" to find a central idea. • Help the student find another central idea in "Through the Tunnel." Here are possibilities: The goal and achieving it are more important than the physical and mental strain experienced to reach the goal. Meeting a tough challenge takes grit and inner resolve and strength. • Review the short story's plot with the student. Help the student use the plot to determine one or more central ideas.

STUDENT'S NEED	POSSIBLE SCAFFOLD
Identifying the climax and figuring out the return to normalcy: Has trouble understanding why the climax comes close to the end of the story; needs help understanding what "return to normalcy" means	• Help the student understand that the climax is always near the end of the story. The climax is the highest point or moment of the plot. After the climax things settle down. The settling down is the denouement, or the return to normalcy for the story. • Have the student skim the last page or two of the completed short story and find the highest point of the plot. To support this, ask the student to show the return to normalcy. • Review the climax and denouement in "Through the Tunnel," if the student needs a concrete example. Then return to the student's completed story.
Inferring a character's personality traits: Confuses physical and personality traits; needs support using story elements to infer personality: dialogue, inner thoughts, decisions, others, and so on	• To help the student figure out a character's personality, look at one of these elements at a time: dialogue and inner thoughts, actions, decisions, interactions with the settings, and interactions with the plot. • Model in a think-aloud how you apply one of the elements, and then have the student try, using the same element but from a different part of the story. • When you see that the student can be more independent, pair him up with a peer expert for more practice.
Figuring out how and why a character changes from the beginning to the end of the story: Needs support figuring out what the character was like at the beginning; has trouble understanding how the setting, plot events, interactions with other characters, decisions, coping with conflicts, and so on can change a character; needs help figuring out what a character is like at the end.	• Help the student infer the protagonist's personality at the beginning of the story and at the end, using what he says, does, inner thoughts, decisions, actions, and so on. • Help the student infer the protagonist's personality at the end of the story and identify any changes. • Show the student how you look at plot events, decisions made, and interactions with others to figure out how the changes developed as the protagonist lived through these events. • Explain that as the protagonist lives through plot events, the events and how he dealt with each one have the potential for changing the protagonist and causing growth and maturity. • Show the student how you identify specific events, decisions, or interactions that changed the protagonist. Then give an event, decision, or interaction to the student and ask her to explain the change in the protagonist.

CHAPTER 8

Reading Texts That Argue

Middle-school students enjoy collecting evidence that supports their arguments and requests for change. For example, when arguing for the creation of a mid-morning snack time, my eighth-grade classes surveyed students in grades six, seven, and eight and called three local pediatricians, who made statements supporting their request. Once students study the art of persuasion, which the CCSS calls "making a claim and arguing for it with evidence," students know that if they're armed with quotes from experts and statistics from reliable sources, they have a better chance of negotiating change. In this chapter, students will study speeches and essays that craft arguments for change.

I've organized the selections in this chapter around the concepts of justice and injustice, themes that resonate with middle-school students as they encounter new and more complex social situations and become more aware of politics, always seeking a just and fair resolution. In this unit, I model how to apply several Common Core State Standards using as the anchor text a speech by Susan B. Anthony that argues for women's right to vote. Below are the Common Core State Standards for reading addressed in this unit:

- determine the central idea and how it develops
- make logical inferences using text evidence
- identify the author's purpose
- discuss the evidence presented that supports the author's claim
- recall details, make logical inferences, and identify themes

The texts in this section are speeches and essays that argue for and/or explain a position or belief. When arguing to convince listeners or readers, writers can use stories, examples, statistics, and accurate information. Often a piece such as President Bush's "9/11 Address to the Nation" weaves explanation and argument. Explanations and background information are frequently needed to understand the main arguments the writer presents.

The Lexile® measures of all the selections in this unit are challenging for developing readers. However, the topics are familiar and the writing engaging, making these complex texts more accessible.

> If you have long blocks of time that allow you to combine lessons, feel free to do so. Here are lessons that you can easily combine:
>
> - Lessons 1 and 2
> - Lessons 5 and 6
> - Lessons 12 and 13

Lessons 1 to 7

Model How to Read Texts That Argue

In this first set of lessons, you will use an anchor text to model the skills and strategies that readers use when tackling complex texts that argue for a claim or position. You will model how to infer, find the central idea, and understand the arguments presented in the text.

Text Complexity Grid

"Woman's Rights to the Suffrage" by Susan B. Anthony
Lexile®: 1040
Text Complexity: 1 = Accessible to 5 = Challenging

QUALITATIVE	1	2	3	4	5
Knowledge demands					X
Author's purpose				X	
Meaning				X	
Text structure				X	
Language/vocabulary					X
Concepts				X	
Inferential thinking demands				X	

LESSON 1

Getting Ready to Read

In this lesson, students will preview the selection to build their prior knowledge and start a concept map on the themes of justice and injustice.

Materials

- "Woman's Rights to the Suffrage," displayed on the whiteboard from the Resources CD
- Students' notebooks
- Students' copies of Building Prior Knowledge handout (see page 261 and the Resources CD)
- Chart paper and markers for taking notes and generating the concept map

Share This Background Knowledge With Students

Susan B. Anthony was fined $100 for casting an illegal ballot in the 1872 presidential election, because women were not allowed to vote. Seething at the injustice, she began a speaking tour in support of female voting rights, during which she gave this speech. The Nineteenth Amendment enfranchised women in 1920. Anthony never paid the fine.

Teaching the Lesson

1. Display the speech and have students take out their Building Prior Knowledge handout. Review how to build prior knowledge; I say something like this:

    Today, I will show you how to build prior knowledge on your own when you are reading a speech like "Woman's Rights to the Suffrage." I preview "Woman's Rights to the Suffrage" by reading the first two paragraphs and the last paragraph, and the five quiz items at the end of the text. Then I list what I have learned from reading the paragraphs and quiz items. Follow along as I read these out loud and then write what I learned.

2. Model how you retell the details you remember from the preview, jotting down notes as you go. Here's my list:

    *   Anthony says she's accused of the crime of voting for president.
    *   The law states that she has no legal right to vote, but Anthony will explain why the law is wrong.
    *   Anthony says that the Constitution gives her the right to vote.
    *   She quotes the preamble to the constitution.
    *   Since women are persons, and the preamble starts with "We the people of the United States," women can vote—legally.

3. Ask students to add any other ideas to the list. Here's what my eighth graders added:

    *   No state has the right to make a law that stops women from voting.
    *   She compares laws made by states to stop women from voting to laws that stop African Americans from voting—both are unconstitutional.

4. Tell students that today the class will start a concept map related to the concepts of justice and injustice. They'll begin by thinking about Susan B. Anthony's "Woman's Rights to the Suffrage," but they will revisit the map as they read other selections in this unit in the coming weeks. Write the words "justice/injustice" on a sheet of chart paper. Explain that justice or injustice can relate to feelings and thoughts of right and wrong within a person as well as legal and civil justice and justice in families and communities. Invite students to turn to a partner and take two or three minutes to discuss justice and injustice, trying to find words and phrases that relate to this concept. It's okay if no ideas come to mind. The class will continue to build the map throughout the unit.

5. As pairs share ideas, accept any word or phrase students offer and add them to the map, as long as students can link the ideas to justice or injustice. Here are three suggestions offered by my eighth graders: *a severe illness that handicaps a person; an unfair and illegal law; dad loses his job.*

6. Read "Woman's Rights to the Suffrage" out loud to help students get the gist of the speech. As you read, help students with the challenging vocabulary by weaving in synonyms. For example, "under indictment," or *accused of*; "our posterity," or *all future generations* or *descendants*; "odious aristocracy," or *hateful rule of privileged men*. Continue to respond to your students' vocabulary needs by supplying alternate words and phrases as you read vocabulary they don't understand.

Wrap-Up

Provide positive feedback to students on their listening skills and their contributions to the concept map.

LESSON 2

Identifying Genre Characteristics and Setting Purposes

In this lesson, students will gain insights into writing to argue and explain and set purposes for reading.

Materials

- "Woman's Rights to the Suffrage," displayed on the whiteboard from the Resources CD
- Students' notebooks
- Prior-knowledge notes from Lesson 1
- "Justice/injustice" concept map started in Lesson 1
- Chart paper and markers

Teaching the Lesson

1. Invite students to work in pairs to identify the characteristics of "Woman's Rights to the Suffrage" that make it a speech. The subtitle is a giveaway, of course, but challenge students to identify other elements that mark the text as a speech.

2. Circulate among students and listen in on their conversations. Responses like those below indicate students have identified the elements of a speech: *It's from first-person. She starts by addressing the audience—"Friends and Fellow Citizens." It's short and sticks to the point of women's right to vote. The subtitle says it's a speech.*

3. Have students reread the building-prior-knowledge notes from Lesson 1.

4. Ask pairs to set a purpose for listening to "Woman's Rights to the Suffrage" a second time. Ask pairs to use the title, information from the prior-knowledge notes, or the concept of justice/injustice, to set a purpose for listening to the speech again. If students have difficulty figuring out a purpose for reading, show them that they can use the title: *My purpose is to find out more about women's rights and suffrage* or *My purpose is to find out why Susan B. Anthony delivered this speech.*

> ### Genre Characteristics: Speech
>
> - Written in the first person
> - Acknowledges/addresses an audience
> - Generally short and focused on one point
> - Usually argues or explains something
> - Uses language that is accessible to the audience

5. Ask students to pair-share and discuss their purposes for listening, then invite a few students to share different purposes with the class.

6. Read the selection out loud and have students follow along. Explain that this is a second reading and that hearing the selection a second time will deepen their comprehension and enable them to recall more details.

7. Return to the "justice/injustice" concept map and invite students to pair-share and add more ideas to the map. Ask them to connect their words and phrases to the concept with specific examples.

Wrap-Up

Point out the positive discussions students had and acknowledge the number of ideas they added to the concept map.

LESSON 3

Identifying the Author's Purpose and Finding the Central Idea

In this lesson, students will determine the author's purpose for writing the speech and pinpoint its central idea.

Materials

- "Woman's Rights to the Suffrage," displayed on the whiteboard from the Resources CD

- Students' notebooks
- Chart paper and markers

Teaching the Lesson

1. Present a think-aloud on identifying Susan B. Anthony's purpose for delivering this speech. Here's what I say:

   Let's think today about the purpose Susan B. Anthony had for writing her speech. We know from thinking about the genre characteristics of speeches that they usually have a specific purpose—often to argue or persuade. That's clearly the case in Anthony's speech. Her purpose is to argue that authorities unlawfully arrested her because women are citizens and therefore entitled to vote; hence, she committed no crime.

2. Ask students to pair-share and add any ideas to your think-aloud that relate to the purpose of this speech. One pair of eighth graders added that a part of Anthony's purpose was to show that the Constitution of the United States supported women's right to vote.

3. Ask students to pair-share and connect the purpose of this speech to the central idea. Explain that a speech's central idea is the fundamental point or points the writer makes. The entire class agreed that the purpose and the central idea were the same in this speech. Several pairs added this idea: Anthony wanted to show that besides her belief that women had the right to vote, the Constitution, the law of our country, proved she was right.

4. Invite students to pair-share to explain how Susan B. Anthony developed the central idea. Tell students to reread the speech and close read to figure out the evidence in the speech that argues for the central idea and to explain how Anthony developed this evidence in a logical order. Here's the reasoning my students offered:
   - First, she claims that she never committed a crime by voting.
   - Next, she reads the Preamble to the Constitution and explains that "We the people" means "the whole people," and not just white males.
   - Having liberty applies to women and men—that's the meaning of "we the people."
   - Being able to vote is the best way to enjoy liberty and participate in our government.
   - When a state stops women from voting, it goes against the Constitution.
   - Those who prevent women from voting do not see our government as a democracy. They don't see government as getting its powers from the people who are governed.

- State laws that prevent women from voting mean that men control women in and out of the home.
- Anthony's final argument is to prove that women are "persons," taking you back to the Preamble and "We the people . . ."

5. Direct students' attention to the "justice/injustice" concept map and invite students to pair-share to find words and phrases from the text to add to the map.

Wrap-Up

Provide positive feedback on students' discussions and their ability to figure out the central idea and arguments that support it.

LESSON 4

Making Inferences Using Text Evidence

The focus of this lesson is making logical inferences and showing the text evidence that enabled students to infer.

Materials
- "Woman's Rights to the Suffrage," displayed on the whiteboard from the Resources CD
- Students' notebooks

Teaching the Lesson

1. Display "Woman's Rights to the Suffrage" and explain that the focus of today's lesson will be using evidence from Anthony's speech to make inferences.

2. Invite students to pair-share and discuss what they recall about making inferences. Circulate and offer support, explaining that a logical inference is an unstated meaning that grows out of text evidence.

3. Model how you use text evidence to make inferences. Here's what I say:

Here's one inference I can make after reading this text: Susan B. Anthony is determined to make women's suffrage legal in every state. To support this inference, I use the fact that Anthony states in the first paragraph that her voting for president is not a crime, but that her ability to vote is a right "guaranteed to me and all United States citizens by the National Constitution, beyond the power of any State to deny." I extend that to mean

she wants women in all states to have the right to vote, so she will fight for
women's suffrage everywhere in the nation.

4.   Have students head a new page in their notebooks with their name, the date, and the title of the speech: "Woman's Rights to the Suffrage." Ask students to fold the page in half lengthwise and on the left-hand side write "Inferences"; on the right-hand side write "Evidence From the Speech."

5.   Ask students to pair-share to make other inferences by discussing possible inferences and finding support for each one in the speech. When they make an inference and can support it with evidence from the text, have students write the inference on the left-hand side of their notebook page and record the supporting details on the right-hand side.

6.   Circulate among pairs and listen in on their discussions. Point students to specific parts of the speech to find support for an inference. Help them make inferences by discussing specific details with them and inviting them to infer. For example, it's possible to use Anthony's citing of the Preamble of the Constitution to infer that she's intelligent and knows what the Constitution says. Here are the logical inferences and text evidence that eighth-grade students shared with their classmates.

INFERENCE	EVIDENCE FROM THE SPEECH
1. Anthony is logical.	1. She starts with "we the people . . ." and uses the "we" to argue that *we* includes all citizens—women and men. She cites Webster's definition of *citizen*.
2. Anthony is brave.	2. She votes, knowing she will be arrested for breaking the law. She includes "Negroes" as citizens along with women.
3. She is passionate about getting the vote for women.	3. She calls it a "downright mockery" to deny women the vote and say they have liberty. She argues we're a democracy, not an aristocracy or oligarchy.

Wrap-Up

Give students positive feedback on their ability to use text details to make logical inferences.

Collaborative Discussions

In this lesson, students will return to Susan B. Anthony's speech several times in order to discuss the questions on page 227. They will continue to make inferences to more deeply understand the text.

Materials

- "Woman's Rights to the Suffrage," displayed on the whiteboard from the Resources CD
- Students' notebooks
- Copies of Discussion Prompts for "Woman's Rights to the Suffrage" (see page 227 and the Resources CD), class set
- Students' copies of Close Reading Guidelines (see page 262 and the Resources CD)
- "Justice/injustice" concept map from previous lessons
- Chart paper and markers

Teaching the Lesson

1. Display "Woman's Rights to the Suffrage." Distribute the discussion prompts to students.

2. Pair students with partners whose instructional reading levels are no more than one year above or below theirs. Form a group of students who cannot read the speech independently; you will work with them.

3. Have students take out their copies of the Close Reading Guidelines handout. Have them reread the guidelines and share how close reading can help when making inferences.

4. Have partners discuss the prompts and find text evidence to support their responses by rereading relevant passages; give them five to ten minutes. Encourage students to use the Close Reading Guidelines for passages that confuse them. Circulate to listen to students' discussions, and extend or shorten the time as needed.

5. Display the "justice/injustice" concept map and have students add words and phrases, inviting them to explicitly connect their ideas to the concepts.

Wrap-Up

Acknowledge the quality of students' discussions and their ability to infer.

1. Why does Anthony refer to the Preamble to the Constitution of the United States?

2. Discuss two arguments that Anthony makes to show that women should have the right to vote.

3. How can you infer from the speech that Anthony has a deep belief in women's right to vote? Find text support.

4. Evaluate the effect that Anthony's use of the Preamble to the Constitution and the dictionary definition of *citizen* has on her argument.

5. Why does Anthony discuss aristocracy and oligarchy?

LESSON 6

Assessment: Test-Taking Strategies

Students will observe how to locate the best answer to a quiz item and then practice with a partner.

Materials

- "Woman's Rights to the Suffrage," displayed on the whiteboard from the Resources CD
- Copies of the "Woman's Rights to the Suffrage" quiz (see the Resources CD), class set
- Copies of the Quiz Answer Sheet (see page 263 and the Resources CD), class set
- Quiz Answer Keys (see page 267 and the Resources CD)

Teaching the Lesson

1. Distribute the quiz. Reread out loud the speech and the quiz items at the end of "Woman's Rights to the Suffrage." Ask students to raise a hand if a passage confuses them and they require a close reading; if so, model how to close read one passage.

2. Show students how you answer the first quiz item. The model is thorough, so you can observe my thinking. Adapt to the needs of your students. Here is my thinking:

   I'll work through the first quiz item, which reads: What is the central idea of this speech? *Let me think about that before I read the answer*

*choices. She said in the beginning that she wanted to prove that she
did not break any laws by voting since the Constitution guarantees
that right. All the arguments she presents relate to that point. Now I'll
read through each of the possible answers.* A: Anthony committed no
crime by voting because she is guaranteed that right by the Constitution.
*That's just what I said! But I'm going to read through all the other
answers to make sure that is the best one.* B: Women are just as good as
men and should do everything men do. *Well, I'm sure Anthony believed
that, but it's not the central idea of this speech; I'll cross it off.* C:
Anthony is willing to go to jail to prove her point that she has the right to
vote in presidential elections. *That may be true, but the text doesn't say
that, and it certainly isn't the central idea of her speech; I'll cross that
off too.* D: The preamble to the Constitution states "We the people." *That
is true, but it is not the central idea of the speech. So A is the best
choice, and the evidence is right in that first paragraph.*

3. If you feel your students need extra support, you can model how you answer
   the second quiz item as well.

4. Give students the Quiz Answer Sheet. Tell them to write their name, the date,
   and the title of the text at the top. Then have them record the answer(s)
   for the item(s) you modeled answering for them, writing in the first column
   the letter of the answer and in the second column the number(s) of the
   paragraph(s) containing the evidence. Note that they will *not* be writing a
   paragraph about one of their answers during this lesson because the focus is
   on helping students practice the test-taking strategies modeled.

5. Pair students with partners and have them complete the last three or
   four questions of the quiz. If you have students who cannot read the text
   independently, work with them in a group, rereading passages for them so they
   can complete the quiz.

6. When students finish, call out the answers as students self-check or collect the
   quizzes to score later yourself.

Wrap-Up

Let students know that you observed how well they reread and skimmed "Woman's
Rights to the Suffrage" to locate the paragraphs that helped them find the best answer.

Writing About Reading

In this lesson, students will identify the arguments Susan B. Anthony makes and the evidence she uses to support them in her speech for women's suffrage. Students will then write a paragraph explaining how Anthony constructed her argument; they will take notes, develop a topic sentence, draft the paragraph, and add a concluding sentence.

You might need two or three sessions for everyone to complete their plans and writing; set aside enough time for students to complete a first draft.

Materials

- "Woman's Rights to the Suffrage," displayed on the whiteboard from the Resources CD
- Students' copies of the Elements of a Paragraph handout (see page 265 and the Resources CD)
- Students' copies of the Rubric: Paragraph (see the Resources CD)
- Students' notebooks
- Additional paper for writing paragraphs
- Sticky notes

Teaching the Lesson

1. Introduce the writing about reading task, explaining how the lesson will work. I say something like this:

   Today we're going to be writing about Susan B. Anthony's speech. Writing about our reading helps us better understand the text; today, we'll take a close look at how Anthony develops and supports her argument that women are entitled to the right to vote. Then, we'll write a paragraph explaining her argument.

2. Have students take out their copy of the Elements of a Paragraph handout and review the guidelines.

3. Tell students that they will support the following statement about the central message of Anthony's speech: *Susan B. Anthony claims that women have the right to vote and that the right is guaranteed in the Constitution.*

4. Have students write the statement in their notebooks and ask them to gather three pieces of evidence from the speech that support it; students should write the evidence in their notebooks.

5. Instruct students to turn their notes into an explanatory paragraph that lays out the arguments Anthony uses to support her claim. Remind students to include a concluding sentence that sums up the evidence and restates how it all supports the thesis statement.

6. As students work, circulate to observe them as they take notes and then begin drafting their paragraph. Remind them to use the rubric to revise their work.

7. Sit side by side with students who require extra support. Acknowledge any successes that students achieved. When possible, use questions rather than statements to address areas that need more work. Questions honor and empower students. Write helpful suggestions on sticky notes and give the notes to students as a reminder of your conversation.

8. Gauge students' progress to determine how much time to allow for the writing and whether it should be completed during the next class.

Wrap-Up

Acknowledge students for taking detailed notes and focusing on writing their paragraphs.

> If you feel students need additional modeling before moving on to the guided practice portion of the unit, work through Lessons 1–7 again using "Packages in Packages" as the read-aloud text (see the Resources CD).

Lessons 8 to 14

Guided Practice With a New Speech

In this next series of lessons, you start releasing responsibility to students, reviewing and coaching as they practice the skills and strategies you modeled with "Woman's Rights to the Suffrage." Assign students a text based on their reading level; text complexity grids for each selection appear on page 231. Then work through the lessons at a pace that's reasonable for your students, allowing one or two weeks, depending on students' needs.

Text Complexity Grids

"Votes for Women" by Mark Twain
Lexile®: 1110
Text Complexity: 1 = Accessible to 5 = Challenging

QUALITATIVE	1	2	3	4	5
Knowledge demands				X	
Author's purpose				X	
Meaning			X		
Text structure			X		
Language/vocabulary					X
Concepts				X	
Inferential thinking demands				X	

"9/11 Address to the Nation" by President George W. Bush
Lexile®: 1040
Text Complexity: 1 = Accessible to 5 = Challenging

QUALITATIVE	1	2	3	4	5
Knowledge demands				X	
Author's purpose			X		
Meaning				X	
Text structure			X		
Language/vocabulary				X	
Concepts				X	
Inferential thinking demands				X	

LESSON 8

Building Prior Knowledge and Setting Purposes

In this lesson, students have the opportunity to build prior knowledge and set purposes for reading with the support of a partner.

Materials

- Copies of "Votes for Women" for students reading at or above grade level
- Copies of "9/11 Address to the Nation" for students reading below grade level
- Students' notebooks
- "Justice/injustice" concept map from previous lessons
- Chart paper and markers or interactive whiteboard

Teaching the Lesson

1. Review the method for building prior knowledge that you modeled with "Woman's Rights to the Suffrage" in Lesson 1.

2. Distribute to students the copies of the texts. Ask students to suggest the number of paragraphs they need to read on the first page; remind them to read the title, the last paragraph, and the quiz items.

> Read "9/11 Address to the Nation" aloud to students who struggle with the text. Follow the directions for working with two groups provided in Chapter 3, page 67.

3. Have students preview their text to build prior knowledge. Remind them to make a list in their notebooks of what they learned from the preview.

4. Ask students to reread their lists and use the information to set purposes for reading. Remind them that to set purposes they can refer to the title, their prior-knowledge notes, or the concept of justice/injustice. Circulate and support students who need extra help.

5. Have students read the selection silently, using their prior-knowledge notes and purpose for reading to get the gist or general idea of the selection.

6. Pair students with partners who read the same passage and ask them to discuss the gist of their selection and connect it to the concept of justice/injustice.

7. Circulate and listen to partner discussions to determine whether students have the overall gist of the speeches. If some students seem confused, support them by helping them close read and/or reread.

8. Display the "justice/injustice" concept map and invite students to add words from their text that relate to the ideas of justice/injustice. Make sure that students explicitly connect their suggestions to the concept.

Wrap-Up

Point out what students did well as they built their prior knowledge and figured out the gist of their texts. Highlight the words and phrases students added to the concept map.

Finding Central Ideas

In this lesson, students practice close reading. Then, they focus on finding their selection's central idea.

Materials

- Students' copies of "Votes for Women"
- Students' copies of "9/11 Address to the Nation"
- Students' copies of Close Reading Guidelines

Teaching the Lesson

1. Have students take out their copies of "9/11 Address to the Nation" and "Votes for Women." Pair students with partners who are reading the same text; gather students who cannot read their text independently; you will work with this group.

2. If needed, refresh students' recall of close reading by reviewing the guidelines sheet with them and discussing how the strategy can help them figure out the meaning of a difficult word or confusing passage.

3. Have students reread their selection silently, keeping their purpose for reading in mind. Read aloud "9/11 Address to the Nation" to students who cannot read it independently. Ask them to raise their hands when they hear a word or sentence that confuses them, so you can model close reading. If no one raises a hand, select a few words and sentences in order to model close reading.

4. Ask pairs to share how close reading helped them figure out a difficult word or a passage that confused them.

5. Invite pairs to discuss what they know about the central idea. Remind students that earlier you modeled how to find the central idea of "Woman's Rights to the Suffrage" (Lesson 3). Circulate and listen as pairs discuss. You might hear comments such as: *It's like theme, but it's the important one. It's an idea that connects to the whole text. There can be more than one. It needs to come from inference because it's not said in the text.*

6. Ask partners reading the same speech to find its central idea and explain how the details in their speech helped them infer and pinpoint it. Circulate and listen in on partner discussions. Prompt students with questions such as: *What are the main events each speech refers to? Why did the author compose this speech? What*

arguments and explanations did the author use to defend his claim? Can you connect the author's purpose to the central idea?

7. Spotlight students who "get it" and have them explain what helped them identify the central idea; this provides the class with additional models. Here's what my eighth graders said about the central idea of "Votes for Women" by Mark Twain:

The central idea of this piece is that women are equal to men and should have the right to vote. Twain explains that he's believed this for 25 years. He points out that his mother knew as much about voting as her son. Then, Twain moves to the need of women to vote in his town to change the "state of things," and he believes that women would vote for an excellent mayor. Twain explains that when making an appeal for money in church, it's best to give today and not wait for tomorrow. He's wanting the same for women's right to vote—pass it today and don't wait for tomorrow. He also relates his experience of wanting to give $400 to the collection plate, but it took so long to come to him that he lost his enthusiasm and kept his money. Twain wants the audience to act now on giving women the vote and not wait for tomorrow, when people might have lost their enthusiasm for the voting issue. Twain supports this central idea all through his speech.

Here's what students said about "9/11 Address to the Nation":

The central idea is that the deadly terrorist attacks might have crumbled buildings and killed innocent men and women, but the attacks cannot shake the strong foundation of the United States. Bush describes the chaos the attacks brought and labels the attacks as evil. Then, he clearly shows how first responders, the military, and ordinary people came to the aid of those hurt in the attack—providing an example of why our strong foundation will not be shaken. Bush assures the American people that the search has begun for those responsible for this horrific act. That he, the Congress, and countless world leaders have condemned these acts of hate and terror. Our allies have joined with our nation to win the war against terrorism—more support to maintain our strength and defend freedom. Bush closes by asking every American to "unite in our resolve for justice and peace." Again, he makes the point that although this day of evil will never be forgotten, it will not damage the American spirit and resolve.

Wrap-Up

Provide positive feedback to students for applying close reading and figuring out a central idea for "9/11 Address to the Nation" or "Votes for Women."

Collaborative Discussions

In this lesson, students will work together to pinpoint the arguments the writers made in their speeches.

Materials

- Students' copies of "Votes for Women"
- Students' copies of "9/11 Address to the Nation"
- Discussion Prompts for "Votes for Women and "9/11 Address to the Nation" (see page 236 and the Resources CD)
- Students' copies of Close Reading Guidelines

Teaching the Lesson

1. Pair students with partners who have read the same text. Gather students who cannot read the text independently and work with them in a group.

2. Display the discussion prompts on the whiteboard or pass out copies to students.

3. Have partners discuss the prompts and then share their ideas with other students who've read the same text, always showing where they found their answer in the text.

4. Ask pairs to review the arguments and explanations in "Votes for Women" and "9/11 Address to the Nation" and share their ideas with another pair that has read the same speech.

5. Circulate among students and help them tease out arguments and explanations from their speech.

> **TEACHING TIP —**
> **SCAFFOLDING**
> **STUDENTS' READING**
>
> *Support students who cannot read "9/11 Address to the Nation" independently, by first pointing to the section in the text that answers the discussion prompt and then rereading that section for them.*

Wrap-Up

Provide positive feedback to students for their detailed discussions and their use of text evidence to support their responses to the prompts.

DISCUSSION PROMPTS FOR "VOTES FOR WOMEN"

1. Explain what Twain means by "it's the widow's mite that makes no noise but does the best work."

2. Why does Twain recount the incident in the Hartford Church?

3. What reasons does Twain offer for being a women's rights supporter?

4. Why does Twain feel that women having the vote could help his town?

5. Evaluate the kinds of evidence Twain provides to support his claim that women should vote.

6. Who provides stronger arguments, Susan B. Anthony or Mark Twain? Give reasons for your choice.

DISCUSSION PROMPTS FOR "9/11 ADDRESS TO THE NATION"

1. Why does Bush say, "A great people has been moved to defend a great nation"?

2. Why does Bush call the acts of terror "despicable"?

3. How does Bush view the American spirit?

4. Evaluate the government's response plans.

5. How does Bush propose to win the war against terrorism?

6. Why does Bush ask for everyone's prayers?

7. What is Bush arguing for in this speech?

LESSON 11

Assessment

Students complete the quiz items that follow their text selection, and choose one of their answers to defend in a brief paragraph.

Materials
- Students' copies of "Votes for Women"
- Students' copies of "9/11 Address to the Nation"
- Copies of the Quiz Answer Sheet (see page 263 and the Resources CD), class set
- Quiz Answer Keys (see page 267 and the Resources CD)

Teaching the Lesson

1. Give students the Quiz Answer Sheet and review the directions. Encourage them to skim and reread parts of their speech so they can note the paragraph or paragraphs they use to answer quiz items.

2. Have students complete the quiz independently. This includes defending one of their answers in a short paragraph; remind them that they may not write about a vocabulary item.

3. Support students who can't read "9/11 Address to the Nation" and the quiz items independently. Reread the selection for them. Then, read the quiz items and the possible answers one at a time and have students select the best answer.

4. When students finish, call out answers to the multiple-choice portion; have students self-correct and turn their papers in to you, or collect the papers and grade them yourself.

5. Separate the quizzes into two piles: students who scored a 4 or 5, and students who missed two or more multiple-choice items.

6. Read the paragraphs students wrote to defend one of their answers. Check to make sure each paragraph contains details from the text. Make note of students who have difficulty and plan time to scaffold their learning.

   Help students who struggled with the paragraph portion of the quiz by working with them in a small group. Show them how to take notes on evidence from the text and then write a brief paragraph that explains their thinking about a question, incorporating the answer from the quiz along with their own text evidence.

> **TEACHING TIP —**
> **SCAFFOLDING STUDENTS**
> **AFTER THE QUIZ**
>
> *Work individually or with small groups of students who missed two or more questions. Do this as the rest of the class reads silently during the second half of your class period. Help students see how looking back in the text can support inferential thinking and recall of text details. These students might benefit from completing an additional practice selection that you choose.*

Wrap-Up

Acknowledge students for returning to the text and skimming or rereading before selecting an answer and for defending one of their answers in a paragraph.

Writing About Reading: Note Taking

In this lesson, students will take notes for a suggested topic that relates to "Votes for Women" or "9/11 Address to the Nation" and record their notes in their notebooks.

Materials

- Students' copies of "Votes for Women"
- Students' copies of "9/11 Address to the Nation"
- Copies of Note-Taking Guidelines for "Votes for Women" (see below) and "9/11 Address to the Nation" (see page 239)
- Students' notebooks

Teaching the Lesson

1. Explain that today students will write about the text they have been reading, either exploring a discussion prompt in greater depth or finding details to answer a question about their text. Distribute the Note-Taking Guidelines for "Votes for Women" and "9/11 Address to the Nation." You may also want to display them on the chalkboard or project them onto a whiteboard.

2. As students working with "Votes for Women" work independently, support students answering questions about "9/11 Address to the Nation." Because this group may consist of developing readers and English language learners, give them the quote based on the first discussion prompt from Lesson 11, so they have background knowledge for note taking.

3. Circulate as students work, supporting students who need help or have questions. Students may need help finding evidence or paraphrasing the text.

Note-Taking Guidelines for "Votes for Women"

Mark Twain believes that women should have the right to vote.

- Write the statement above in your notebook.
- Find three details from "Votes for Women" that support Twain's claim that women should have the right to vote. Write them in your notebook.

> ### Note-Taking Guidelines for "9/11 Address to the Nation"
>
> *"A great people has been moved to defend a great nation."*
>
> - In your notebook, write this quote from President George W. Bush's speech.
> - Find three or four supports for this quote in the speech; write them in your notebook.

Wrap-Up

Provide positive feedback on students' use of the text to take detailed notes.

LESSON 13

Writing About Reading: Drafting

In this lesson, students write an explanatory or informational paragraph about their text, drawing on the notes they took in the previous lesson and consulting the Elements of a Paragraph handout. Students will need more than 20 minutes to complete the writing; I suggest allowing 30 to 45 minutes for the task on each of two days.

Materials

- Students' copies of "Votes for Women"
- Students' copies of "9/11 Address to the Nation"
- Students' notebooks
- Students' copies of the Elements of a Paragraph handout (see page 265 and the Resources CD)
- Students' copies of the Rubric: Paragraph (see the Resources CD)
- Additional paper for drafting a paragraph

Teaching the Lesson

1. Have students take out their copies of the Elements of a Paragraph handout and review it. Tell them they will be writing a paragraph to explain the speaker's argument as presented in his speech.

2. Students who are writing about "Votes for Women" can use the statement they took notes on in the previous lesson as their introductory sentence, or they can craft an original one. Their task is to explain the argument Twain develops for giving women the right to vote. Remind students to include the speech's title and author in the introductory sentence.

3. For students who are writing about "9/11 Address to the Nation," write a model topic sentence to help them get started: *In "9/11 Address to the Nation," President Bush claims that "A great people has been moved to defend a great nation."* Students can opt to use this introductory sentence or craft one of their own. Their task is to explain what Bush means by the quote.

4. Instruct students to use their notes from the previous lesson to write a complete paragraph, following the guidelines on the Elements of a Paragraph handout. Remind them to use the rubric to revise their writing.

5. Circulate and support students as necessary. Always begin by noting the positives a student has achieved, and remember to phrase suggestions as questions to honor and empower your students.

6. Collect the paragraphs and assess them using the rubric. You can note errors in spelling, usage, and punctuation and use this data for writing mini-lessons and in one-on-one conferences.

Wrap-Up

Provide positive feedback to students on using their notes to craft their paragraphs.

WRAPPING UP THE UNIT

Independent Practice and Assessment

In the last part of this unit, students work with a text independently, so you can assess their progress, scaffolding or extending their learning as appropriate.

Text Complexity Grids

"Unsafe Behind the Wheel" by Kate Zernike

Lexile®: 1280

Text Complexity: 1 = Accessible to 5 = Challenging

QUALITATIVE	1	2	3	4	5
Knowledge demands				X	
Author's purpose				X	
Meaning				X	
Text structure			X		
Language/vocabulary					X
Concepts				X	
Inferential thinking demands				X	

"Head Trauma" by Lauren Tarshis

Lexile®: 950

Text Complexity: 1 = Accessible to 5 = Challenging

QUALITATIVE	1	2	3	4	5
Knowledge demands				X	
Author's purpose				X	
Meaning			X		
Text structure			X		
Language/vocabulary				X	
Concepts				X	
Inferential thinking demands				X	

ASSESSMENT

Reading a New Text Independently

Have students work on their own, as this is an assessment that will help you determine students' strengths and needs. They will build prior knowledge and read the text independently. For the assessment, you have three options: students can write a summary, compose an explanatory paragraph, or complete a Word Map about the unit's concept. I recommend that each student do at least one writing activity and complete the Word Map.

Set aside five or six consecutive days for the assessment. You will probably need two 30- to 45-minute classes for students to build prior knowledge, read for the gist, reread for deeper understanding, and complete the Word Map. Over the next three or four days, take about 35-45 minutes to have students complete the writing. If a few students need more time for taking notes and writing, give them the extra time.

Materials

- Copies of "Unsafe Behind the Wheel" for students reading at or above grade level (see the Resources CD)
- Copies of "Head Trauma" for students reading below grade level (see the Resources CD)
- Students copies of Building Prior Knowledge Handout (from Lesson 1; see page 261 and the Resources CD)
- Students' copies of Guidelines for Writing a Summary
- Copies of the 5W's Organizer (see the Resources CD), for students writing summaries
- Students' copies of the Elements of a Paragraph handout

- Copies of Writing Topics for each assessment text (see the Resources CD), for students writing paragraphs
- Copies of the Word Map (see the Resources CD), class set
- Students' copies of the Rubrics for Informational Text Summary and Paragraph
- Students' notebooks
- Additional notebook paper for writing summaries and/or paragraphs

TEACHING TIP — PEER ASSESSMENT

Have students give their plans and first drafts to a writing partner. Ask the partner to use the rubric and the Guidelines for Writing a Summary or Elements of a Paragraph handout to make sure all elements have been included. Partners give each other feedback that can improve their summaries or paragraphs. Have students write a second draft based on peer feedback. Collect and read the drafts.

Teaching the Lesson

1. Have students take out their copy of the Building Prior Knowledge handout while you distribute the assessment texts and copies of the Word Map.

2. Remind students to use the strategy they have practiced to build their prior knowledge and jot down a list of what they learned from their preview in their notebook. Tell them that on the first two days of the assessment, they should preview the text to build prior knowledge, then read for the gist. Encourage them to reread the text for deeper comprehension before they complete the Word Map.

3. Invite students to complete the Word Map, specifying how many characteristics and examples you want them to provide to demonstrate their understanding of the concept.

4. On the next day, ask those students who will be writing a summary to take out their Guidelines for Writing a Summary handout. Give them a 5W's Organizer and the rubric you will use to assess the summary.

5. Ask those students who will be writing a paragraph to take out their Elements of a Paragraph handout. Distribute the Writing Topics list and the rubric you will use to assess the paragraph.

6. Invite students to reread and take notes for their summaries or paragraphs. Have them work through the writing process outlined on the Guidelines for Writing a Summary handout or the Elements of a Paragraph handout, consulting the corresponding rubric to check their work.

7. When students finish, have them turn in their work. Assess it using the rubric.

Wrap-Up

Give students lots of positive feedback for utilizing the strategies you've been teaching them to boost their comprehension.

Interpreting Assessments

The paragraphs can show you whether students can make logical inferences and find specific text details from the selection. See the Scaffolding Suggestions chart on page 245 to help you support students with reading issues.

To scaffold students who require writing support, use the Scaffolding Suggestions for Helping Students Write Summaries and Paragraphs chart on the Resources CD.

Following Up the Assessment

Based on your assessment of students' writing, you can determine how many days to spend scaffolding and extending their learning. I recommend allowing at least one day for students to revise their writing based on your feedback; during that time, you can meet with your most struggling readers. Then, you may choose to spend additional days working in small groups, scaffolding students who need it and extending the learning of those who are ready for more challenge.

Supporting Students Who Require Scaffolding

The chart on page 245 offers scaffolding suggestions based on students' writing, your observations as they read and discuss texts, and your conferences on independent and instructional reading. Support students with similar needs by working with groups of two or three. When students struggle and are unsuccessful with the assessment, work one-on-one with them.

At first, when you scaffold, you might do all or most of the modeling and thinking aloud. Follow-up conferences should gradually turn over to the student the responsibility for learning. You can do this gradual release by pairing the student with a peer, by continuing to confer with and observe the student's thinking, or by having the student work independently and then share her thinking with you. This can occur in two or three short conferences (see forms on the Resources CD). However, some students will need several conferences, and you might have to return to the skill as you move on to another unit.

Texts to Use for Scaffolding

Students can use the text they read for their independent assessment or a text you have selected. You'll find excellent texts in these Scholastic magazines: *Action*, *Science World*, *Scope*, and *Storyworks*. For speeches, check out these URLS:

- *http://www.ranker.com/list/famous-short-speeches/william-neckard*
- *http://www.emersonkent.com/famous_speeches_in_history_presidents.htm*

Suggestions for Helping Students Think Across Texts

After students who were successful on the assessment revise their writing, you may want to follow up their learning by challenging them to think across the texts they have read during the unit; this task supports the Common Core State Reading Standards 7 to 9 for informational texts. Once students have read, discussed, and analyzed each text in this unit, they will be able to find common themes and ideas among them. You can use the suggestions below to help students complete across-text thinking.

- Study the speeches in this unit and compare what motivated two of the speechmakers to argue for their point of view.

- Compare two speeches and discuss whether the opposite point of view has convincing and justifiable arguments. If so, try to formulate arguments for these.

Ideas for Inquiry and Problem Solving Beyond the Text

If you have time to extend the unit, ask students to devise questions based on their reading, or use the prompts below to spark an inquiry.

- Have students study how one of these countries—China, Russia, Afghanistan, or Iran—has violated human rights. Have them develop arguments that ask American citizens and the federal government to intervene on behalf of the people in these countries.

- Ask students to collect newspaper articles that show violations of human rights and develop a plan for addressing these violations.

- Why are human rights so important to people all over the world? What did you learn from the selections you read that can help people who live in countries where their rights have been violated?

Students can write a short speech to share their results, participate in a class discussion or debate, create posters displaying what they've learned—there are many possibilities, and I find that allowing students to choose their mode of presentation motivates and engages them.

CLOSING THOUGHTS AND QUESTIONS TO DISCUSS

You can continue professional study by discussing with a peer partner or a group of colleagues the parts of the lessons that worked and the parts that need refining. Here are some questions to guide your conversations:

- Discuss how you might include in your curriculum the writing and performing of speeches that argue or persuade. Invite the social studies and science teachers to attend and discuss so they can have students develop a position related to their subject and support it in a speech.

- Share scaffolds you used to help students pinpoint and evaluate the arguments for a claim in one or more pieces in this chapter.

- Discuss other forms of writing you can introduce to students that will enable them to make a claim and support the claim with evidence. Consider thinking about a newspaper editorial, a blog, or an op-ed piece that contains solid evidence.

- How can you use the Internet to develop students' ability to support claims with evidence?

Scaffolding Suggestions for Helping Students Read Texts That Argue

STUDENT'S NEED	POSSIBLE SCAFFOLD
Identifies arguments: Finds selecting the arguments that support a position a challenge	• Reread aloud and then model how you first figure out the author's position, using Susan B. Anthony's speech. • Ask the student to find the author's position in the selection they read in Lessons 8 to 13. If the student has difficulty with this, point to the section in the text that states the position and have him paraphrase it. • Have the student find arguments that support the position. Continue practicing until the student can work independently.
Understands why writing to explain and argue work together: Is unable to show why it's important to include an explanation with some arguments	• Use the Susan B. Anthony speech (or another selection) and point out explanatory and informative parts such as the paragraph on oligarchy and the quote from the Preamble. Explain how these sections support the argument. • Have the student select explanatory and informative parts of a selection she's read and discuss how these sections support the arguments.
Author's purpose for arguing for a position: Has difficulty explaining how the author's position shapes the content	• Explain the author's purpose in Bush's speech or another selection and show how the purpose determines the information included and arguments presented. • Have the student explain the author's purpose in the selection he read for the assessment in Lessons 2. • Model and then ask the student to select details that relate to the author's purpose, so he sees how these work in concert.

CHAPTER 9

Reading Poetry

As a reading-writing workshop teacher, I view poetry as one of the most important genres for students to read. Because poets choose every word with care, heart, and thought, poems are an ideal way to teach figurative language, connotative meanings, rhythm, sound, imagery, and the importance of precise language.

Poems should be heard many times, and enjoyed for the emotions and images they evoke within us and for the rhythm of language. Poems speak directly to our feelings; it's the stirring of these feelings that then becomes each reader's entry into the poems' meaning. Before analyzing a poem's structure and meaning or identifying the devices the poet used to share his or her vision, it's important to allow students to play with the poem (Heard, 1998), to explore the language and imagery.

Often, poems use everyday language to express complex themes, making this an ideal genre for developing readers to improve reading fluency, make logical inferences, and practice pinpointing themes. Use short poems like those by Langston Hughes and Sandra Cisneros to involve developing readers with complex themes that grow out of accessible language. With time to read and reread, discuss and write about poems, all students can dig deeply into poetry and develop their awareness of and appreciation for the richness of language and thought.

In fact, studying poetry is an excellent way to meet the Common Core Craft and Structure standards for middle-school reading, which ask students to

- determine the connotative and denotative meanings of words
- analyze figurative language such as simile and metaphor
- analyze the impact of rhyme and of the repetition of sounds, such as alliteration, on the meaning of a specific stanza of a poem or in the entire poem
- compare theme and central ideas in multiple texts such as stories, myths, memoir, and poems

All this thinking is a natural outgrowth of thoughtfully reading, discussing, and writing about poetry, and you'll see how smoothly it fits into the teaching you'll do in this unit.

The poems I've selected for this unit relate to the natural world; students can complete some across-text thinking after they have read, discussed, and responded to two or three poems. I have organized this unit differently from the others because I believe that poetry should be read aloud to best enjoy the poet's language and ideas. Instead of lessons, I have provided a routine for reading a new poem. I encourage students to read and reread poems, talk about them, and write about them; I provide discussion and writing prompts for each poem in this unit. If you'd like to teach a mini-lesson on figurative language or poetic structure, I recommend doing so after the students have read or heard a poem multiple times. I've included a list of types of figurative language you can share with students or use as a basis for mini-lessons; see page 249 and the Resources CD.

Routine for Reading a Poem

Here's what I recommend you do to encourage and develop students' enthusiasm for the poems in this unit and other poems you study.

- Read the poem aloud to the class, so students can hear a fluent, expressive reading.
- Pair students with partners and give each student a copy of the poem.
- Have partners take turns reading the poem aloud several times to one another. Invite them to listen to and enjoy the language, rhythms, and images the poem

evokes. Repeat this shared partner reading two or three times on different days, allowing students to grow familiar with the words, images, and rhythms.

- Invite each student to complete an initial, nonanalytical response to the poem by trying one of the response strategies on page 250.

- Have students pair-share their responses and then discuss what the poem means to them, citing specific words, figures of speech, and lines that helped them explore and discover meaning.

- Develop a mini-lesson on figurative language that relates to the poem, the organization of the poem, the rhyme scheme, or the theme. Feel free to present specific mini-lessons targeted to students' needs to help them appreciate the poem's language, structure, and meaning.

- Move partners more deeply into the poem by having them discuss questions for each poem and then write an informal response based on their discussions. I have included discussion prompts for each of the four poems in this unit.

- Invite partners to select three or four key words in a poem and discuss the denotative and connotative meanings of each word.

TEACHING TIP —
STRATEGY FOR STUDENTS

After students answer questions for the poems in this unit, invite partners to create questions for a poem and then give the poem and questions to another pair. Doing this can deepen students' understanding of and connections to the poem and also provides the extra time you need to scaffold those who require support.

Assessing Students' Knowledge of Poetry

Students' written responses to poems are ideal for assessing their comprehension of a discussion question or a prompt you ask them to explore. You can also ask students to compare how two different poems on the same topic treat similar themes.

For me, the guiding rule for assessing students' understanding of poetry is to assess what has been taught to and practiced by students. You can ask students to show how figurative language enhances the meaning of a line or stanza in a poem or discuss how the connotative meaning of a word or phrase impacts the poem's meaning.

Ten Types of Figurative Language

For each term that's listed in this box, you'll find a short definition and an example from the literature used in this book. Help your students understand that in addition to poets, writers of literature and informational texts also use these devices.

Simile is a figure of speech that compares two unlike things that have something in common. A simile uses *like* or *as* to make the comparison. *Example*: From "La Bamba" by Gary Soto: "The sheets were as cold as the moon that stood over the peach tree in their backyard."

Metaphor is a figure of speech that compares two unlike things that have something in common. Metaphor doesn't use *like* or *as* but equates the two unlike things, often using a form of "to be" as the verb. *Example*: From "The Highwayman" by Alfred Noyes: "The moon was a ghostly galleon tossed upon cloudy seas."

Personification is giving human personality traits, emotions, and qualities to inanimate objects or abstract ideas. *Example*: From "The Tyger" by William Blake: "When the stars threw down their spears, / And water'd heaven with their tears, "

Alliteration is the repetition of the same sounds at the beginning of words or in stressed syllables. *Example*: From "Crystal Moment" by Robert Peter Tristram Coffin: "He leaned toward the land and life."

Onomatopoeia is using words that imitate the sounds associated with the objects or actions of the words. *Example*: From "Dust Bowl Disaster" by Alex Porter and Kristin Lewis: "Suddenly, Ike felt a powerful jolt. Bzzt! Electricity shot through the car, shorting it out."

Oxymoron is a figure of speech that combines two contradictory terms. *Example*: From "The Runaway" by Robert Frost: "We heard the miniature thunder where he fled."

Assonance is also referred to as "vowel rhyme." It's the repetition of similar vowel sounds in adjacent words. *Example*: From "A narrow fellow in the grass" by Emily Dickinson: ". . . a transport / of cordiality."

Repetition is the repeating of a word within a sentence or a poetical line within a stanza or throughout a poem. *Example*: From "The Day I Walked and Walked" by Ahmon'dra (Brenda) McClendon: "Well, we walked and we walked, and it seemed like we walked around that building for a long time."

Initial Responses to Poems: Four Options

After students have read aloud or listened to a poem several times, invite them to complete an initial, nonanalytical response to draw them more deeply into the poem. Here are four response options that have been successful with my students.

Four Words: Ask students to write in their notebooks the first four words that come to mind after hearing the poem. Next, have students choose one of the words that resonated with them and write about how the word connects to the poem. Partners share and discuss their written responses.

Visualize and Draw: Have students draw the images they see after reading and/or listening to a poem.

Word Choice and Mood or Tone: Have each student reread the poem silently and then choose four to ten words and short phrases that contribute to the mood or tone of the poem. Partners share their lists and discuss the mood or tone the words imply or suggest.

A pair of eighth graders collected these words from "The Runaway" by Robert Frost: *snorted, bolt, miniature thunder, running away, clatter of stone, alone, shudders.* The pair decided that the mood reflected the colt's fear of snow—something new to him. The poet's choice of these words helped reinforce the idea of the colt's fear of winter and snow and being out alone and also suggest that the owner was not a good caretaker because the colt was alone.

Feelings: Have students jot down two feelings they experienced while listening to the poem. Invite students to compare their feelings to the feelings they believe are part of the author's purpose. Are they alike? Different? Explain.

Poetry Lessons

I've selected four poems related to nature for students to explore in this unit along with discussion prompts for each poem. I recommend following the routine on pages 247–248 for each one, allowing three or four days for each exploration. After students have read and responded to at least two poems, you may choose to have them work on the Thinking Across Texts activities on page 252.

You'll find images of the four poems I've included for this unit on page 251; the reproducible versions and discussion questions are on the Resources CD. The questions will enhance students' understanding of each poem and serve as models for questions student might ask about other poems they read.

A narrow fellow in the grass

by Emily Dickinson

A narrow fellow in the grass
Occasionally rides;
You may have met him—did you not?
His notice sudden is,
The grass divides as with a comb,
A spotted shaft is seen;
And then it closes at your feet
And opens further on.

He likes a boggy acre,
A floor too cool for corn.
Yet when a boy and barefoot,
I more than once, at noon,
Have passed, I thought, a whiplash
Unbraiding in the sun—
When stooping to secure it,
It wrinkled and was gone.

Several of nature's people
I know and they know me;
I feel for them a transport
Of cordiality.
But never met this fellow,
Attended or alone,
Without a tighter breathing,
And zero at the bone.

The Tyger

by William Blake

Tyger! Tyger! burning bright
In the forests of the night,
What immortal hand or eye
Could frame thy fearful symmetry?

In what distant deeps or skies
Burnt the fire of thine eyes?
On what wings dare he aspire?
What the hand dare seize the fire?

And what shoulder and what art,
Could twist the sinews of thy heart?
And when thy heart began to beat,
What dread hand and what dread feet?

What the hammer? what the chain?
In what furnace was thy brain?
What the anvil? What dread grasp
Dare its deadly terrors clasp?

When the stars threw down their spears,
And water'd heaven with their tears,
Did He smile His work to see?
Did He who made the lamb make thee?

Tyger! Tyger! burning bright
In the forests of the night,
What immortal hand or eye
Dare frame thy fearful symmetry?

The Runaway

by Robert Frost

Once when the snow of the year was beginning to fall,
We stopped by a mountain pasture to say, "Whose colt?"
A little Morgan had one forefoot on the wall,
The other curled at his breast. He dipped his head
And snorted at us. And then he had to bolt.
We heard the miniature thunder where he fled,
And we saw him, or thought we saw him, dim and grey,
Like a shadow against the curtain of falling flakes.
"I think the little fellow's afraid of the snow.
He isn't winter-broken. It isn't play
With the little fellow at all. He's running away.
I doubt if even his mother could tell him, 'Sakes,
It's only weather.' He'd think she didn't know!
Where is his mother? He can't be out alone."
And now he comes again with a clatter of stone
And mounts the wall again with whited eyes
And all his tail that isn't hair up straight.
He shudders his coat as if to throw off flies.
"Whoever it is that leaves him out so late,
When other creatures have gone to stall and bin,
Ought to be told to come and take him in."

Crystal Moment

by Robert Peter Tristram Coffin

Once or twice this side of death
Things can make one hold his breath.

From my boyhood I remember
A crystal moment of September.

A wooded island rang with sounds
Of church bells in the throats of hounds.

A buck leaped out and took the tide
With jewels flowing past each side.

With his head high like a tree
He swam within a yard of me.

I saw the golden drop of light
In his eyes turned dark with fright.

I saw the forest's holiness
On him like a fierce caress.

Fear made him lovely past belief,
My heart was trembling like a leaf.

He leaned towards the land and life
With need above him like a knife.

In his wake the hot hounds churned
They stretched their muzzles out and yearned.

They bayed no more, but swam and throbbed
Hunger drove them till they sobbed.

Pursued, pursuers reached the shore
And vanished. I saw nothing more.

So they passed, a pageant such
As only gods could witness much,

Life and death upon one tether
And running beautiful together.

Suggestions for Helping Students Think Across Texts

Once students have read and discussed two or more of the poems in this unit, they will be able to find common themes and ideas among them. You can use the suggestions below to help students complete across-text thinking.

- How are the poems you read in this unit relevant to your life today? Is it their subject matter? Is it the themes they contain? Explain.

- How did the poems you selected change or make you adjust the way you view animals and the natural world?

- Use what you learned from the poems and research a present-day environmental issue. Then compose a letter about the issue to the editor of a newspaper, or write an article that argues for protecting the environment and the habitat of animals.

- The tiger is an endangered species today. Read about this on the Web site below and report to your classmates or give a speech that argues for protecting tigers. *http://www.buzzle.com/articles/endangered-tigers.html*

CLOSING THOUGHTS AND QUESTIONS TO DISCUSS

You can meet with colleagues to share how the poetry routines worked for you and exchange suggestions with them for more formal lessons and other routines. Here are some questions and prompts to guide your conversations.

- How does figurative language impact the meaning of a poem? Of other genres? Find an example of figurative language in one of the selections in this book or another text you choose, and discuss it with colleagues.

- What lessons did you develop to help students absorb the figurative language explanations and examples on page 249? Explain why you believe these were successful or invite colleagues to offer suggestions to improve the lessons.

- Discuss how you might direct pairs or small groups of students to create questions relating to a new poem. How might this support students' understanding of the structure of poems and figurative language? How can you borrow what students developed and put it to use in your classroom?

- How can poetry support students' understanding of the denotative and connotative meanings of words?

CHAPTER 10

Reflecting on Reading Complex Texts

It may be that reading achievement is less about ability than it is about the opportunity to read. Only with the practice and the expertise that comes from sufficient opportunities to engage in independent silent reading will students reach their full literacy potential.

—Gambrell, Marinak, Brooker, & McCrea-Andrews (2011)

I have opened this final chapter with a quote from "The Importance of Independent Reading," a chapter in *What Research Has to Say About Reading Instruction* (2011), because I want to focus attention again on the necessity of independent reading. For students to meet the Common Core State Standards, they must have differentiated instruction targeted to their areas of need—that's what the lessons in this book offer.

But equally important is that they read a wide range of materials independently—and regularly. This is the only way students can sufficiently develop their background knowledge, vocabulary, and comprehension skills to become college and career ready. Providing students with access to books and opportunities to read is crucial to helping them develop a meaningful personal reading life. Students need well-stocked classroom libraries and school libraries with rich and varied collections, staffed by a certified school librarian who can order books, advise teachers, and help students find engaging reading materials. Moreover, recent research shows that independent reading for developing readers should consist of materials they can read with 99 percent accuracy (Allington, 2009; Torgenson & Hudson, 2006), so we must have age-appropriate books at all reading levels.

As we foster the independent reading lives of our students, we must also encourage them to stop and think about their reading, something many readers, especially developing ones, might not do. It's impossible for one teacher to monitor every independent reading book a student completes, but we can put in place several routines that build in accountability and reflection. Here are four student practices I recommend incorporating into your reading program:

- Entering completed or abandoned books on a reading log (see the Resources CD for a reproducible form)
- Presenting one book talk a month (see the Resources CD for guidelines)
- Writing a book review three or four times a year (see the Resources CD for guidelines)
- Discussing a book with a partner and documenting the conversation (see the Resources CD for a discussion form)

In addition, I recommend that three or four times a year you confer with each student about his or her independent reading; you'll find a form to guide these conferences on the Resources CD. Encouraging a "stop to think" pattern in students can lead to their being self-reflective about their reading and can even inspire them to seek out a peer for a brief book discussion. You may also consider establishing voluntary monthly lunchtime book clubs, which I've found are a great way for students to eat together, discuss books, and still have some time to go outside and play.

Building Students' Vocabulary

In addition to a strong independent reading program, building students' vocabulary through a study of roots, prefixes, and suffixes is essential to developing proficient readers who can tackle complex texts.

Middle-school students need to improve their academic vocabulary—words related to specific disciplines—as well as develop fluency reading the 5,580 words that constitute

90 percent of the words they'll encounter in texts for grades three to nine (Carroll, Davies, & Richman, 1971). The most effective way to build this vocabulary is to select and teach roots that relate to the texts students are reading and to the disciplines they are studying.

To this end, all disciplines—social studies, mathematics, science, and English—need to include the study of roots and affixes (see the Resources CD for a list of Latin and Greek roots, prefixes, and suffixes). A science teacher might select the Greek root *geo,* meaning "earth," and have students generate a list of related words such as *geography, geophysical, geology, geometry, geophysicist, geologist, geomagnetic, geocentric, geode.* This list could lead students to the study of words that build on *graph, centric, ology,* and *phys* and enable them to define unfamiliar words using their knowledge of roots.

In language arts classes, I recommend that teachers spend three or four minutes a day each week building words using roots and affixes. I include on pages 255–257 a sample five-day teaching routine that you can use with any root.

Teaching Roots: A Five-Day Vocabulary Routine

DAY 1

Write the root, the language it derives from, and its meaning on chart paper or the whiteboard. Here's what I write before studying the poem "Crystal Moment" (see page 251 and the Resources CD).

spec, Latin, means "to see"

Have students pair-share for two minutes and generate words they think come from the same root. Record the list on chart paper or the whiteboard. Here's the list my students suggested for *spec*:

spectacle	**respect**
spectacular	**respectable**
spectator	**disrespect**
spectacles	**inspect**
	inspector

DAY 2

Read the list of words out loud and ask students to pair-share to see if they can find additional words. Students added these words to the list for *spec*:

inspection
inspected
special

Explain that students can challenge a word to make sure it comes from the root under study. If a word is challenged, look it up in the dictionary, showing students the word origin. For *spec*, students challenged *special*. Using a document camera, I displayed the dictionary entry so students could see the origin of the word. *Special* comes from old French *especial* and from the Latin *specialis*, meaning individual or particular. I help students understand that even though a word contains the root, it's important to consider the word's meaning, and *special* does not relate to the meaning of *spec*, to see

DAY 3

Invite students to work with a partner and use their knowledge of the root to define the words the class generated. Here's the list of words with students' definitions for words containing *spec*.

spectacle: something amazing to look at

spectacular: related to spectacle

spectator: person who sees

spectacles: eyeglasses to help a person see

respect: to look up to

respectable: someone or something worthy of respect

disrespect: opposite of respect; looking down upon

inspect: look closely

inspector: a person who looks closely at something

special: challenged word—not from *spec*

inspection: the act of seeing into or looking closely at something

inspected: past tense of "inspect"

In their notebooks, have partners compile a list of prefixes used with the root and use their dictionaries (print or online) to define each prefix.

DAY 4

Discuss with students various situations in which a word might be used, and refine the definitions. Model how to use the word and situation to compose a sentence that shows an understanding of the word.

WORD	SITUATIONS WHEN YOU MIGHT USE THE WORD
spectacle: something amazing to look at	to describe a pageant, circus, parade, show, opera, concert, or other performance
spectator: a person who sees	to name a person or critic observing a show, parade, circus, pageant, concert, etc.
spectacles: eyeglasses to help a person see	to describe how a person looks; to show that a person cannot see well
respect: to look up to	to show that one person honors another
respectable: someone or something that is worthy of respect	to describe an authority figure, such as a parent or police officer
disrespect: to look down on, refuse to value	to describe negative behavior
inspect: to look closely at	to describe what someone does with a microscope; to a building; to clothing
inspector: a person who looks closely at something	to name someone who checks safety in buildings, restaurants, or hospitals
inspection: the act of looking closely at something	to describe how a parent checks a room; how someone might look at a used car

Sample sentence: The show's finale was a *spectacle,* with dozens of students dressed in colorful costumes dancing, singing, juggling, and doing gymnastics in a carefully choreographed, fast-paced performance.

DAY 5

Partners select two words and write sentences that reflect a true understanding of the word and not simply the word's definition. Pairs share their sentences. Here are two student sentences:

- Every time my mom reads a book or magazine she puts on her *spectacles.*
- The class showed *respect* for the visitor by offering a seat, listening to her talk, and asking thought-provoking questions.

Working with one root over a series of days helps students learn several words as well as prefixes and suffixes. Teach a few prefixes a week because prefixes change the meaning of a word. Use prefixes from the words students generate, or choose ones that will be highly useful for students to know.

Avoid having students copy the list of words the class generates, because many have visual discrimination difficulties and will copy them incorrectly. I do not have my students memorize the list for spelling or vocabulary quizzes. I prefer to work on about 15 roots with each grade level during the school year and revisit these lists and add words and situations each time. By designing lessons that actively involve students and deepen their knowledge of words related to a root, I can enlarge their vocabulary.

Middle-school teaching teams can work together to select ten to 15 roots that are related to the disciplines that they plan to teach. I suggest that teams meet annually, before school starts, to revisit and adjust their selection of roots.

Professional Learning Improves Instruction

Working together to maximize students' vocabulary learning is important, and I urge you to extend your collaboration with colleagues to include professional learning, a key factor in developing the skill and expertise needed to teach reading effectively. When teachers read and discuss the pertinent research found in professional books and journals and on blogs, they can continually evaluate and adjust their practice, always keeping in mind students' diverse needs and varied literacy experiences (Allington, 2002b, 2007).

Bringing in literacy experts for multiple hands-on learning workshops and having teachers attend conferences sponsored by their states is one part of professional study. For teachers to gain the background knowledge necessary to respond to students' needs and to apply the demanding Common Core Standards to reading and writing, schools need to develop and provide time during the day and at scheduled faculty meetings for the following professional learning experiences.

Peer Coaching: Yearlong teacher-learning partnerships can provide support through discussions and peer observations and planning. Teachers should choose their partner so they feel comfortable sharing what works and what needs adjusting.

A principal might want to suggest a partnership between a teacher who has little to no training with analyzing texts and a teacher who has greater knowledge and experience. Such a pairing can ease the frustration and anxiety of the less-experienced teacher.

Bimonthly Conversations: These can occur during team, grade-level, or departmental meetings. Participants can include teachers, administrators, and resource specialists, all of whom read an article or chapter in a book and use prompts to spark meaningful conversations. Here are some ideas:

- Discuss the points that apply to your teaching and how each might affect your practice and students' learning.
- Discuss how you might integrate these teaching ideas into the curriculum.
- Explain why you disagree with elements the author presented.

Sharing Resources: This can be done between peer partners, among members of a grade-level team or department, among the entire faculty, or with teachers in other districts. Teachers can bring resources to a meeting or post them online in a shared file. Resources can include professional books, articles, and blogs; adolescent literature; materials discovered at a conference or workshop; and lessons that proved successful in the classroom. Sharing lessons that worked can improve the instruction of teachers with little to no training in an area. (See my *Redefining Staff Development*, 2000.)

Peer Observations: These work well once partners have established a trusting and mutually beneficial relationship. Partners observe one another to learn, to troubleshoot, and to adjust their teaching of a lesson. These observations are kept between partners and aren't written up for administrators; the purpose is growth and not evaluation.

Assessing Students' Writing: Share with peers samples of students' writing about reading and discuss so you can understand students' reading and writing strengths and needs. Studying students writing can inform the lessons we present and the interventions and scaffolds we plan. (For more information, see my *Teaching Middle School Writers* [2010a].)

Teachers Make the Difference

Research shows that it's teachers who make the most difference in students' reading achievement. Effective teachers offer their students personalized instruction, embed skills in meaningful contexts, collaborate to learn the best literacy practices and apply the latest research to their lesson planning, develop interactive lessons, encourage creativity and collaboration, and provide students with more reading and writing opportunities (Allington, 2002a; Allington, Johnston, & Day, 2002; Ferguson, 2010; Taylor, Pearson, Clark, & Walpole, 2000).

I have faith in the power of teachers to inspire their students to reach for the sky and become the creative thinkers and problem solvers our world needs. Emily Dickinson captured this belief in the following poem:

I GAINED it so,
By climbing slow.
By catching at the twigs that grow
Between the bliss and me.
  It hung so high,
  As well the sky
Attempt by strategy.

I said I gained it,—
  This was all.
Look, how I clutch it,
  Lest it fall,
And I a pauper go;
Unfitted by an instant's grace
For the contented beggar's face
I wore an hour ago.

Yes, help your students' reach exceed their grasp, and each time they slip, support them, lift them up, motivate them so that learning matters. A tall order—but I have faith that you are up to the challenge!

Building Prior Knowledge

Directions: Follow these steps to familiarize yourself with the topic of a text and build some prior knowledge to prepare yourself for reading and understanding the text.

- Read the title. Ask yourself, "What do I know about this topic?" If you know little to nothing, make sure you tell yourself to read slowly and thoughtfully. Be prepared to reread parts and close read to make sense of words, sentences, and paragraphs. If you know something about the topic, take the time to compare what you read to what you know and note and adjust any differences.

- Read the first paragraph if it is long. If it is short, read the first two paragraphs.

- Skip to the end and read the last paragraph. **Note:** *If it is a short story, do* not *read the end!*

- Read any questions or discussion prompts that follow the text.

- Tell a partner everything you learned from reading the opening and closing paragraphs. When you work alone, think to yourself about everything you learned.

- In your notebook, jot down in your own words what you learned. This is your prior knowledge of the text. You may reread your notes to remember what you've learned.

- Set a purpose for reading. Think about questions you have, based on your prior-knowledge list. You may use the text's title or the unit's concept as well. Then create one question or statement to describe your purpose. As you read, keep in mind your purpose for reading.

Close Reading Guidelines

Close reading is a strategy that can help you figure out a difficult word or understand a challenging piece of text. When you're reading a text, assume that every word and phrase carries meaning. If you're unsure of what something means, pause and do a close reading.

If it's a difficult word . . .

- Look carefully at the word. Are there any prefixes, suffixes, or roots you recognize?
- Reread the sentences before and after the one containing the difficult word. Do they contain any clues to what the word means?
- Is there a glossary you can consult? Are there any text features, such as charts or illustrations, that provide clues to the word?
- Have you seen or heard the word or phrase? In what situation? Can you recall what the word or phrase meant in the specific situation?

Dig Deeper

- Can you connect the word or phrase to information that came before it? To what you know and have learned from the preview?
- Why do you think the writer uses this particular word or phrase?
- How does this word or phrase relate to the tone, mood, or theme of the text?
- What is the connection between this word or phrase and others within the text?
- What is the significance of this word or phrase in relation to other ideas in the sentence or paragraph?

If it's a difficult sentence, paragraph, or section . . .

- Read each sentence word-by-word, chunking phrases and making sure you know what each one means. If a particular word gives you trouble, use the strategies above to figure it out.
- Paraphrase each sentence by saying it in your own words.
- Continue rereading and paraphrasing each sentence. When you get to the end of a paragraph, retell it for yourself. If you can't retell several details, then reread the paragraph.
- Continue rereading and retelling paragraphs. When you get to the end of a section, retell it for yourself.

Dig Deeper

- Consider the themes of the text. How does the sentence, paragraph, or section relate to them?
- Why did the writer include this sentence, paragraph, or section in the text?
- How does this sentence, paragraph, or section connect to the title?
- How does this sentence, paragraph, or section connect to other parts of the text?
- What inferences can you make from this sentence, paragraph, or section?

Name _____ Date: _____

Quiz Answer Sheet

Title of Text _____

Directions

1. Answer the multiple-choice items that follow your text; record the letter of the *best* answer below.
2. For each item, write the number of the paragraph(s) that contains the evidence you used to determine your answer.
3. Then select one answer to defend in a short paragraph—do not choose a vocabulary item. Use text details and logical text inferences to support your point.
4. Use the checklist to make sure you include all the required elements in your paragraph.

ANSWERS	EVIDENCE FROM TEXT (*Put # of paragraph(s)*)
1.	
2.	
3.	
4.	
5.	

GUIDELINES FOR PLANNING A PARAGRAPH

For your introductory sentence, restate the quiz prompt along with your answer. Then jot down details from the text and logical inferences you made that provide support for the answer.

Draft your paragraph on a separate sheet of paper. Include your introductory sentence and evidence from the text that supports your answer. Wrap up your paragraph with a concluding sentence.

Check Your Work!

_____ Notes: details and inferences from the text

_____ Title

_____ Introductory Sentence

_____ Evidence: details and inferences from the text

_____ Concluding Sentence

Name _____ Date: _____

Word Map

Directions:

1. Under "What is it?" write the concept.
2. Come up with a similar word of phrase and write it in the box at the left.
3. Under "What is it like?" write four to six of its characteristics. Then write some examples in the space below.
4. After you complete the map, use the word in a sentence that shows you understand its meaning.

What is it?   *What is it like?*

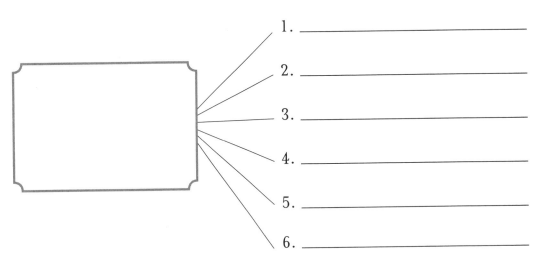

Examples:

My Sentence:

Elements of a Paragraph

Directions: Making your point in writing is a powerful skill. When you argue, inform, or explain a point about a text you've read, use these steps to craft an effective paragraph so readers understand and agree with your perspective.

Title

Capture your reader's attention. Introduce the topic. Keep it short!

Introductory Sentence

Write a topic or introductory sentence that gives the title and author of your text and expresses the point you want to make about the text.

Text-Based Evidence

Supply two or three pieces of evidence from the text that support your main point. These may be facts, examples, or descriptions written in your own words, or a summary of the content of dialogue. You may also include inferences that you make from key details.

Concluding or Wrap-Up Sentence

Reiterate your position and add details that leave the reader thinking about your ideas.

Check Your Work!

_____ *Notes: details and inferences from the text*

_____ *Title*

_____ *Introductory Sentence*

_____ *Evidence: details and inferences from the text*

_____ *Concluding Sentence*

Guidelines for Writing a Summary

The 5W's and Somebody-Wanted-But-So Organizers

Directions: Follow the guidelines for taking notes on your text to write a summary. Use the checklist to make sure you include all the required elements.

Guidelines for Taking Notes

- Use the 5W's Organizer to take notes on informational texts. Use the Somebody-Wanted-But-So Organizer to take notes on literature.
- Read the directions on the organizer carefully.
- Skim the text to find specific details related to each prompt on your organizer.
- Jot down notes in your own words on the organizer.
- Reread your notes to make sure they are detailed and complete.
- Add more details if you find some.

Guidelines for Writing a Summary

- Give your summary a title.
- Reread your notes and craft an introductory sentence.
- Include the title and author of the text in your introductory sentence.
- Use your notes to compose sentences for the summary.
- Write a concluding sentence.
- Read your summary out loud and listen for missing words, the flow of sentences, and unwanted repetitions.
- Revise the summary.
- Check for spelling.
- Turn in your organizer and summary.

Checklist for Summary

____ *Title*

____ *Introductory sentence with author and title*

____ *Summary sentences with text details*

____ *Concluding sentence*

Quiz Answer Keys

Note: Use the Check Your Work! checklist on the Quiz Answer Sheet to evaluate students' paragraph.

CHAPTER 3

The Great Fire

1. C, 1, 4
2. C, 6
3. D, 1
4. B, 4
5. B, 5

Blizzard!

1. B, 1, 2
2. A, 4, 5
3. D, 5, 6
4. C, 8
5. A, 6

Dead Men Floating

1. D, 1–4
2. D, 1
3. A, 6–8, 10–12
4. B, 13
5. B, 14

CHAPTER 4

"Woodrow Wilson"

1. C, 4
2. C, 2
3. D, 2
4. A, 5
5. A, 3

Idi Amin

1. A, All
2. D, 15
3. C, 12, 13
4. B, 7
5. A, 15, 16

Napoleon Complex

1. A, 1, 2
2. B, 3
3. B, 10
4. B, 7, 10
5. C, 8, 9

CHAPTER 5

"The Opening of a New World"

1. C, 2–8
2. B, 2
3. B, 3, 4, 13–15
4. D, 8
5. B, All

"Helen Keller and Anne Sullivan"

1. C, 1, 3, 7, 9
2. A, 5, 6, 7
3. B, 6
4. B, 7, 8
5. D, 3

"Tickling a Trout"

1. B, 3, 5
2. C, 3, 11–16
3. D, 3–16
4. D, 3
5. B, 14, 15, 16

CHAPTER 6

"Helios"

1. B, 5
2. A, 6–8
3. D, 5–8
4. C, 7, 8
5. C, 5

"Twin Titans and the Creation of Man"

1. C, 5
2. C, 4, 5
3. A, 2
4. B, 2, 3
5. D, 4

"Athena and Arachne"

1. C, 1
2. A, 3, 4
3. B, 2
4. D, 7, 8
5. B, 3–8

CHAPTER 8

"Woman's Rights to the Suffrage"

1. A, 1
2. D, 4, 5, 8
3. C, 8
4. B, 4, 5
5. D, 5

"Votes for Women"

1. C, 2
2. A, 5
3. C, 3
4. D, 3
5. A, 4, 5

"9/11 Address to the Nation"

1. C, 5
2. D, 1, 2, 8
3. D, 3, 8
4. B, All
5. A, 4

Bibliography

Professional References

Alliance for Excellent Education (2010). *High school dropouts in America.* (http://www.all4ed.org/files/HighSchoolDropouts.pdf).

Allington, R. L. (2002a). What I've learned about effective reading instruction. *Phi Delta Kappan, 83*(10), 740–747.

Allington, R. L. (2002b). You can't learn much from books you can't read. *Educational Leadership, 60*(3), 16–19, Alexandria, VA: ASCD.

Allington, R. L. (2007). Effective teachers: Effective instruction. In K. Beers, R. E. Probst, & L. Reif (Eds.), *Adolescent literacy: Turning promise into practice.* Portsmouth, NH: Heinemann.

Allington, R. L. (2009). If they don't read much . . . 30 years later. In E. H. Hiebert (Ed.), *Reading more, reading better*, pp. 30-54. New York: Guilford.

Allington, R. L. (2011). *What really matters for struggling readers: Designing research-based programs* (3rd ed.). Boston: Allyn & Bacon.

Allington, R. L., & Cunningham, P. M. (2002). *Schools that work: Where All children read and write* (2nd ed.). Boston: Allyn & Bacon.

Allington, R. L., Johnston, P. H. and Day, J. P. (2002). Exemplary fourth-grade teachers. *Language Arts, 79*(6): 462–466.

Allison, B. N., & Rehm, M. L. (2007). Effective teaching strategies for middle school learners in multicultural, multilingual classrooms. *Middle School Journal, 39*(2), 12–18.

Allison, N. (2009). *Middle school readers: Helping them read widely, helping them read well.* Portsmouth, NH: Heinemann.

Anderson, R. C. 1984). Role of reader's schemas in comprehension, learning, and memory. In R. Anderson, J. Osborne, & R. Tierney (Eds.), *Learning to read in American schools.* Hillsdale, NJ: Erlbaum.

Anderson, R. C., & Pearson, P. D. (1984). A schema-theoretic view of basic processes in reading comprehension. In P. D. Pearson, R. Barr, M. L. Kamil, & P. Mosenthal (Eds.), *Handbook of reading research* (pp. 255–291). New York: Longman.

Bear, D. R., Invernizzi, M. R., Templeton, S., & Johnston, F. R. (2011). *Words their way: Word study for phonics, vocabulary, and spelling instruction* (5th ed.). Boston: Allyn & Bacon.

Beck, I. L., & McKeown, M. G. (2006). *Improving comprehension with questioning the author: A fresh and expanded view of a powerful approach.* New York: Scholastic.

Brozo, W. G., Shiel, G., & Topping, K. (2008). Engagement in reading: Lessons learned from three PISA countries. *Journal of Adolescent & Adult Literacy, 31*(4), 304–315.

Brozo. W. G., Valtin, R., Garbe, C., Sulkunen, S., Shiel, G., & Pandian, A. (2012). Member country highlights from PISA 2009. *Reading Today, 29*(6), 11–13.

Burke, J. (2010). *What's the big Idea? Question-driven units to motivate reading, writing, and thinking.* Portsmouth, NH: Heinemann.

Carroll, J. B., Davies, P., & Richman, B. (1971. *The American Heritage word frequency book.* Boston: Houghton Mifflin.

Common Core State Standards Initiative (2010). *Common Core State Standards for English Language Arts.*

Duke, N. K. (2003). Informational texts? The research says, "Yes!" In L. Hoyt, M. E. Mooney, & B. Parkes (Eds.). *Exploring informational texts: theory to practice* (pp. 2–7). Portsmouth, NH: Heinemann.

Duke, N. K. (2004). *The case for informational text.* Alexandria, VA: ASCD.

Duke, N. K., & Pearson, P. D. (2002). Effective practices for developing reading comprehension. In A. E. Farstrup & S. J. Samuels (Eds.), *What research has to say about reading instruction* (3rd ed.). Newark, DE: International Reading Association.

Ferguson, R. F. (2010). *Exemplary high schools.* http://www.journalism.columbia.edu/system/documents/351/original/Ferguson.pdf

Fountas, I. C., & Pinnell, G. S. (2006). *Teaching for comprehending and fluency: Thinking, talking, and writing about reading, K–8.* Portsmouth, NH: Heinemann.

Gambrell, L. B., Marinak, B. A., Brooker, H. R., & McCrea-Andrews, H. J. (2011). The importance of independent reading. In S. J. Samuels & A. E. Farstrup (Eds.), *What research has to say about reading instruction* (4th ed., pp. 143–158). Newark, DE: The International Reading Association.

Graham, S., & Harris, K. R. (2005). *Writing better: Effective strategies to improve the writing of adolescents in middle and high school.* Baltimore, MD: Brookes Publishing.

Graham, S., & Harris, K. R. (2007). Best practices in teaching planning. In S. Graham, C. A. MacArthur, & J. Fitzgerald, (Eds.), *Best practices in writing instruction.* New York: Guilford.

Graham, S., & Hebert, M. A. (2010). *Writing to read: Evidence for how writing can improve reading.* New York: Carnegie Corporation.

Graves, D. H. (1989). *Discover your own literacy: The reading/writing teacher's companion.* Portsmouth, NH: Heinemann.

Guthrie, J. T. (2003). Concept-Oriented Reading Instruction. In A. P. Sweet & C. E. Snow (Eds.), *Rethinking reading comprehension* (pp. 115–140). New York: Guilford.

Guthrie, J. T., Wigfield, A., & Klauda, S. L. (2012). *Adolescents' engagement in academic literacy* (Report No. 7). Retrieved from: www.corilearning.com/research-publications

Guthrie, J. T., Wigfield, A., Metsala, J. L., & Cox, K. E. (1999). Motivational and cognitive predictors of text comprehension and reading amount. *Scientific Studies of Reading, 3*(3): 231–256.

Heard, G. (1998). *Awakening the heart.* Portsmouth, NH: Heinemann.

Jensen, E. (2012). Keynote on June 8, North Texas Literacy conference, Dallas, TX.

Kindig, J. S. (2012). *Choosing to read: Connecting middle schoolers to books.* Portsmouth, NH: Portsmouth.

Krashen, S. D. (2004). *The power of reading: Insights from the research* (2nd ed.). Westport, CT: Libraries Unlimited.

Lipson, M. (2007). *Teaching reading beyond the primary grades.* New York: Scholastic.

Marzano, R. J. (2004). *Building background knowledge for academic achievement: Research on what works in schools.* Alexandria, VA: ASCD.

National assessment of educational progress. (2008). *NAEP, Reading Report Card for the Nation and the States.* Washington, DC: U.S. Department of Education, Office of Educational Research and Improvement.

Ogle, D. (2011). The promises and challenges of the CCSS. Keynote Session at Conference at Valparaiso University.

Ogle, D., Klemp, R., & McBride, B. (2007). *Building literacy in social studies: Strategies for improving comprehension and critical thinking.* Alexandria, VA: ASCD.

Robb, L. (2000). *Redefining staff developments.* Portsmouth, NH: Heinemann.

Robb. L. (2008). *Differentiating reading instruction: How to teach reading to meet the needs of each student.* New York: Scholastic.

Robb, L. (2009). *Assessments for differentiating reading instruction.* New York: Scholastic.

Robb, L. (2010a) *Teaching middle school writers.* Portsmouth, NH: Heinemann.

Robb, L. (2010b). *Teaching reading in middle school: A strategic approach to teaching reading that improves comprehension and thinking* (2nd ed.). New York: Scholastic.

Robb, L. (2012). *Smart writing: Practical units for teaching middle school writers.* Portsmouth, NH: Heinemann.

Rosenblatt, L. M. (1978) *The reader, the text, the poem: The transactional theory of the literary work.* Carbondale, IL: Southern Illinois University Press.

Rosenblatt, L. M. (1983). *Literature as exploration* (4th ed.). New York: The Modern Language Association.

Taylor, B. B., Pearson, P. D., Clark, K., & Walpole, S. (2000). Effective schools and accomplished teachers: Lessons about primary-grade reading instruction in low-income schools. *The Elementary School Journal, 101*(2), 120–165.

Tierney, R. J., & Readence, J. E. (2000). *Reading strategies and practices: A compendium.* Boston, MA: Allyn & Bacon.

Tomlinson, C. A. (1999). *The differentiated classroom: Responding to the needs of all learners.* Alexandria, VA: ASCD.

Torgeson, J. K., & Hudson, R. F. (2006). Reading fluency: Critical issues for struggling readers. In S. J. Samuels & A. E. Farstrup (Eds.), *What research has to say about fluency instruction* (pp. 130–158). Newark, DE: The International Reading Association.

Children's Literature

Anthony, S. B. (1873). Woman's Rights to the Suffrage. Retrieved from: http://www.nationalcenter.org/AnthonySuffrage.html

Baca, J. S. (2010). *Stories from the edge.* Portsmouth, NH: Heinemann.

Baicker, K. (2012). *Napoleon complex: A young general takes France by storm.* New York; Scholastic.

Barrett, S. M. (Ed.) (1906). *Geronimo's story of his life.* New York: Duffield and Co.

Blake, W. (1997). The tyger. In *The complete poetry & prose of William Blake.* New York: Anchor.

Bruchac, J. (2001). Tickling a trout. In B. Sizoo (Ed.), *Teaching powerful writing: 25 short read-aloud stories and lessons that motivate students to use literary elements in their writing.* New York: Scholastic.

Bush, G. W. (2001). 9/11 Address to the Nation. Retrieved from http://www.johnstonsarchive.net/terrorism/bush911a.html

Byars, B. (1992). *The Moon and I.* Winter Haven, FL: Messner.

Coffin, R. P. T. (1924). Crystal moment. Retrieved from http://www.marymaclane.com/elisabeth/crystalmoment.html

Collins, S. (2008). *The hunger games.* New York: Scholastic.

Dahl, R. (2001). *Boy: Tales of childhood.* New York: Puffin.

D'Aulaire, I., & D'Aulaire, E. P. (1962). Helios. *D'Aulaires' book of Greek myths*. New York: Dell Yearling.

D'Aulaire, I., & D'Aulaire, E. P. (1962). Orpheus. *D'Aulaires' book of Greek myths*. New York: Dell Yearling.

Delacre, L. (1996). Manco Capac and the rod of gold. *Golden tales: Myths, legends, and folktales from Latin America*. New York: Scholastic.

Denega, D. (2012). *Dead men floating: A small town is awash in skeletons*. New York: Scholastic.

Dickinson, E. (2008). Narrow fellow in the grass. In F. S. Bolin & C. Chung (Eds.), *Poetry for young people: Emily Dickinson*. New York: Scholastic.

Dougherty, S. (2010). *Idi Amin (wicked history)*. New York: Franklin Watts.

Douglass, F. (1845). *Narrative of the life of Frederick Douglas: An American slave*. Boston: Anti-Slavery Office.

Frost, R. (2002). The runaway. In L. Untermeyer (Ed.), *Robert Frost's poems*. New York: St. Martin's.

Jiménez, F. (1997). The Circuit. *The circuit: Stories from the life of a migrant child*. City NM: University of New Mexico Press.

Hopkins, L. B. (1995). *Been to yesterdays: Poems of a life*. Honesdale, PA: Boyds Mills.

Keller, H. (1997). Helen Keller and Anne Sullivan. In J. Canfield, M. V. Hansen & K. Kirberger (Eds.). *Chicken soup for the teenage soul*. New York: Scholastic.

Krull, K. (2000). Cleopatra. *Lives of extraordinary women: Ruler, rebels (and what the neighbors thought)*. New York: Harcourt Children's Books.

Krull, K. (2011). Woodrow Wilson. *Lives of the presidents: Fame, shame (and what the neighbors thought)*. New York: Harcourt Children's Books.

Lessing, D. (2008). Through the tunnel. *Stories* (Everyman's Library). New York: Knopf.

Lewis, K. (2011). "The fury of fire." *Scholastic Scope* Vol. 60, No. 2, pp. 4–9.

Lowry, L. (2000). *Looking back: A book of memories*. New York: Delacorte.

Lowry, L. (2012). *The giver*. New York: Laurel Leaf.

Marrin, A. (2012). *Years of dust: The story of the Dust Bowl*. New York: Puffin.

McLendon, A. (2004). The day I walked and walked. In J. Canfield, M. V. Hansen, L. Nichols & T. Joyner (Eds.), *Chicken soup for the African American soul*. New York: Scholastic.

Murphy, J. (2000). *Blizzard!* New York: Scholastic.

Murphy, J. (1995). *The great fire*. New York: Scholastic.

Noyes, A. (1913). *Collected poems*. New York: Frederick A. Stokes Co.

Okita, D. (1995). In response to Executive Order 9066: All Americans of Japanese descent must report to relocation centers. In *Crossing with the light*. Chicago, IL: Tia Chucha Press.

Porter, A. & Lewis, K. (2012). "Dust bowl disaster." *Scholastic Scope* Vol. 60, No. 10, pp. 4–9.

Rooney, A. (2002). Packages in packages. *Common Nonsense Addressed to the Reading Public*. New York: Public Affairs.

Rozett, L. (2012). *Ice queen: Catherine the Great seizes power in Russia*. New York: Scholastic.

Soto, G. (2000). La Bamba. *Baseball in April and other stories*. New York: Sandpiper.

Tarshis, L. (2011). "Head trauma." *Scholastic Scope* Vol. 60, No. 4, pp. 4–10.

Twain, M. (1901). Votes for women. Retrieved from: http://www.famousquotes.me.uk/speeches/Mark_Twain/index.htm

X, Malcolm, & Haley, A. (1964). The opening of a new world. *The autobiography of Malcolm X*. New York: Random House.

Zernike, K. (2012). "Unsafe Behind the Wheel?" *New York Times Upfront*, Vol. 145, Issue 3, pp. 6–7.

Text Credits

Every effort has been made to secure permission for the texts included with this book. We gratefully acknowledge the following:

"Helios" and "Orpheus" are reprinted from *D'Aulaire's Book of Greek Myths* by Ingri and Edgar Parin D'Aulaire. ©1962 by Ingri and Edgar Parin D'Aulaire. Used by permission of Doubleday, an imprint of Random House Children's Books, a division of Random House Inc. Any third party use of this material, outside of this publication, is prohibited. Interested parties must apply directly to Random House, Inc. for permission. Excerpt from *Blizzard!* by Jim Murphy. Text ©2000 by Jim Murphy. Reprinted by permission of Scholastic Inc. "The Circuit" by Francisco Jiménez is reprinted from *The Circuit* by Francisco Jiménez. ©1997 by Francisco Jiménez. Reprinted by permission of the University of New Mexico Press. "Cleopatra" from *Lives of Extraordinary Women* by Kathleen Krull. ©2000 by Kathleen Krull. Reprinted by permission of Harcourt Children's Books, an imprint of Houghton Mifflin Harcourt Publishing Company. All rights reserved. "Cut Anchor Line" by Donald Graves. Reprinted by permission of Mrs. Betty Graves. "The Day I Walked and Walked" by Ahmon'dra (Brenda) McClendon is reprinted from *Chicken Soup for the African American Soul.* ©2004 by Chicken Soup for the Soul Publishing, LLC. Published by Backlist, LLC, a unit of Chicken Soup for the Soul Publishing, LLC. Chicken Soup for the Soul is a registered trademark of Chicken Soup for the Soul Publishing, LLC. Reprinted by permission. All Rights Reserved. Excerpt from *The Great Fire* by Jim Murphy. Text ©1995 by Jim Murphy. Reprinted by permission of Scholastic Inc. Excerpt from *Idi Amin* by Steve Dougherty. Text ©2010 by Scholastic Inc. Used by permission. "La Bamba" by Gary Soto. From *Baseball in April and Other Stories* by Gary Soto. ©1990 by Gary Soto. Reprinted by permission of Harcourt Children's Books, an imprint of Houghton Mifflin Harcourt Publishing Company. All rights reserved. "Manco Capac and the Rod of Gold" from *Golden Tales* retold by Lulu Delacre. ©1996 by Lulu Delacre. Reprinted by permission of Scholastic Inc. "Packages in Packages" by Andy Rooney. Reprinted from *Common Nonsense* by Andy Rooney. ©2003 by Andy Rooney. Reprinted by permission of PublicAffairs, a member of the Perseus Books Group. "Through the Tunnel" by Doris Lessing. From *The Habit of Loving* by Doris Lessing. ©1955 by Doris Lessing. Originally appeared in *The New Yorker*. Reprinted by permission of HarperCollins Publishers. "Tickling a Trout" by Joseph Bruchac. Reprinted by permission of the author, c/o Barbara Kouts Literary Agent. "Woodrow Wilson" from *Lives of the Presidents* by Kathleen Krull. ©1998 by Kathleen Krull. Reprinted by permission of Harcourt Children's Books, an imprint of Houghton Mifflin Harcourt Publishing Company. All rights reserved. Excerpt from *Years of Dust: The Story of the Dust Bowl* by Albert Marrin. ©2009 by Albert Marrin. Used by permission of Viking Children's Books, a division of Penguin Young Readers Group, A Member of Penguin Group (USA) Inc. "Prison Studies" from *The Autobiography of Malcolm X* by Malcolm X and Alex Haley. ©1964 by Alex Haley and Malcolm X. ©1965 by Alex Haley and Betty Shabazz. Used by permission of Random House, Inc. Any third party use of this material, outside of this publication, is prohibited. Interested parties must apply directly to Random House, Inc. for permission. Excerpt from the Scholastic XBOOKS title *Dead Men Floating* by Danielle Denega. Copyright © 2012, 2007 by Scholastic Inc. All rights reserved. Used by permission. Excerpt from the Scholastic XBOOKS title *Napoleon Complex* by Karen Baicker. Copyright © 2012, 2010 by Scholastic Inc. All rights reserved. Used by permission. Excerpt from the Scholastic XBOOKS title *Ice Queen* by Louise Rozett. Copyright © 2012, 2009 by Scholastic Inc. All rights reserved. Used by permission. Excerpt from "Train of Death: Sonia Nazario" from the Scholastic ON THE RECORD title *Reporting Live* by John DiConsiglio. Copyright © 2012 by Scholastic Inc. All rights reserved. Used by permission. Excerpt from "Bird in a Cage: Maria Reyes" from the Scholastic ON THE RECORD title *Life and Death* by Candace Jaye and John Malcolm. Copyright © 2012 by Scholastic Inc. All rights reserved. Used by permission. For more information about ON THE RECORD go to www.scholastic.com/ontherecord. For more information about XBOOKS go to www.scholastic.com/xbooks.